From Communism to Community

From Communism to Community
Memoirs of a Diplomat and Teacher

Selby Martin

Dedication

To my wife Rachel

Book Design and Production by YouCaxton

ISBN 978-1-911175-31-5

Contents

Forewords

In this delightful memoir Selby Martin sets out not to impress, nor necessarily to amuse, but to tell the story of his life exactly as it took place, and to share those things that have most shaped his extraordinarily diverse and interesting career and given him the most fulfilment. Throughout his tale the facts are made all the more fresh and convincing by brief excerpts from his own diaries and from weekly letters home from abroad which his mother dutifully kept, numbered and archived until he should need them. Between the lines, one senses a number of personality traits in competition – explorer, linguist, limnologist, and teacher, all bound by a strong set of values – not least among them modesty and scrupulous honesty.

Selby's story starts in 1939 with him being packed off at the age of six to join his two elder brothers at a boarding school in Sussex. A year later, by which time the threat of invasion must have seemed all the more menacing, the whole family uprooted itself and moved to a shooting lodge far away in the Central Highlands of Scotland where there was no electricity, no central heating and no telephone. The shooting lodge was within two miles of a large and well-known prep school that had already been evacuated to Rannoch.

It was in this remote mountainous land of moor and lakes that Selby was not only launched on a first-class education that led on to a scholarship to Marlborough and a place at Cambridge to read modern languages, but was also inducted by his father into those country pursuits and enthusiasms – most of all fishing – that have possessed Selby ever since.

When the war in Europe came to an end, the family was able to return home to Broadstairs, much to his distress. He moved on to the rough and tumble of a house at Marlborough College and then into the Royal Air Force for National Service where he was based at a radar station in East Anglia; and then on to take up his place at Clare College, Cambridge to read modern languages, specifically German and French.

Whilst at Cambridge he fell in love with Scandinavia. He therefore decided to drop French as his second subject after German, and take up a Scandinavian language instead. Finnish would have been his first choice but this turned out not to be an option at Cambridge. So he settled for Swedish instead and during his second long vacation went off alone on a three month tour of Scandinavia and with little but his fishing equipment to keep him company.

After Cambridge it was time to decide what career to go for. Unlike today, the problem then was the wide array of career opportunities available for emerging graduates. After a couple of false starts at interviews, with a nudge from MI6 he put himself in for the diplomatic service exam to see what happened. Not everyone, including himself, might have thought at the time that he was suited for life as a diplomat with all its pretensions, conventions and restrictions. Nor was he at all happy at the thought that a significant part of his life in the Foreign Service would be spent in London. Selby was offered a place and decided to give it a try. A year was spent in a department in the Foreign Office occupying himself with the less than riveting task of defending Britain's territorial claims in Antarctica. He then arrived at the British Embassy in Moscow at the height of the Cold War to take up his first posting abroad.

The job he was to fill was that of Private Secretary to an extremely able, well liked, but very demanding Ambassadorial couple who spoke little if any Russian and had been in Moscow barely a year themselves. This was a daunting challenge to say the least but whatever the difficulties, it offered a brilliant start to a diplomatic career and gave Selby enviably wide opportunities for travel with the Ambassador across the Soviet Union, through Soviet Central Asia and Siberia. To this, during a brief period of détente, Selby contrived to add some challenging private journeys on his own initiative, going off the beaten track into north-west Russia to have a look at his beloved Finland from the Soviet side of the border, and then to the North German and Scandinavian parts of the Soviet Union in Estonia, Latvia and Lithuania where he could already sense and report back to London the growing resistance to Russian dominance and exploitation.

The next ten years took him on typically testing foreign service postings from extreme cold to the tropics, covering two new continents, and three different language groups as well as a three year spell back in London to learn the ropes for policy-making at an intermediate level. Halfway through the decade, Selby met and married Rachel, who was herself from a British colonial service family. Thus reinforced, Selby set out for his third foreign posting at the new capital of Pakistan, Islamabad. But this posting was cut in half because after the first two years Selby's experience of working in a communist regime was needed to fill a slot in Bulgaria where he was to be deputy chief of mission and therefore definitely on the way up.

By the end of two years in Bulgaria, now with two small children, Selby had begun to feel an increasingly strong impulse to put diplomacy behind him and become a teacher. He applied to take a year's sabbatical leave to enable him to put this impulse to the test and see if he could obtain teaching experience before making up his mind. His request was not surprisingly turned down. But his mind was by then made up and he resigned much to the regret of his many friends in the Foreign Service.

I would like to conclude with the observation that he was by no means my only colleague with promising prospects who took the decision to quit in mid-career and move on to another profession or calling. Some moved into politics, some into the home civil service, some into banking, some just to write. However, reading this book has convinced me that few chose a route as challenging, as fulfilling or as rewarding for others as Selby Martin, and we owe him a considerable debt for being willing to share the whole story with us.

Sir Derek Thomas (Foreign Office)

*****

Selby and Rachel Martin have been friends of mine for over forty years; and for exactly twenty of those years he and I were colleagues on the full-time staff of Shrewsbury School. Selby was appointed to Shrewsbury by the great reforming headmaster Donald Wright, one of whose aims was to recruit men who were well established and experienced in another profession, in order to introduce and encourage awareness of a wider dimension. The account of the second half of Selby's career very clearly reveals how faithfully and successfully he has fulfilled that aspiration; and his career as a whole may be seen as a reciprocal movement from the world-wide sphere of diplomacy, first to the much narrower world of one particular school and then out again to the service of the civic community and the preservation of the local environment.

In all his activities, as a teacher of modern languages, as a form master, house tutor and as a senior instructor in the School's outward-bound scheme, Selby has been concerned to introduce that wider dimension, as the following examples indicate. As a language teacher he carefully assessed the merits of the various techniques available and willingly assisted pupils who wished to explore languages not included in the formal time-table; as a form master he took the social dimension into account, by teaching them how to write a gracious and appropriate thank-you letter; as a tutor he taught his charges how to read clearly and intelligently on public occasions. He was a strong advocate of the importance of 'minority time' in the school curriculum, believing that such time spent positively, freed from the constraints of the classroom and the strait-jacket of specialization, provided an opportunity to develop an interest which could bring life-long pleasure and enrichment. He shared his devotion to bee-keeping and to trout-fishing and his interest in freshwater biology with his pupils; he encouraged musical appreciation and he endowed a prize for the most entertaining contribution to the annual inter-house singing competition. His book reveals how his diplomatic training stood him in good stead in negotiations with Welsh farmers and in moderating the heated disputes of competing rowing coaches; and there are many delightful practical tips gleaned from his own personal experience, such as how to deal with aggressive dogs! Selby's love of the countryside, demonstrated in the examples given above, was an important factor in his change of career; and it was matched by his concern for the preservation of the local heritage, seen, in its most powerful expression, in his sterling work for both Shrewsbury Civic Society and the Campaign to Protect Rural England, as recorded in the later chapters of the book.

Although this is primarily a personal story, Selby is careful to place each of its stages in a wider and informative context, both in the fields of diplomacy and of education; and he brought a civilised, dedicated and tenacious approach to all his enterprises in these fields. His account is notable for its honesty both of opinion and of self-assessment, though his colleagues would certainly consider the latter to be far too modest. These admirable qualities, together with the rich variety of experience which they record, combine to produce a fascinating book.

Dr David Gee (Shrewsbury School)

Acknowledgements

I am grateful to friends and colleagues for their help in putting together these memories and accompanying illustrations. There are many of them since experiences recounted in this book range over a wide field.

Wellesley House School and Marlborough College have provided material from their archives and I am particularly indebted to Shirley Tudor-Evans for permission to reproduce extracts from the diary of her mother, Barbara Boyce, who was the headmaster's wife at Rannoch. A Rannoch and Marlborough friend Brian Gotto was most helpful over the description of our wartime experiences. Mike Digby contributed to the section on National Service in the RAF, while Bjørn Sørheim commented on language teaching.

For my years in the Foreign Office, I have been helped by Derek Thomas and John Ure, colleagues in Moscow; Jane Holliday in Bolivia and Alan Burner in Bulgaria; Canon Michael Bourdeaux and Martin Nicholson advised on Soviet matters. I would like to thank the Foreign & Commonwealth Office and the Information Management Department which agreed to certain passages. I was grateful for contact with Alan Shave and Rene Botelho who brought me up to date on fishing in Bolivia, while David Adams, cartographer, has worked hard to produce two maps. Wikipedia has been a valued source for background information.

Numerous Shrewsbury School colleagues have also assisted in compiling the chapters covering the years spent there and after retirement, notably Andrew Allott, Chris Conway, David Gee, Chris Minns, Gilbert Roscoe, Robin Trimby and Mark Twells. My daughter Jessica also advised on teaching matters. Shropshire Museums and Shropshire Newspapers Ltd. gave permission to reproduce photographs.

I am particularly grateful to Derek Thomas and David Gee for writing a joint Foreword, to proof-reader Peter Cartledge and to my son David, himself an author, for his advice on editing content, proof-reading the text and providing invaluable help at all stages in operating the computer. Without his help it is doubtful whether the book would ever have been published.

Introduction

A chance event led to a lifetime's memories being put onto paper. Some years ago my wife Rachel and I had arranged to go to a meeting of the Shropshire branch of the National Association of Decorative and Fine Art Societies. We were about to leave the house when the Programme Secretary telephoned. She had a problem. The lecturer, an art historian from Keele University, had been delayed and would be a few minutes late; would I be prepared to fill the gap until he arrived to take over?

My first reaction was to say 'No'. How could I address the meeting with no time to prepare? However, I had spoken briefly to a meeting of the Shrewsbury Campaign for the Protection of Rural England a few weeks earlier on my time as a diplomat at the British Embassy in Moscow, so I agreed. At the meeting, the chairman introduced me and I began. As the lecturer failed to show up, I had to keep going until, after forty minutes, I had to confess that I had nothing more to say. Such an unconventional appearance at the NADFAS meeting was well received and someone suggested that I should write a book.

I had arrived in Moscow in 1958 on my first posting abroad with the Foreign Office and every week without fail would send a letter home to my parents through the Diplomatic Bag with an account of what I had been doing. My mother kept all these letters, numbered them and stored them away. I continued to write from later postings in La Paz, Rawalpindi and Sofia. Years afterwards I came across them, along with diaries, in suitcases in the attic. I felt I owed it to my mother to make use of them.

Because I left the Foreign Office in 1972 to teach, the memoirs fall into two distinct sections; the first is about life abroad in the embassies, the second covers experiences as a master teaching at Shrewsbury School and involvement in local organisations campaigning to protect the environment. I am fully aware that none of this is exceptional, nor can it compare with the life stories of so many others, particularly those involved in the Armed Forces during the war.

PART 1

Chapter 1

Broadstairs

It is a curious fact that one remembers where one was as momentous news broke. My first such memory reaches back to September 3, 1939, the day that the Second World War broke out. I was playing in the sand on the main beach in Broadstairs when a siren sounded across the bay, announcing the outbreak of war with Germany. I must have been there with my nanny, Minnie, as I was only six at the time; it was Minnie's job to look after me, push me around in a pram and later in a push-chair while my parents got on with their work. The outbreak of war determined the direction of my life from then on.

I had been born at home in Broadstairs, the youngest of three sons. At the age of six one accepts the circumstances of one's family as normal and at the time I would have had no idea at all just how privileged was the background which surrounded me, least of all the rigid conventions of the time.

My father, Archibald William Martin, ran a building business in Ramsgate, along with my uncle Charles. The firm had been founded by my grandfather William Woodgate Martin in 1877. He had begun as an apprentice carpenter in High Halden at the age of fourteen and as the years went by expanded his skills to become a builder. He had arrived in Ramsgate from Cobb's Wood near Tenterden on the advice of his doctor who claimed that the sea air would help him with the asthma from which he suffered. He might in a sense have been coming home for legend has it that the family is descended from a Huguenot exile from France who had come to Ramsgate to escape persecution after the revocation of the Edict of Nantes in 1685. This edict had provided freedom of religion in France but its revocation had led to the oppression of Protestant minorities. Our ancestor is thought to have become harbour master of the port of Ramsgate, which at that time handled a large volume of trade with the continent. On my grandfather's death in 1934, the firm was taken over by his two sons, Charles and my father, Archibald. The business continued to flourish, employing around one hundred staff.

Our mother, Magdalene Ranger, was from a very different background, also from West Kent. She had married Frank Haslam but the marriage ended in double tragedy when her husband died of tuberculosis and she lost their baby in an accident; a pan of boiling water fell over the baby girl and she died. Mother decided to stay in Broadstairs with her brother, Edgar Ranger, who designed a house for her in the Arts and Crafts style which was then fashionable. The contract for its construction was awarded to W. W. Martin & Son of Ramsgate. This was how our parents met and they were married on February 27, 1924. The house was named 'Little Chart' after the village where she had previously lived.

This was an area of Kent which was rapidly being developed by incomers as well as by local families. There were several reasons for this. The climate was considered healthy and the railway line along the north coast of Kent brought it to within commuting distance of London involving a two hour journey. There were seven boys' preparatory schools in Broadstairs, a concentration which encouraged inter-school sports as many were in walking distance of each other. The popularity of the cliff-top area between the town and North Foreland led to the construction of many luxurious houses, some even with tunnels leading down to the beach. Beyond the lighthouse were open fields, a golf course and Joss Bay, with its row of bathing huts, some modest, like ours, others more pretentious. Beyond that stood the imposing Kingsgate Castle, which was not at all ancient, having been built in the eighteenth century and so named because King Charles II had landed here in 1683.

Because of the area's reputation for good health, it also became a home for the less privileged. There were three large orphanages in the immediate vicinity of our house, including one run by Barnardo's, and we would see crocodiles of small children being taken for walks along the esplanade. It never occurred to us boys to question where they had come from or why they were there, still less what happened to them when they grew up. My parents were no doubt aware that many were the offspring of London prostitutes; certainly they were happy to hand on surplus fruit and vegetables to these homes, particularly the Wainwright, which was almost next door.

It was at 'Little Chart' that my eldest brother, David, was born in 1928. Clearly the house was too small for a growing family served by resident domestic staff and again Uncle Teddy was commissioned to design a larger house on a plot of over an acre in extent, for which my parents paid £2000. As with Little Chart, it was in the Arts and Crafts style, featuring

2

wooden beams externally and internally, with diamond leaded windows. My other brother John and I were both born here. Downstairs we had a large drawing room, a dining room and kitchen. An integral double garage was reached through a cloakroom, with W.C. The telephone was on a shelf beside the basin; one had to wind a handle vigorously to attract the attention of the telephonist, while power for the instrument came from two large Leclanché cells in a cupboard below the sink.

On the first floor were three bedrooms: our parents' with a dressing room leading off it, which doubled up as a bedroom for myself, a spare room for guests, a children's room and a nursery. There was just the one bathroom with WC, although the nursery had a small bathroom attached to it, but no WC. The nursery later become a cosy sitting room. On the second floor was an attic with two bedrooms for resident staff, for a cook cum housekeeper as well as a nanny. The house was named Barnjet.

There was no central heating. A coal and log fire in the drawing room and a gas fire in the dining room kept us warm; there was also a fireplace in the nursery. A coal-fired boiler in the kitchen supplied hot water but this was lit only once or twice a week on bath-night. Beside the back door, on one side was a lavatory for the cook, on the other two large bunkers, one for coal and one for coke. Beyond these was a roomy larder. There was no refrigerator until later, nor of course, any other equipment such as a washing machine. Clothes were washed in a large pan and put through a mangle before going out to dry on the line.

The gardens were extensive. My father was a passionate gardener and much of the garden was planted out with apple trees of several varieties and two walnut trees; these yielded a goodly quantity of nuts in the autumn but also formed a strong visual feature in the centre of the orchard. The apple trees also cropped well; indeed, far more than we could possibly eat. Certain varieties were kept in an apple store which also housed two bee hives for my father kept bees. Beside it was a pond with a cascade of water running down through a rockery and a sitting out area where we drank early-morning tea on fine summer mornings.

Bordering the drive was an expanse of flower beds on which our mother spent much time and energy. The results were impressive; passers-by in the road would stop at the entrance to look in and admire the wealth of colour. Further down were the vegetable beds and greenhouses, for cucumbers, grapes and tomatoes, each offering a different environment. We also had a tennis court bordered by a row of tall cherry trees; they produced lots of cherries but we seldom gathered any, for the birds got there first and in any case, most of the cherries were high up out of reach. To the north, the site was bounded by a tall brick wall, separating the garden from Stone Gap, a path which led down through a cleft in the chalk cliffs to the beach. A gate in it gave us access to the path and we would occasionally use it to go for a quick swim. My father would also go that way to fetch up sea weed to spread onto the asparagus bed in the autumn. The corner at the top between the path and Stone Road was a favourite spot for an ice-cream seller to park his tricycle to offer refreshment to those who had climbed up from the beach on a hot afternoon. Needless to say he also refreshed me when I could get hold of the odd sixpence to pass over the fence.

Running such an establishment must have been very demanding and called for a number of servants and gardeners. The position of resident cook/housekeeper appeared difficult to fill to my parents' satisfaction. My nanny Minnie kept a diary, one entry in which was a sketch showing a procession of applicants coming and going for interview. It was about 1936 that my mother received a visit from a north-country girl, Lilian Dickens, who had been driven from home by an oppressive step-father and had come south in search of employment and a home. She turned out to be a loyal and hard-working housekeeper, to remain with us, during the war in Scotland and after. She was also a superb cook.

This was an ideal and stable environment for us three boys in which to grow up. It was not to last however as the area between North Foreland and Sandwich could well be chosen as a bridgehead for a German invasion. All was to change; the population needed to move out, not least the schools. Meanwhile it was prudent to send me away for security reasons and it was decided that I should accompany my two brothers, David and John, to their preparatory school, Temple Grove, in Sussex. Although there were six or seven good schools in Broadstairs my parents had a very high regard for the Temple Grove headmaster, Mr Batchelor, and had decided to send my brothers there. It made sense for me to go there too, although I was only six and up to that time had had no school experience apart from attending a pre-prep day school in Margate.

Temple Grove was a large stone building at the end of a long drive, with extensive grounds which included a wood and three lakes. It was probably here that my interest in nature and wildlife began, for we often played round them; certainly the smell of rotting vegetation even now reminds me of those lakes and my brief spell at the school.

This was my first experience of boarding and I did not settle in well. Both David and John were in their last years there and enjoying positions of trust and responsibility. Perhaps this led me to think that I could do as I liked and I was soon in trouble for playing with fire extinguishers. I was also caught smuggling wild strawberries, decorated with some

4

kind of make-believe garnish, up to the dormitory; these were hidden in my Wellington boots, which along with our gas-masks we had to take up with us. I was not caned for these offences but I do remember frequently having to stand in the corridor outside Mr Batchelor's study for reprimands. I even remember the lay-out in the study – the magisterial desk on the right, with a big bookcase behind and the bay window beyond.

Due to the threat of German air raids, we had the occasional practice air-raid alert. There was at least one practice at night, when we had to put on our Wellingtons and carrying our gas-masks we assembled on the lawn outside in the moonlight, no doubt to be counted and checked before returning to our beds.

I left the school after only one year, not for reasons of misconduct but because we had to leave Broadstairs as the threat of invasion became more likely.

Chapter 2

War Years in Scotland

One of the several Broadstairs schools to be evacuated was Wellesley House. The headmaster, John Boyce, was a friend of the Cobbold family, wealthy East Anglian brewers whose boys attended the school. Not long before the war the Cobbolds had bought the Rannoch estate in Scotland from the Menzies and were able to offer its lodges to the school for the duration of the war.

Rannoch is a remote part of Perthshire with rich landscape features and a turbulent history. At its eastern end is Loch Rannoch, ten miles long and bordered on its southern shore by the remnants of the ancient Caledonian Forest, recognised as a World Heritage site and overlooked by the impressive peak of Schiehallion. From the village of Kinloch Rannoch at its eastern end, roads run along both shores of the loch before joining at Bridge of Gaur and climbing six miles up to the Moor of Rannoch and its station on the West Highland railway. Since the road ends there, traffic is comparatively light and the road remains much the same now as it was in the 1940s. A footpath continues down the shore of Loch Laidon to Glencoe. Apart from the construction of holiday chalets in the grounds of the Loch Rannoch Hotel in Kinloch Rannoch and a hydro-electric station on the river Gaur, there has been little development to despoil its magnificent scenery.

Perhaps because of its remoteness, Rannoch was a refuge for those wishing to escape the attentions of authority for whatever reason and for centuries different clans were in conflict. Christianity arrived in the 5th and 6th centuries with missionaries from Iona setting up cells. Among these was St Chad who had many cells in different parts but came to Rannoch once a year to help the people scraping a living from the soil and later became Bishop of Lichfield. A. D. Cunningham in his comprehensive *History of Rannoch* gives a detailed account of the area and of the decline in the population over the last two hundred years. In 1755 there had been 2,500 inhabitants living in thirty-five villages, whereas in 1984 there were only 400 residents and three villages. There are many reasons for this, variously changes in agriculture, the economy, highland clearances and the establishment of sporting estates in Victorian times. Despite, or perhaps because of this decline, Rannoch is now a vibrant and hard-working community serving an increasing number of tourists.

The Rannoch estate covered a large area at the western end of Loch Rannoch, extending up towards the Moor of Rannoch. It included three shooting lodges round the shores of the loch, the largest being Rannoch Lodge at the head near where the river Gaur flowed in. About two miles from Rannoch Lodge and higher up the river was a fourth lodge, Dunan. When the school moved in September 1939, it was intended that Dunan should be used to house members of staff. It was not long before this idea was dropped for two good reasons – it had no electricity nor telephone, an unreliable water supply, and its distance from Rannoch Lodge made teaching and supervision at the school impractical for staff living there.

It so happened that the headmaster, John Boyce, knew my father well since the latter had carried out various building and decorating jobs for the school over several years. He was pleased to offer him the lease of Dunan for our family to live in for the duration of the war. It was an arrangement that fitted in well with our needs; David and John would go to the Leys School, Cambridge, which had been evacuated to the Atholl Palace Hotel in Pitlochry. I had been sent to Temple Grove in Sussex in September 1939 and would transfer to Wellesley House at Rannoch. This school had been founded in 1866 in Ramsgate and in 1898 moved to its present location in Broadstairs. The school was typical of many such established in the town and elsewhere when the benefits of living in the countryside or by the sea, rather than in London smog, became almost a matter of fashion. It was privately owned and in the 1930s run by two partners, Shirley Russell and John Boyce who had joined the staff in 1928. The school aimed to achieve the highest standards in academic studies as well as in sport and education in general; many boys went on to leading independent boarding schools such as Eton, Harrow and Winchester. Discipline was firm, but not excessively so.

Dunan was a sporting lodge of characteristic Scottish style and lay-out, well suited for the fisherman, shooter or deer stalker. It stood on high ground above the river Gaur, looking east over pasture land and behind it lay a fir-tree plantation sheltering it from the prevailing wind and rain. Behind the house were two keeper's cottages and a garage, the whole set back from the road that led from Bridge of Gaur to Rannoch station, high up on the Moor of Rannoch.

Accommodation comprised a dining room and sitting room each side of the front porch, a kitchen with two doors, one opening onto the corridor to the dining room, the other to the pantry, store room and the back door. In the same area was a large room, looking out to the front; this became a playroom for us children and alongside was a smaller room, my father's workshop where he practised carpentry, including the construction of boats and a bridge with gate over the ha-ha between the house and the field in front. Upstairs there were four bedrooms and a lavatory. At some date an extension had been added at one side to provide a bathroom off the stairway landing and below a further lavatory and cloakroom.

While the accommodation suited our family perfectly, the standard of services did not. The lack of electricity meant that we had to rely on paraffin lamps for all lighting. With the house came two Aladdins, impressive lamps with a tall glass chimney and a circular wick; the flame from this heated a mantle which gave out a bright light, quite up to the standard of a 100 watt bulb. But there were problems. With these lamps the wick has to be adjusted to the exact height for the flame to light up the mantle, too low and there was little light, too high and the mantle became encrusted with soot, which spread also to the glass chimney. The flame would increase in height as it warmed up and you could not leave the lamp to look after itself. If the lamp smoked, it took time for the soot on the mantle to burn off, once the wick had been turned down. Also, mantles were brittle; they broke easily and had to be replaced. Despite all this, the lamps gave out plenty of light and imparted a sense of cosiness as we sat round the fire on a cold and stormy night.

The rest of the house was lit by simple paraffin lamps, less bright but adequate, and positioned where needed. One was left in the passage outside my bedroom next to my parents' room since I was afraid of the dark. These lamps too made for a lot of work; if the wick was not lowered within a few minutes of being lit, the lamp began to smoke and the glass chimney would have to be scrubbed clean the next morning.

Similar difficulties arose with the paraffin cooker on which our mother prepared the meals. There were three burners in a row, fed from a single fuel tank. On one occasion, our mother had put on the lunch to simmer while we all went off to the river to fish. On our return some time later, we discovered that one of the burners had been too high; it was not just a matter of a sooty chimney – the entire kitchen was filled with smoke and every inch of the walls and ceiling was blackened with soot.

Water came from a tank on the hillside above the house, fed by a small stream. The water was clean but from time to time long thin worms would come out of the taps, as they bred in the tank and got drawn down into the house. We tried putting a trout in there in the hope that it would eat up the worms but that did not work. In winter the pipe down to the house froze and my father had to draw water from the river in a bucket, breaking the ice to get at it. On one occasion the hole had frozen over and was covered with a layer of snow; he fell in but fortunately the water was quite shallow.

Running the household imposed much stress on our parents, although, as far as I can remember, they never lost their tempers, still less vented their frustration on us boys. At some stage Lilian, our housekeeper from Broadstairs, came to us after working for a while in a munitions factory and this was a great help. Without electricity there was of course no fridge but during the war, supplies of perishable food were in any case very limited. There were two grocers in Kinloch Rannoch, both of whom had mobile shops delivering once a week. Their vans would stop in the road outside and my mother would go out to obtain whatever was on offer within the limits of the ration cards. Yet we were not too dependent on the grocery vans. Milk was delivered daily by Donald who ran a bus service from Kinloch Rannoch up to Rannoch Station. The milk arrived in metal churns and the cream was skimmed off to be turned into butter; to start with it was shaken by hand in a Kilner jar, later in a contraption designed and built by my father which required no more than turning a handle.

A butcher from Aberfeldy delivered meat once a week and with his supplies coming from local farmers, one suspects that the rationing system was applied flexibly. The same van served the school and I would await its arrival to beg for feathers from pheasant, woodcock and grouse which I needed for tying flies. My father was a good shot and there was plenty of game to be had, especially rabbits but also grouse and woodcock. On one occasion he incited my sorrow, even anger, by shooting a snipe which seemed to me so small and pitiful a bird – although, as he told me later, I had no scruple in eating it.

We kept chickens and for most of the year had our own eggs. At times of abundance they were put down in buckets of a preservative called isinglass and as a last resort my mother would use powdered egg. The chickens were also pets and I cannot recall how we resolved the conflict between our affection for them and the opportunity for a tasty meal. A further source of food, at least in summer, was fish from local rivers and loch, which were rich in trout and the occasional pike and perch which could be caught when trout were out of season.

This was after all a sporting estate. In 1913 when the Camuserricht Farm and Dunan were put on the market, the Game bags for that year were 2,295 grouse, 35 Black Game, 50 Ptarmigan, 25 stags and various other creatures. By 1940 there was less game around but two keepers were employed to manage the estate and control predators. One of them, Alastair Dow, had gone off to join the army, but the second, Crockett, was past call-up age and still did his best to maintain the estate and its game. Opposite the house and in full view of the road was his gibbet, a large board to which he nailed the corpses of predators he had managed to despatch, either shooting them or by means of spring-loaded traps. I was fascinated by the evil-smelling collection which included foxes, wild cats, stoats, weasels and the odd crow. It never occurred to me at the time nor to many others that these creatures, some now very rare, should not be hunted down almost to extinction to protect a part of local wildlife for shooting to gratify man's lust for sport.

Of wildlife there was an abundance. Capercaillie nested in the wood on the way to Bridge of Gaur and my mother when cycling past was alarmed by their screeching call. It was reported that Archie the road man had been attacked and had to beat the bird off with his shovel.

The river Gaur, which flowed past Dunan into Loch Rannoch and out as the river Tummel, was a major feature in our lives. The river offered a wide variety of habitats beginning at Loch Laidon on Rannoch Moor, it dropped gently through a succession of large rocky pools for a mile to Loch Eigheach. These pools held very large ferox trout which could be caught on spinners, particularly in the early season. Ferox trout inhabit many Scottish lochs, feeding on small trout or char; the ones caught in the viaduct pools near the railway bridge would have dropped down in the autumn to spawn in the rapids and probably swam back to the loch in the following summer for they could not have found enough feeding in the river to maintain their unusual size.

Loch Eigheach was in two main parts, joined by a deep and rather sluggish channel flowing between steep banks and in places quite weedy. This too was a venue for large ferox trout of between four and twenty pounds in contrast to the usual fish six inches or so in length. They were extremely difficult to catch and would only take a fly in stormy weather. For my mathematics teacher at Wellesley House, Frank Fraser, this was his favourite spot; he was often to be seen there, fishing in a gale force wind and driving rain, having cycled five miles from school to get there. He was a skilful and experienced angler and used salmon flies to good effect, catching several trout up to nine pounds in weight. My father, albeit less experienced, was also successful, catching a fish of 6 lbs 4oz. This was on a worm fly to which had been attached a Blue Zulu, his favourite for normal fishing in the loch. It took a long time to land – just as well, for he had not taken a landing net with him and one of us had to dash back to Dunan by bicycle to fetch it.

Most of our trout fishing was on the lower loch, which held numbers of quite small fish. It was difficult to fish from the bank because of weeds and rushes, so my father built a punt large enough to carry two or three people. It was square at both ends and consisted of a sturdy wooden frame and solid floor, the whole covered in thick canvas. To make it waterproof, he applied linseed oil and two coats of grey paint. In the middle was a large wooden drum holding a hundred yards of rope. The anchor was dropped at the top of a drift and the rope was let out when needed to ensure that the water was fished thoroughly: even the angle of the boat to the wind could be adjusted by fixing the rope into whichever one of several slots on the gunwale provided the best position. The boat was propelled with simple wooden paddles, also painted grey.

The lower part of Loch Eigheach flowed out through just one pool to the top of the Rannoch Falls. These were spectacular, especially in a spate when the water thundered over them. Salmon could only jump them at certain water levels and were a wonderful sight which we enjoyed as we pushed our bikes up the steep hill alongside. Sometimes we approached the pool below the falls with awe trying to lure them with a bunch of worms but we never had a bite.

A short way downstream the river was joined by a small burn crossed by a red iron bridge and below that was a long gravel reach where salmon spawned. We knew that because from time to time we would find a dead salmon, with a chunk bitten out of it by an otter. Then came a holding pool, Collie's Pool, which offered the best chance of a salmon. In August 1944 my brother John caught one on a prawn weighing 6lbs 10oz; it took half an hour to land.

After further rocky pools the river meandered slowly through flat pastures in front of Dunan. This environment was well suited to pike and perch, although there were also some good trout which we caught on night-lines baited with bits of pike. Below this and a few more pools was a stretch of gravel and small stones with a population of freshwater mussels. From time to time it would be visited by a family of gypsies who collected the mussels in the hope of finding pearls in them. To locate the mussels in the rapidly flowing water, they used upturned buckets from which the bottom had been removed; when held close to the surface, it was possible to see the riverbed without the interference of reflections.

Below a large pool by the Bridge of Gaur, the river flowed into Loch Rannoch, a stretch much visited by us boys at Rannoch Lodge. An effective method was to stand under the bridge and let out a line baited with a worm and a cork to indicate a bite. Where the river finally entered the loch there was slack water holding large numbers of pike. We fished for these so successfully that we were able to send a sackful by train to a fishmonger in Glasgow; there was a demand for pike among refugees from Eastern Europe. An unusually large specimen, weighing around 12lbs was caught in a trap by a teacher at Rannoch Lodge; it was served up for tea and was much enjoyed by us all.

There were good reasons for the pike to congregate in this area. In the first place, salmon smolts from the spawning grounds upstream would drop down on their way to the sea and offer the pike an easy meal. Only later did I learn on a visit to the Faskally Fish Research Centre at Pitlochry about the char in Loch Rannoch. There are in fact two distinct species of char. They live and feed at great depth, which accounts for the fact that we never knew of their existence, let alone caught one. In October, they migrate up the river Gaur at night to spawn, returning at once to the loch. The eggs hatch out in the river and the baby char soon drop down to the deep waters of the loch. Another opportunity for the pike to feed.

There were other distractions in summer. We played a kind of golf using hockey sticks owing to the lack of golf clubs and we played table-tennis. David and John built model aircraft and I may have joined in in some way. The ping-pong table in the playroom was converted into a runway, with the net removed, the elastically-driven plane would take off and with luck fly out through the open sash window. We knocked up with a tennis racket against the garage wall and we sawed up logs to keep us warm in the winter holidays; there was little coal.

I cannot recall much about how we passed the time in the long winter evenings. We did not have a library and I don't think we read much, if at all. Nor did we listen to the wireless except for news bulletins and Churchill's speeches. There was no television or other distraction, yet I do not remember being bored. But holidays were relatively short and at school we were always kept busy.

How we managed to celebrate Christmas I do not know. Shopping for presents was impossible; our parents sometimes returned to Broadstairs in term-time because my father was running his business as well as he could, and doubtless they brought things back with them. I do not believe we ever reached a church to celebrate Christmas, despite the church at Bridge of Gaur being within easy cycling distance. Mother was an Anglican and may have had reservations about taking us to the local Scottish church. However, we were brought up as Christians and generally on Sundays we would gather in the sitting room to read the service of Holy Communion, although of course there were no sacraments, with each of us taking a part. Mine was to read the Lord's Prayer kneeling at a leather armchair.

One curious memory remains with me. Twice on New Year's Eve as we sat round the fire in the sitting room, we distinctly heard the sound of bagpipes from the chimney. Rushing outside to see who was playing, we found nothing but darkness and the stillness of the night and our nearest neighbours were two miles away at Bridge of Gaur.

Another strange story was told to us by the keeper Crockett, who was too old to be called up for military service. When the West Highland Railway was being planned, a ball of fire was seen one night sweeping across Rannoch Moor on the line which the railway eventually followed. Crockett was approaching eighty when he told us this. The railway was built in 1889, so he could have been alive at the time and related what he had seen or had been told by a contemporary eye-witness rather than repeating a local legend.

In 1950 my parents rented Dunan for a month. By then electricity had been introduced and we enjoyed once again the delights of fishing the Gaur and several hill lochs in the area. My next visit was in 1992 when I arranged a reunion of former pupils at Wellesley House during the war. By then the river had been transformed. Scottish Hydro had built a dam across the bottom end of Loch Eigheach and diverted the water through a pipe to a hydro-electric plant beside Collie's Pool. The effect was disastrous. The water level in Loch Eigheach had risen by several feet; the two separate parts and the adjoining Dairy Pool had become a wide and featureless expanse of water. The narrow channel between the two parts – the home of large trout – and the marshy ground were all lost. The falls, once so dramatic, are now no more than a trickle. Collie's pool is dominated by the outflow from the power station on its further bank and no longer exists as we had known it. The gravelly levels above Collie's Pool are silted up and it is inconceivable that salmon would still be spawning there. Even the Red Bridge burn has been diverted into Loch Eigheach to increase flow to the power station.

It was not just the damage to the loch, the river and the surrounding landscape that so upset me. The power station is not run on a continuous flow of water to generate a steady current as one might expect. Rather it is used intermittently to meet peak demand: at some times, there is virtually no water in the river, at others it appears to be in full flood. The impact on the general ecology of the river must be very great; it is no longer a natural habitat and as a fishing venue it is virtually ruined. It is hard to imagine a greater violation of the environment than the abuse which has been inflicted on a beautiful area of the Scottish countryside. Moreover, it is dangerous. Anyone wading in the river downstream would have no warning of a sudden surge in the flow of water. Not long before our visit, a boy paddling in the river above Bridge of Gaur had been swept away and drowned. The owner of Dunan had asked for a bell or siren to be installed to give warning of a sudden flood but received no reply to his request. At the time of the power station's installation, there was none of the present-day pressure for renewable energy and the need to mitigate the effects of global warming and climate change. It was purely a question of commercial profit.

*****

Wellesley House had moved to Rannoch in September 1939, very soon after the outbreak of war. A special train was hired from the railway company and took the necessary furniture; desks, chairs, beds and all the paraphernalia needed by the school, along with the boys and staff, to Rannoch station. From here it was taken by truck and bus to the several lodges around Loch Rannoch. The school's arrival is recorded in a postcard sent by the headmaster's wife, Barbara Boyce, to her aunt in Broadstairs: 'The chickens and dogs travelled well – boys well-behaved.' Not all the lodges were ready and some of the party had to stay at the Loch Rannoch hotel in Kinloch Rannoch for a couple of weeks.

Rannoch Lodge is an imposing granite building in a commanding situation at the head of the loch with magnificent views eastwards towards the triangular peak of Schiehallion. Two reception rooms on the ground floor were turned into classrooms, and another into a dining hall. Upstairs were bedrooms converted into dormitories and staff accommodation. The kitchens, larder and storerooms were in the basement.

A mile down the north side of the loch was another lodge, Camusericht, with five or six bedrooms; the house was used by the school solely as dormitory accommodation, with boys being sent by bus back and forth for lessons and other activities. Two miles further on was Talladh-a-Bheith, a lodge of similar design with an extensive walled garden and grounds. This became the senior school for the top two years, run by Billy Williamson. On the opposite side of the loch was a fourth lodge, Finnart, rented from the Dall estate. This was the junior school, where I went in September 1940. There was a long shingle spit stretching out into the loch where I first began fly-fishing; so clear is my memory of it that I recall the three flies I first used – Blue Zulu, Cinnamon & Gold and Peter Ross.

Splitting up the school into three separate parts was necessary in order to accommodate some seventy boys and staff. Whether this was a good thing from an educational point of view is debatable. I think it was. Each house had its own particular syllabus, style and organisation. The academic pressures and discipline in the senior house were quite distinct from the requirements in the junior house, and this arrangement did not prevent the whole school or, if appropriate, just the senior two houses from getting together for special occasions. Administratively it must have been a nightmare.

It is probably the final two years at Talladh-a-Bheith which left the strongest impression on us. We studied hard and Latin seemed to dominate our lives. The day began with a lesson before breakfast when the gender rhymes from the back of Kennedy's Shorter Latin Primer or irregular verbs and paradigms were learnt by heart. The gender rhymes were sung at lights-out time to melodies from Gilbert and Sullivan when Billy Williamson came round the dormitories. Looking back, it is strange to reflect that so much effort should have been dedicated to learning, for example:

'Many nouns in - is we find
To the masculine assigned;

amnis	*current*
axis	*axle*
caulis	*cabbage*
collis	*hill*
clunis	*haunch, buttock*
crinis	*hair'*

And so on. Was this recondite learning of Latin words a waste of time? I don't think so. We learnt to learn and enjoyed it.

This is not to say that other subjects were neglected – far from it. I recall that our mathematics teacher Frank Fraser taught us to calculate the height of Schiehallion by using trigonometry, the height 'x' over the distance 'y' (taken off a map) in relation to the 'Tan' of the angle of elevation taken with a protractor. It is curious that the Astronomer Royal, Nevil Maskelyne, had used Schiehallion in the 18th century in an experiment to measure the density of the earth, something of which we were not aware at the time. Other subjects were taught by a variety of people; how they came to be at Rannoch is hard to say – it cannot have been easy to recruit assistant masters in wartime and it is a noteworthy achievement that all subjects were covered throughout the school for the whole of the war years, and to the highest standard. Billy Williamson was an outstanding teacher and many boys won scholarships to leading public schools.

At the end of the summer term in 1943, my parents were asked to decide during the holidays what subject I should take in an additional class; there were three options – Advanced Mathematics, German or Greek. I cannot remember whether I was consulted on this, but my parents decided it should be Advanced Mathematics.

As the first leaves on the birches were beginning to turn yellow, my trunk and tuck-box were loaded into the car and we drove off to Talladh-a Bheith, some six miles away on the north shore of Loch Rannoch, the senior of the three parts of the school then evacuated to Rannoch. The headmaster, Billy Williamson, was there to welcome us:

> *'We would like Selby to take Advanced Maths,' said my father.*
> *'I'm sorry,' replied the headmaster, 'the boys on the train from London have already arrived and the Maths class is full. He'll have to do either German or Greek.'*
> *'Since we're at war with Germany,' said my father, 'he'd better do German.'*

Once or twice in one's life a small incident occurs which, although insignificant at the time, is seen in later years to have had far-reaching consequences. This was certainly the case in this instance. Had I got back to school an hour or so earlier, I would have taken Advanced Mathematics and would certainly have followed a very different career.

While the standard of academic teaching was outstanding, it was much more difficult for the school to provide a range of sports simply because there were no playing fields apart from one at an Army base near the Ericht power station and a field at Rannoch Lodge. So far as I can remember, we played only one away soccer match, against a school which had been evacuated to Blair Atholl Palace near Pitlochry. A sports day was held at Rannoch Lodge each summer, in effect a fête to which local children and their parents were invited. This was also a fund-raising event with a national theme: 'Wings for Victory' or 'Salute the Soldier', with donations attributable to specific items – so many shillings for a hand grenade, up to £8 million for a battleship. Deficiencies in the provision of formal sports were made up for by Physical Exercise, wide games on the hills behind and military drill. We were also taken on walks along the road. At any time a blast on a whistle would send us scurrying into the bracken to hide as if the Germans had invaded and were about to attack us. We never saw an aeroplane but were constantly reminded of the war as news came through. Across the loch there was a training camp for Norwegian and Canadian soldiers who would occasionally stride past on training exercises. We did however contribute to the war effort by picking potatoes and gathering sphagnum moss which was to be used to make dressings for treating wounded soldiers.

Less formally we were left to our own devices. We all had bicycles and in the absence of traffic could ride up and down the loch side. Fishing was popular at Bridge of Gaur, within walking distance of Rannoch Lodge and in the loch itself from Talladh-a-Bheith. For me this became a lifelong hobby and I learned to tie my own flies; indeed I supplied flies to Fosters, a fishing-tackle firm in Derbyshire, earning 2/6 (13 pence) for a dozen. It doesn't sound much now but it all helped and most importantly I enjoyed doing it in winter during the close fishing season. We also had occasional lectures by visiting speakers many of whom were distinguished in their respective fields.

School life at Rannoch was not as idyllic as nostalgic memories might suggest. We had to work hard to stand a chance of winning a scholarship or passing Common Entrance. There were also the pressures and conflicts of growing up, the suffering of being teased, rivalries and jealousies, homesickness and unhappiness. At least one boy ran away from Rannoch Lodge; he was recaptured in the Rannoch station toilet six miles away, whither he had walked in an attempt to take the train home. My reports indicated some academic ability but also shortcomings. I was spending too much time fishing, and not enough reading; I was very untidy and at times badly behaved. The worst comment was probably that in another boy's report, which pointed out that he was well-behaved 'except when under Martin's influence.'

Despite such unhappy moments, we had a wonderful time even if the facilities available could not stand comparison with those on offer nowadays. We did not appreciate at the time just how difficult it must have been to run the school in so isolated a location. Engaging teaching and domestic staff, laying on meals when food was rationed, health care, organising activities, all presented huge problems for the headmaster, John Boyce, and his wife Barbara. Many years later, as a result of organising a reunion dinner, I met the Boyces' daughter Shirley, who showed me a diary which her mother had kept from 1942. I am grateful for her permission to include some extracts which illustrate how things were for them rather than for us:

17

February 2, 1942

'Rather an odd day to start a diary perhaps, but after all I suppose one day is as good as another and the beginning of a term as good as the beginning of a year. The Lent term is now 4 days old – seems more like four weeks. Heavy snow. A busy morning writing letters to parents so that they could go with the boys' letters. Six of them in bed today with sickness and diarrhoea. Seems to be going about the neighbourhood so can't be the food, a good many now recovering and appetites returning thank goodness. Suppose I should be thankful when they don't eat so much, but find I worry far more when they ask for small helpings.

'Water none too hot for boys' baths this evening. Had to fetch kettles from the kitchen and even then had to give our Viscount a choice of cold and clean bath or hot and dirty left over from the last boy. He chose hot and dirty! If only Mrs Waller did not think she could manage the hot water and take it as a personal insult if we suggest anybody else stoking it, we might get some hot water.'

February 3,

'A knock on the door at 3a.m. 'Please sir, Stewart mi [minor] has been sick.' John [Barbara's husband] went to investigate while I lay in my warm bed feeling horribly guilty and fervently hoping that no changing of bed clothes would be necessary. Luckily for me he returned shortly and said all was well. Knew we were in for some bad news this morning when matron announced that she wishes to speak to us both directly after breakfast. Stewart mi has measles – damn!

'Heavy fall of snow in the night, no chance of getting Mrs Blond to the station for the morning train........Stewart feeling rather sorry for himself this evening and Matron is sitting up with him tonight. Offered to do half the night, and was very relieved when she refused the offer. Have a nurse coming tomorrow thank goodness.'

February 8,

'Soap rationing announced on the wireless tonight which should please the boys! It also suits me as instead of going into every Woolworths and pleading to buy more than one tablet, to say nothing of writing to various suppliers every week, I shall now get a monthly permit which will mean far less work.'

February 25,

'Colonel Radford called in this evening with a week's growth of beard.

He is camping out with a mule battery on the road up to Ericht.'

February 26,

'*Boys had a marvellous morning being shown over Colonel Radford's Mounted Regiment, 400 mules, 50 horses and 1300 men. They saw guns being fired and were taken all round the camp, which then packed up and went off to lake Ericht. A casualty, Major A, who fell 200 feet off Ben Alder two days ago and cut his head and arm came in to telephone and after almost blistering the mouthpiece – thank goodness the boys were out of earshot! - had his cuts dressed by Matron.'*

I have no memory of military incident at Rannoch but as the following entry in Barbara Boyce's diary shows, it could happen and when it did the relevant authorities were quick to turn out:

March 2,

'*Just when we were frantically writing the last few letters to catch the post this afternoon Miss Ewen came in and told John that a man wished to see him, to which John replied it was quite impossible till after the mail had gone. Miss Ewen continued to bleat pathetically that she thought it might be important and something about an unidentified aeroplane which had crashed in flames until at last John took the written message and suddenly leaped up and said: 'By Jove you're right, it is important.' Within 10 minutes he had successfully informed Dundee Air Observer Corps and had unsuccessfully tried to inform the Black Watch and Home Guard. He then jumped into the lorry which had brought the man down from the station – their telephone being out of order. Tommy and I followed in Tommy's car. We arrived at the station to find the Home Guard there all dressed up and armed to the teeth, headed by Mr – I beg his pardon – Sergeant Young, looking ten years younger and obviously hoping to arrest Hitler. The aeroplane was seen on fire about seven miles from the station by a shepherd on the other side of Loch Laidon about 11a.m. Through a telescope a man had been seen walking about by it, but had since disappeared. John set out with the search party and I decided to walk home, leaving Tommy at the station to bring John back in the car. [The distance from the station is six miles] On my way back I was passed by various officials of the Home Guard including the doctor, a detachment of the Black Watch, and Hughes, the policeman from Kinloch Rannoch, who all whizzed past in their cars, the light of battle gleaming in their eyes! Part of the Black Watch had been in such a hurry that they collided with the Canadians' ten ton truck, fortunately without casualties on either side. John and Tommy returned about 8p.m. The search party had walked about fourteen miles and found the aeroplane, but no sign of the airman. By that time it was known that the aeroplane was an Oxford Training plane – a great blow to everybody. Just as we were going to bed about 10.30 Lieutenant Marr phoned and said that the airman had still not been found, but that his tracks had been followed going in a circle and the Home Guard would be required to make another search at dawn, so John and I had to go out and rouse McMartin and MacPhee [gamekeepers], who of course were all sound asleep and warn them to be ready to catch Balfour Beatty's lorry at 6.30a.m.'*

March 3,

'The indefatigable Marr phoned at 6a.m. to say that Hughes had tracked the pilot to within one and a half miles of King's House. He burbled on for about a quarter of an hour about nothing at all, much to my wrath as I was quite certain that by this time somebody must have found the man and I dislike being roused by the telephone at that hour of the morning. Later in the day of course it was discovered that the man had been picked up at Bridge of Orchy having spent the night in a shepherd's house. Rather a blow for the unfortunate Hughes who had tracked him almost to Glencoe! However it gave everybody a little excitement including Mrs Young who had 'come all over queer inside' and been unable to cook the dinner.'

March 5,

'Was ordered to rise this morning so that the boys on our wing who were coming out of quarantine today could come into my room to dress after their disinfectant baths. Got eight more downstairs today. Spent part of the morning cutting their hair which is now very shaggy as MacIntyre [estate ploughman] is still too frightened of the measles to come in and do it. Frightful blizzard today and had a frozen pipe which burst when being thawed out, so we are now without cold water on our side of the house.'

March 6,

'The blizzard continues and is said to be the worst in living memory round here. I can well believe it. About 3 o'clock there was a telephone call from the plumber who had got as far as Camusericht, asking if we could bring a horse to pull him out. Set off with MacIntyre, a horse, Mr

Kupp and four boys armed with shovels. We couldn't see where we were going and the wind was so cold it cut our hands and faces and made me almost sorry for the Nazis in Russia. The drifts were so deep in places that it was soon over the tops of my Wellingtons. The boys thought it grand fun and one of them said 'Now we shall have something to put in our Sunday letters'. The horse decided he preferred a warm stable and would not play, so we had to push as well as shovel, but the snow was very light and in most cases the car pushed it away in front of the bonnet and we were back here by five o'clock. Decided it would be impossible for the boys to return to Camusericht by car so arranged for them to walk over with the masters directly after High Tea, taking their breakfast with them. This they thought great fun and they set off in high spirits, muffled up to the eyes.'

My experience of school at Rannoch and that of my fellow pupils was so memorable that many years later I decided to hold a reunion dinner. This took place at Davy's wine bar in St James's and was the first such reunion attended by a significant number of colleagues whom I had been able to trace. Further reunions took place in later years and in 1991, while preparing for one at Rannoch, I called in at Talladh-a-Bheith to arrange for our party to visit. It was now a guesthouse owned and managed by some Germans. We were warmly welcomed and I was handed a letter they had received from one of my best friends, Simon Becker, dated March 12, 1991. He recalled a bitterly cold winter night at Talladh-a-Bheith when suddenly there was a tremendous clattering at the windows.

'This was several hundred sparrows trying desperately to get in,' he wrote. Billy Williamson, headmaster, instructed the boys to let them in; willing hands rushed to the windows to let in an absolute avalanche of sparrows, none other birds, who then settled on every available perch. The following morning, they opened the windows and the birds flew off – several thousand of them.

The bizarre element is what followed, twenty-seven years later. My son was having some difficulties with his primary education and I read that Billy Williamson was now headmaster of a well-known school, Ashdown House in the Ashdown Forest. My son was enrolled at the school where he was later to become head boy. My brother visited me from America and we decided to go down to the school and take Billy out to dinner and reminisce about our Rannoch days. We had a delightful dinner at Gravetye Manor and over brandy and cigars we began to swap stories about the war years. Then came the bombshell.

'Do you remember the night of the sparrows?' he said.

'Yes, of course I do,' I said. 'What about it?'

'Well, it's the most extraordinary thing. Of course at the time, we had to keep quiet about it in case we upset any of you and we were not a little disturbed ourselves, but it is the most remarkable tale. The following evening, Violet [his wife] and I went out for a drink at the Kinloch Rannoch Hotel and we were discussing the sparrow incident at the bar when someone picked up what we were saying and stopped us dead in our tracks'.

'That's happened up at Talladh-a-Bheith before,' he said.

'What do you mean?' I asked him.

'I dunno know exactly, but I'm certain it's happened up there before, many, many years ago, you'll have to go down to Kinloch Rannoch to examine the records and find out.'

Billy Williamson continued, 'Our curiosity at this point was insatiable and so we went down to Kinloch Rannoch to examine the records. There we found the chilling answer. 100 years previously, to the day, a young girl had committed suicide in Kinloch Rannoch and on that same day thousands of sparrows had besieged the windows of Talladh-a-Bheith.'

'Well, so what?', I countered, 'nothing more than a strange coincidence.'

'Except for one thing,' said Billy

'What's that?' I said sceptically.

'The fact that on that night in question that you remember so well, a young girl committed suicide in Kinloch Rannoch.'

Simon Becker continued his letter to the owners of Talladh-a-Bheith by asking if they could corroborate his story. He was himself doubtful. Billy was a master storyteller and it occurred to him that this might have been some kind of grown-up prank.

We were fascinated by this story. I did not myself remember the sparrows but then I had been unwell and was sent home to Broadstairs a week or so before the end of term. All the same, I wanted to pursue it and so delivered a copy of Simon's letter to a local historian, Alan Cunningham, an expert on Rannoch and author of a couple of historical books on the area.

A few days later, we moved to the Rannoch Station Hotel and had enjoyed a generous dinner with the Somervilles, the owners of Rannoch Lodge. At breakfast, the waitress brought to our table a small piece of paper with a handwritten note:

'Mary Elizabeth McPhee
died 6th Dec 1945 (aged 32) (she committed suicide)

Gravestone in KR graveyard
5th on right of the gate (new cemetery)
from

Alan Cunningham
Dalbruch Dall'

Alan told me later that he searched records for 100 years earlier but had been unable to find any account of a suicide in Kinloch Rannoch at that time.

This really took us aback. We visited the Kinloch Rannoch cemetery and found Mary McPhee's grave exactly as indicated by Alan Cunningham. At subsequent reunions I asked fellow pupils who would have been at Talladh-a-Bheith at that time, but none could remember the sparrows. It is a puzzle and strongly suggests that Simon had entered into the realm of the supernatural; had he, perhaps, dreamt about sparrows? How come, then, that Billy Williamson had raised the matter twenty seven years later? Was the whole story Simon's invention? If so, is it not odd that Mary McPhee had taken her life at exactly the date when the sparrows incident allegedly occurred? Elizabeth Sutherland in her book *Ravens and Black Rain* tells how Scots, and more especially the Picts, are gifted with powers of second sight and she gives numerous examples. I have also learnt (possibly from this source) that McPhees are particularly inclined in that direction. It remains a mystery.

Wellesley House returned to Broadstairs in January, 1946 and I was appointed head boy. Our family also returned at the same time. It was a big change to be returning into town and the school in Kent. I remember bursting into tears when my mother told me the summer before that we were going to leave Scotland. Although we were very privileged to live in a big house with a tennis court and garden and had lots of fun, I did not like going from school to the local church in a crocodile and above all I missed the wide open spaces and the wonderful landscapes of Rannoch.

Chapter 3

After the War: Marlborough and National Service

The return from Rannoch to Broadstairs was tinged with sadness but opened up a wide variety of activities different from those enjoyed in Scotland. Our house Barnjet was still standing, despite the one next door getting a direct hit from a German bomb and a V1 falling on the beach just below, both of which had blown out the windows. Life continued much as it had before the war but without so many staff. There were still tennis parties and the garden was gradually restored. We kept a couple of pigs and an underground air-raid shelter, with access from the house down a stairway and through a tunnel from the garden, was used to grow mushrooms.

Just how I became interested in fireworks I cannot recall. Amongst the rubble of the bombed-out house next door was a strange kind of firework; I do not know whether it was for a Guy-Fawkes-Night entertainment or some kind of military or naval warning flare. It consisted of two parts, a globe halfway in size between a grapefruit and a football, filled with gunpowder around a number of small cylinders of some kind of compressed powder; when ignited they burnt with a bright red flame. The globe had a fuse hanging from it and rested on a cone-shaped receptacle filled with gunpowder. When lit, this would propel the globe into the air, and it would explode high up, sending down a shower of red balls of fire.

This object gave me an unusual toy to play with and before long I was setting about making my own gunpowder. Arrowsmiths, the chemists in Broadstairs, sold me charcoal powder, sulphur and saltpetre (sodium nitrate). Equal parts carefully mixed together made a gunpowder good enough for simple fireworks. I recall just one which was very successful. You take a piece of iron pipe about six inches long, fill it with gunpowder, block up the ends as tightly as you can and set it on a cradle a few inches off the ground. You put a lighted candle underneath and stand clear. It goes off with a bang and the pipe flies off in one direction or the other, depending on which plug had blown out.

Interest in fireworks was further stimulated by a discovery of quantities of cordite on the beach below the house. During the war, a ship carrying munitions had been sunk somewhere out at sea and sticks of cordite had been washed ashore. They were about four inches long, similar in thickness to spaghetti and a deep yellow colour. Careful beach combing along the high-water line resulted in a fair enough supply of cordite sticks. When lit, they burnt with a fizz but lacked any explosive element. The best way to use them seemed to me to cut them up into little pieces and mix them in with gunpowder.

At this time my brother John was doing his national service in the Royal Engineers and one week-end brought home a couple of thunderflashes. These are used in training exercises to simulate explosions and go off with a very loud bang. This offered a welcome opportunity to make an even more spectacular firework. Powdered milk was sold in tins about seven inches tall with a rectangular cross-section and a lid on top. We cut a hole in the lid big enough to fit over a thunderflash. This was held upright in the tin and the space around filled with a mixture of gunpowder and cordite. We set it up at the end of the tennis court under a wall and members of the family assembled at a safe distance. John set off the thunderflash fuse and ran back. The explosion was quite impressive but perhaps less grand than I had hoped for. I do not think the powdered milk tin was as stout a container as should have been used and I doubt whether we had bound on the lid tightly enough.

On entering Marlborough College in the autumn of 1947, I browsed in the Encyclopaedia Britannica in the school library to find out more about fireworks. I was fascinated to discover how a rocket is made. The gunpowder is compacted into a cardboard tube in a cone so that on ignition the greater surface area would give more immediate thrust. I also learnt that certain chemicals could be added to produce colour – strontium for red, barium for green, etcetera; I had already used iron filings for sparks. I must have written home enthusiastically about all this, for it was at this stage that my father put his foot down and forbade me to continue pyrotechnic experiments. Just as well! Indeed, looking back on all this I feel I was lucky not to have injured myself. And I doubt whether any pharmacist nowadays would be happy to sell a small boy the wherewithal to make gunpowder.

Another less noisy activity, again promoted by John, was the construction of hot-air balloons. Nowadays Chinese lanterns appear to be quite straightforward, but we had to use available materials light enough to enable the balloon to take off. Four sheets of tissue paper were glued together, with a top closing one end. Very thin pieces of bamboo were tied together to form a square frame to which the tissue paper envelope was attached. A wad of cotton wool was tied to wires stretched from each corner of the frame. To combine resistance to heat with lightness, the centre section of each wire was made of steel wire used for traces when fishing for pike, the rest being thin copper wire; of this we had a limitless supply from a massive loudspeaker picked up in the ruins of the house next door.

On a calm evening, the cotton wool wad was doused with methylated spirits and lit. It was a minute or so before the air in the balloon was warm enough to give lift-off and the balloon would then rise high into the sky. Once the methylated spirit began to run out, the balloon would drift down, usually into some one's garden. On one occasion it reached a field of ripe corn a few hundred yards away and we were worried that it might set off a fire. Fortunately it did not; part of the fun was running after the balloon as it sailed off and on this occasion we reached the spot in good time.

We had had no mains electricity at Dunan where we lived during the war, so our wireless set was powered by batteries. It contained a two volt lead accumulator and a 120 volt battery. The former heated the cathode of the valves within, while the latter powered the electrons which rectified the received radio signal from AC to DC and amplified it before passing it to the speaker. The lead accumulator could be recharged and we had two or three of them. When one had gone flat, it was sent with the local bus to Kinloch Rannoch to be recharged. The 120 volt battery lasted longer but had to be thrown away and replaced when no longer working.

I must have questioned the logic of this arrangement, not understanding the chemistry that lay behind it. I had taken an expired high-tension battery back to school with me and one night, after lights out, took it down to the little lavatory which was reached off a landing between the first and second floors of Talladh-a-Bheith, the senior part of Wellesley House at Rannoch. I unscrewed the lid on the light switch and with a couple of wires, connected the battery to the terminals. Not surprisingly, this didn't work. The current was AC and the cells of the battery were not rechargeable. The only result was a humming vibration from the battery and a flickering of the light. This lavatory was also used by me in pursuit of another of my interests which was astronomy. It had a roof-light and by standing on the lavatory pan I was able to get a much better view of the night sky than was possible from the dormitory. My contemplation of the stars must have been noticed by the matron as there were concerns that I might be very sick.

So when we came back to Broadstairs, I continued my interest in wireless. John taught me how to make a crystal set, using a cardboard lavatory roll former wound with a few turns of cotton-insulated copper wire for the primary coil and about ninety turns for tuning, a variable condenser, a crystal and a pair of headphones. Such a contraption requires a very long aerial high up, and this was strung between the attic window and a walnut tree in the orchard. It worked quite well, but only, of course, for headphones. Many years later, I was invited to preach at a Wellesley House service and recalled the function of a crystal set receiving radio waves to illustrate a person tuning in to the Holy Spirit. I am not sure that the boys knew much about crystal sets and I doubt whether the message of my sermon got across.

The next step was to construct a wireless using valves. A local shop sold me a small lead accumulator and this I was able to recharge since the local electricity supply, from a diesel generator up near Broadstairs station, was DC; by connecting the supply current to the battery via a 40 watt bulb, it was possible to charge it, providing you got the wires the right way round and if the positive element produced bubbles of hydrogen, it was OK.

This led to making a two valve radio which would be strong enough to power a loudspeaker. The basic crystal-set circuit was replaced with one published in the magazine *Practical Wireless* using two pentode valves. Amongst the few letters my mother kept from my time at Marlborough is one containing an urgent request to send on a certain copy of *Practical Wireless*. I joined the Wireless Society at the college but eventually I gave it up. I have noted elsewhere how odd it was that the Royal Air Force put me onto radar in my national service but dabbling in wireless after the war must have given me some understanding of how radar worked.

It had not been my parents' intention that I should go to Marlborough College, but rather that I should follow my two elder brothers, David and John, to the Leys School, Cambridge. Nor had that been their intention either, so far as I know; it just so happened that during the war the Leys had been evacuated to the Atholl Palace Hotel in Pitlochry, not all that far from Rannoch where the family was living and where I was going to Wellesley House, also evacuated. Evidently John Boyce, my headmaster, felt that Marlborough would suit me better and so put me in for the scholarship examination in the summer of 1946. I went there with another boy, Macmillan, escorted by his parents and we stayed at the Aylesbury Arms Hotel. My results were good enough for me to be awarded a minor scholarship, although, sadly, I was let down by an abysmal mathematics performance (marked 'gamma' rather than 'alpha'); had these grades been higher, I might have gained a major scholarship. This was what was clearly expected of me, for I well remember the headmaster, John Boyce, expressing his disappointment at the result with little suggestion of congratulation in his voice, although his end of term report was more positive.

Of the boys who attended Wellesley House at Rannoch during the war, almost a third went to Eton, with the rest divided more or less equally between Dartmouth, Marlborough, Stowe and Rugby. Four went on to Glenalmond reflecting the intake of Scottish boys. Neither my parents nor I had visited the school and in a time of petrol rationing and limited communications, it was scarcely possible for parents to accompany their son to a number of different schools so as to come to an informed decision.

I have no memory of my arrival at Marlborough, nor whether I was taken there by my parents in a car or more likely sent off by train, with the inevitable trunk and wooden tuck box despatched Passenger Luggage in Advance a few days before. Marlborough was exclusively a boarding school and I do not recall any day boys from the local area. It had been founded in 1843 for the sons of the clergy by a group of clergymen, who took over the lease of the Castle Inn just outside the town on the London to Bath main road. Much building took place round the courtyard, principally boarding houses, classroom blocks, a library, a dining hall and the chapel. As the school grew in numbers, health problems arose, with too many boys dying from scarlet fever or other diseases in the congested quarters. It therefore became necessary either to acquire premises which could be converted into boarding houses by the addition of a wing, or to build new ones from scratch. In this way, the school became split between in-college and out-college houses. There was also a split by age, with junior houses for new arrivals who then moved on to a senior house at the end of their first year. The purpose was to enable boys to settle down and gain confidence in a forbidding environment and possibly to protect them from abuse.

In college, there were two junior houses, A1 and A2, with six senior houses, named just as unromantically B1, B2, B3, C1, C2 and C3. The A and B houses were said to have been designed by a specialist in prisons; certainly that was their feeling, with a central well and floors surrounded with high iron railings. There were three junior out-college houses, Priory in the town centre, with Barton Hill and Upcot along the Bath Road a couple of hundred yards and half a mile from the school gates respectively. These fed the out-college senior houses of Cotton, Littlefield, Preshute and Summerfield; the first two were on the Bath

Road, with Preshute on the water meadows the other side of the Kennet. Summerfield was up a side road a similar distance away.

While the college as a whole created an overarching loyalty in relation to other schools, there were differences in outlook distinguishing the types of house, not to mention rivalry in sport. I felt that life in the in-college houses was tougher and physically more demanding, particularly for the lower years who had no study rooms and worked and played in Upper School, a long hall of desks. John Betjeman had been at the school shortly after the First World War and in *Summoned by Bells* recalls his intense dislike of Upper School and the bullying that went on there:

> *'There was a building known as Upper School*
> *(Abolished now, thank God, and all its ways),*
> *An eighteen-fifty warehouse smelling strong*
> *Of bat-oil, biscuits, sweat and rotten fruit'.*

Things had improved by the 1950s but the reputation of Upper School lived on. The principle of 'By the boys for the boys' described by John Betjeman in *Little Innocents* still prevailed in Upcot when I went there.

Central feeding encouraged cohesion between the in-college houses and it seemed to me that, notwithstanding the hard conditions, there were more opportunities for cultural activities such as music, singing, art and societies; boys living in-college had these activities to hand, those in out-college houses had to come in to take part. Out-college houses also seemed to me to be more enthusiastic and competitive in sport, less inclined towards culture. However, generalisations of this kind are not always valid. Much more important were the attitude and interests of the housemaster; some favoured sports, others music and art, and it was this which set the tone of the house.

Many boys arriving at Marlborough had been entered from an early age and put down for a particular house if their fathers had been there themselves. This was not the case for boys like myself entering on a scholarship without any previous association with the school. We went where there happened to be vacancies and for me this was the out-college houses of Upcot and Littlefield.

The housemaster at Upcot at the time, Bernard Newman, was a distinguished former hockey player. He intervened little in the detailed running of the area beyond the green baize door, appearing only in the evenings to take prayers and make announcements. Our part of the house consisted of a large 'L' shaped hall with desks along three sides for the twenty-six boys and an open fireplace in one corner. In later years an application had been filed to demolish the whole building. There was

29

some concern among neighbours and in the end the housemaster's side of the building was saved and converted into flats for members of the college staff. New houses were built on what had been the boys' part of the house.

To begin with, supervision was in the hands of two second-year boys who stayed on for an extra term to maintain order and organise our activities. I have evil memories of them. They encouraged bullying and were themselves immature, with no senior boys over their heads to keep them in their place and ensure that they did not exceed the limits of their responsibilities. I lacked self-confidence to stand up to them and suffered. My unhappiness stands out in parts of a letter I wrote home at the time:

> *'I am afraid I do not like this place as much as Wellesley. Certainly I get more freedom but I do not appreciate this in the least; I never have any spare time. For instance, this afternoon I very much wanted to write some letters but we had to have a 'burr', which means we had to have an all-in fight, and then single fights, which have been going on now for an hour and a half. Of course, I had to have a go with the only result that I got a bruised knee and a bleeding nose. In one of the fights, now going on, one of the boys was jolly nearly knocked out. He was staggering around the room, on the floor every now and again, with blood dripping about the place. If that is the school's idea of a quiet half-holiday, I am afraid I cannot agree with it.'*

and in another letter:

> *'Please do you think you could address my letters in future to S.W. Martin rather than Selby Martin, for at the present, every one calls me Silly Martin as a result. People here are so jolly unkind to me, constantly calling me names and being nasty to me. It is so annoying...*
>
> *'When I am not at Upcot I feel none too happy, but when I am in my house, I feel absolutely awful. It is entirely the fault of these beastly boys.'*

and I went on to ask my parents not to mention this to Ben Newman. 'I think it might be better if you did not write to him about anything, as I would only be called silly names even more if the boys got to know as they definitely would.' and I later suggested that my birthday should be postponed by a couple of months as I was frightened to receive parcels. 'I am always teased by everyone whenever any thing arrives for me. The result is that I dread the post instead of looking forward to it.'

After leaving Marlborough, I remained in touch with my senior housemaster, Reginald Jennings, and must have mentioned all this to him. In 1959, by which time he had retired from house-mastering and was the college Registrar, he wrote about both the difference between in-college and out-college houses, and bullying. He suggested that boys in his out-college house were just as nice as those in-college but if a boy was independent-minded and had lots of admirable side lines, out-college was probably better as he would get a study much younger; a shy boy would be better off in-college. Bullying in junior houses he described as a recurrent plague and the price that had to be paid for the almost complete absence of bullying in senior houses. As a housemaster in four different houses, he had dealt with one or two sharp outbreaks of junior house bullying and thought I had experienced bad luck in having 'one of these maddening little epidemics in Upcot.' For me it had not been little.

Not everything was negative. In the same letter as that quoted in the first one above I noted: 'One thing good about this place is that the food is absolutely excellent. For lunch today we had roast beef, 'tatos, beans, chocolate ice cream and dates in custard. Another, there is no personal fagging, which is a good thing.' It was not all Tom Brown's Schooldays. I was not hungry, but a friend from Wellesley House days, Brian Gotto in Preshute, certainly was. He wrote to me:

'Both in Hall for lunch and at supper in house I never got enough to eat. No complaint about quality, although I didn't take kindly to whale meat. It was normal for the senior boys to help themselves first and so copiously that meagre were the leavings for the juniors at the bottom of the table. I felt the real pangs of hunger and one day was driven to theft, helping myself to the tea-time bun of a boy who could afford a 'brew' in town. To fill the void, I consumed beech-mast, hazel nuts, birds' eggs (moorhen and jay) and cooked up Cremola, a disgusting custard substitute containing cornflour.'

Was it right for me to complain to my parents in a way that must have deeply upset them? Perhaps they should have complained to Ben Newman; maybe they did and he took no notice, maybe they didn't, reckoning that all this was part of education and would make a man of me. I shall never know. I was clearly unhappy, but a lot of this was the kind of teasing which goes on in any such community and perhaps I was just a wimp and should have shown more guts.

Fairly soon after our arrival, all new boys were summoned by Ben Hylton-Stewart (the 'Stag') for a voice test with a view to being enrolled into the chapel choir. Such activity did not fit in with the ethos of the house and I definitely did not want to take part in something which would certainly have been the pretext for even more teasing. The test consisted of reproducing three notes played on the piano. The first two I hit spot-on but the third I deliberately sang wrong. I had committed a lie, one which I have regretted all my life. The training and experience of singing in the chapel choir would have been invaluable as part of my overall education and a help when later I took up singing and joined choirs. Nevertheless I several times attended voluntary evensong on a Sunday, mainly to get away from the violence and oppression in the house. It has left me with a great affection for evensong and its part in my spiritual life. Many years later when teaching at Shrewsbury, I noted in my diary:

> 'I like the service of Evensong – it is nice to say 'Thank-you' after a good day; and I like the casual and friendly atmosphere – as near as you will get to a voluntary service.'

An odd thing about the Marlborough chapel is that the pews are set along the length of the nave cathedral-fashion rather than across it. This fits in well architecturally but perhaps is less encouraging for boys' attention to what is going on in the service; one could easily be distracted by gazing at those sitting opposite or at the fine paintings above the back row, occupied by members of staff who kept an eye on us all.

One unusual incident remains in my memory from this time. A master had told a boy, probably also in Upcot, about an abandoned cottage high up on the downs not far from Marlborough, said to be haunted. He invited the boy to go with him on a Sunday afternoon to have a look. Several of us heard of this and were attracted by the idea of going out there on our bicycles the day before to set up a few hauntings, for example balancing things on the top of doors which would drop off when the door was pushed open. One such prank was to line up a few bottles on a chimney piece with a string behind them attached to a fixed object at one end and to the handle of a door at the other. When the door was pulled open it would bring down the bottles with a shattering crash.

There was a well in front of the cottage and to this we then turned our attention. How deep was it? Could we find out its depth by dropping down stones and measuring how long it took for them to splash at the bottom? It was deep – we could not see the water below by peering down. Some one suggested lighting a bonfire and dropping down burning sticks. This we did, gathering together a few bits of old furniture and dropping them down once they were well lit. It was fun and we happily returned to Upcot later that afternoon. We never heard whether the master had in fact gone up there the following day. However, one evening that week, Ben Newman came in to take evening prayers, announced that a complaint had been received about damage to the property and ordered all those involved to come to his study immediately afterwards. I expected a thrashing with his cane but this did not happen. Instead we each had £1 9s 6p deducted from our reserve of pocket money. Since then, if I hear of youths vandalising property, I soberly recall that I too had been guilty of the offence.

Life in Upcot changed for the better in the Lent term of 1947. The two older boys had moved on and their tasks were taken over by two boys from our year. We ran our side of the house happily even if with the occasional dispute. Yet the weather was not kind; it was one of the coldest winters for years. One afternoon some friends and I went off to explore the countryside not far from Upcot. A hollow tree-lined lane was completely covered over in snow and somehow I twisted my ankle in the branches of a tree and had difficulty limping home. I was sent off to the sanatorium for further examination for what turned out to be a greenstick fracture. A day or two later I felt unwell and for a time sat huddled in front of the fire. I had a high temperature; it was scarlet fever, probably picked up on the earlier visit to the San. It was a cold and dreary afternoon, beginning to get dark and I was sent back with my suitcase to spend two or three weeks there, first recovering and then in quarantine. It was boring. I do not recall any work being sent in. There were seven of us and we passed the time doing jigsaw puzzles, playing board games and cards, including strip poker. It was still bitterly cold when we came out but I found refuge in a lavatory above the boiler room at Upcot, despite smoke and fumes from the fire below. Food rationing, shortages of fuel caused by the miners' strike, the weather and an epidemic of scarlet fever must have been a severe challenge for the school administration. The Headmaster, Frank Heywood, was away on sabbatical leave, leaving Arthur Robson, his deputy, as stand-in. Conditions became so severe that he ended the term early and sent us all home.

By the summer term, the weather had improved and we were able to play outside. With a friend, Timothy Woods-Ballard, I would go trout fishing in the Kennet downstream of Marlborough with occasional success. I cannot recall whose water we were fishing, or even whether we had permission to fish there. So my stay in Upcot ended as happily as it had started with misery.

My first year in Littlefield, a senior out-college house, went well. It had been built in 1872 specifically as a boarding house to ease congestion in the college. Littlefield and Cotton Houses were designed by George Edward Stewart, a distinguished architect who had also been responsible for the Law Courts in London. It accommodated about forty-eight boys, later increased to fifty-seven with the conversion into dormitories of servants' quarters above the housemaster's side of the house. Adjoining the latter was the house library and down a few steps, the dining room and serving area, with the kitchen below in the basement. Then came the boys' entrance from a steep path up from the Bath Road. We had a small kitchen with gas rings and a wash basin. From this a boot room, changing room and showers led off in one direction, the lavatories in another. The latter were basic, with a urinal along one wall and a row of lavatory seats opposite, low slung in compartments without doors. Between the kitchen and the lavatories was a photographic darkroom for developing and printing films. It may originally have been intended as a storage cupboard but was now equipped with developing trays, an enlarger and a wash basin. It served its purpose well. One tray would be filled with developer, another with fixer. By a dim red light to which black and white film was not sensitive, one would remove the film from the camera, unroll it and taking the ends of the celluloid twelve-exposure film, one in each hand, dunk it back and forth in the developer until the images appeared, rinse it, do the same in the fixer, rinse again and hang up to dry. Contact prints or enlargements could then be made.

An advantage of this house, compared with those in-college, was that from the outset we had individual studies shared between two. The studies were on both sides of a central corridor on the ground and first floors, with fourteen studies on each. Stairs led up from an area of notice boards with details of teams and other instructions to dormitories on the second floor. This was also a punishment area; the penalty for minor offences was to be set a poem to learn by heart and recite to the monitor or prefect in question. There were two dormitories with beds along each side and washbasins in a row down the middle. Each bed was in its own partition to provide some measure of privacy; the windows were high above and always open at night. There was no heating and in cold weather flannels in the basins might be frozen stiff by the morning. The boys' side of the house was burnt down in April, 1962, to be rebuilt two years later to a rather dull design.

Dormitory life was regimented. At three minutes to ten, a bell was rung and we would kneel at our beds to say prayers in silence until the bell was rung again at ten. Talking after lights-out was not permitted except on Saturdays. In the morning the bell was rung again to get us out of bed; we would wash, dress and go down to breakfast which began punctually at 8 o'clock. This was usually a good meal of eggs and bacon, even if the standard of cooking left something to be desired. Lunch was taken centrally in the college but supper back in the house was less appetising and gave rise to complaints. Our housemaster, Arthur Titley, once responded in the manner of Marie Antoinette: 'Count your blessings and eat cheese.' Also in the dining room was a wind-up gramophone with a steel needle picking the music up from a 78 rpm record. There were few records to choose from; the most popular was Elgar's *Pomp & Circumstance March No 4*.

In my first year and throughout my time at Littlefield I shared a study with Peter Glossop, a good friend with whom I got on well. Neither of us was any good at sport but we frequently played tennis with two other friends, Andrew White and Roger Gonin. The only sport I was any good at was football; I liked the game and had played in the Wellesley House First XI. Unfortunately Marlborough is a rugby school – rugby in the Michaelmas term, hockey in the Lent and cricket in the Summer. An older boy in the house, John Tyzack, also keen on football, organised a team of enthusiasts to play on Sundays and this I enjoyed. The authorities did not approve and it was banned, without any reason being given. I did not like rugby and so played on the wing as this was where I was least likely to get involved. Hockey I had to learn and enjoyed it; indeed, I did well enough to be put in charge of it during my national service at a Norfolk radar station. Preparatory school at Rannoch had been a wonderful experience but we played very little sport simply because there was not much in the way of playing fields. Had this not been the case, I might have done better at sport at Marlborough and become involved in sport's social pleasures by belonging to a team, even if not a distinguished one, and I regretted this.

Military training at the school was taken seriously and membership of the Corps was compulsory for all boys. Drilling and ground combat training were practised each week and much attention was paid to smartness. Belts had to be blancoed and boots polished; it was here that I learnt the art of securing a hard-polished toe-cap, putting on successive layers of Kiwi wax polish to be rubbed in with a spoon heated over a candle. There were voluntary night exercises and once a year we had a field day, often a long way from college, for which we carried Lee Enfield .303 rifles with blanks. The instruction 'Down! Crawl! Observe! Sights! Fire!' is burnt into my memory.

In the Sixth Form, however, one had other options and I was attracted to the Air Section. In this we learnt the Morse Code, semaphore, recognition of aircraft such as Wellington, Halifax and Lancaster bombers and of course, how to distinguish between Spitfires and Hurricanes. For field days we were taken to an airfield and taught to fly in Tiger Moth biplanes and also went up in Ansons and Dakotas. It was fun to go flying in a

Tiger Moth and learn to navigate using a circular calculator strapped to my knee. The war had ended only three years before and a military ethos still prevailed.

Needless to say, German as well as the obligatory French were among the subjects I pitched into on arrival at Marlborough in the autumn of 1946. At some stage, I must have been asked in which direction I wanted my studies to go, for soon after the beginning of term, I mentioned in a letter home that I had done well in French and was coming top in German; my reports confirmed this. Some ability in other subjects is reflected by the fact that I took School Certificate at the end of my first year, with distinctions in English Language, Latin and Elementary Maths and Credits in English Literature, Geography, French, German and Additional Maths and the following year I was entered for Higher Certificate in French, German and English. If I had passed this, I would certainly have changed over to the Sciences. This was a relatively new department; it did not matter that a boy had done no science in the Lower School. I did not pass that year and had to retake the exam a year later; by then it was too late to change over to Science and I had to repeat the Higher Certificate in languages the year after, and the year after that, hardly exciting or a challenge but I do not remember getting bored with it all. In fact, I enjoyed it and did well. My bookcase includes several books awarded as prizes in French and German; they are all about fishing.... salmon, trout and coarse fishing in the Lonsdale Library series, also an encyclopaedia on trout flies and how to dress them.

Teaching was based on the form system for a boy's main subject, with sets for subsidiary ones. There was greater flexibility in the settings than is the case nowadays; in my first term I was moved up a year in German because of my previous studies, but not in other subjects. The school list, published each term, was much concerned with exam orders. A single exam would have been set for all boys in that year and they were listed by order of result; the set master for each was shown by an initial. The school list also included the names of prize winners and details about the prize itself, after whom it was named and exactly what it was for. Lower School boys were (and still are) in arcanely named forms, starting with Shell, then Remove and finally Hundred, at which point the School Certificate exam was taken. In the Fifth and Sixth Forms, boys were in 'Sides' denoting the area of subjects for Higher Certificate such as Classics, Mathematics, Science, History, Modern and Modern Languages. This specialisation did not however, exclude continuing studies in other matters, for example, when I was on the Modern Languages side in my second year, I still had lessons in History,

English and Mathematics. I regretted that I had had no lessons in Science in my first year and so had missed the opportunity to take Science for Higher Certificate. The change had been expected as my reports at the end of that year anticipated a move to the Science side the year after. It seems extraordinary that there was no provision for science lessons of any kind in the Lower School apart from a sex lesson given by the head of biology.

The School List then, as now, gave provisional dates for the following three terms. It also supplied parents with remarkably detailed information about train services according to region. Under Western Region appeared the following information:

> 'The 11.5 a.m. from Penzance; Plymouth (North Rd) 1.55p.m.; Exeter (St David's) 3.30p.m. connects at Westbury with the 6p.m. thence due at Savernake 6.42p.m. The next train from Savernake to Marlborough is 7.50p.m.'

Under London Midland Region the notice about the 12.55p.m. train from Newcastle-on-Tyne to Birmingham had all main intermediate stations listed with the times for catching it. At Birmingham one had to change to catch the 6.5p.m. to Cheltenham and change again for the 8.10p.m. due in Marlborough at 10.8p.m. (To-day's time for the journey from Newcastle to Birmingham is only seven minutes shorter). This was before Beeching; there is no longer a rail link to Marlborough. At the end of term, the school had a special train laid on from Marlborough via Swindon to London. It had a reputation for rowdiness and some friends and myself preferred to share a taxi to Hungerford to take an express direct to Paddington.

The school's emphasis was on academic studies and sport but there were opportunities for pursuing other interests out of school. I had arrived with three main hobbies; fireworks, fishing and making wireless sets – and an interest in astronomy. I soon gave up fireworks at my father's behest. I pursued wireless with some enthusiasm; my letters home requested copies of the magazine *Practical Wireless* and suggested components such as radio valves and variable condensers for birthday presents. I joined the school Wireless Society for a time but dropped out when the subject matter at meetings became too technical and beyond my comprehension.

My passion for fishing continued unabated and in this a boy in the year ahead of me, Michael Coates, gave me valuable advice on how to get permission to fish for trout in the river Kennet below Marlborough, possibly one of the finest chalk streams in the country. One had to find out who were the owners of certain stretches, look up their addresses in *Who's Who* and then write politely enthusing over the joys of dry-fly fishing in chalk streams and ending with a request to be allowed to fish in that person's water. Several responded positively and I enjoyed some happy trips to the river on my bicycle. These were always in the afternoon, not the best time of day for hatches of fly, but even if the fish were not rising, the beauty and tranquillity of the landscape were a joy. In addition, one of Peter Glossop's relations owned fishing on a mill pool in town associated with a tannery; he kindly gave me permission to fish there whenever I wanted.

By the time we returned to school after the summer holidays, the trout season was almost over and I turned to spinning for pike and perch in the Kennet-Avon Canal at Great Bedwyn and Savernake. This involved a ten-mile cycle ride along the main A4 road towards London, turning off after a couple of miles into narrow lanes leading through open fields and forest. The pike were not very large and I usually put them back; just occasionally I would keep one to fry up in the house kitchen. Once I caught myself. The spoon had been hung up in some rushes near the bank. I jerked hard to clear it, whereupon the spoon flew back at my face. I ducked but it caught in the lobe of my right ear. I enquired in the village after the local doctor and went to see him. Fortunately he was at home; he removed the spoon, patched up my ear and generously sent me off with a couple of books on fishing.

Another hobby new to me was metal-work. The school had a small workshop with several lathes. We were taught how to make and sharpen lathe tools and then how to use them. I was pleased with my creation of a simple oscillating single-cylinder steam engine which I proudly took home with the idea of connecting it to a model steam-engine boiler. This never came about because I carelessly left it on the train and never saw it again.

One of the masters, John Thompson, ran a music appreciation group in his rooms in the college. We met on Saturday evenings with orange squash and biscuits provided for our refreshment. Mr Thompson would explain the structure of classical compositions and play them to us on his gramophone. It made for a pleasant and relaxing evening, an arrangement which I later adopted on joining the staff at Shrewsbury School.

I appreciated the variety of opportunities for hobbies at Marlborough, which included photography, printing, carpentry, dancing, natural history and much more besides. These are a boy's formative years. He will have arrived from his preparatory school with hobbies often picked up from his parents, teachers or siblings; some will be taken further, others dropped and new ones acquired. The most important thing is that a pupil will leave school with a keen interest in some extra-curricular activity, be it sport or a hobby, which will provide interest and relaxation in later life. Pressure from studies and sport should not squeeze this out, nor should an obsession with computers and other electronic devices. Just what activity is offered by a school will depend ultimately upon the interests of staff members and their willingness to pass them on.

I also enjoyed going down town to look into antique shops and book stores and attend auctions. At the other end of town up a dingy side street was a scrap-metal merchant who also dealt in ex-government equipment left over after the war. One day I noticed a number of dynamo/alternators used for converting AC to DC (or it may have been the other way round) still in their original packing. On reading *Exchange & Mart*, I discovered an advertisement from a firm in Cheltenham wanting such equipment. I bought one for 10/- and sent it off to them. They were interested and wanted to buy thirty at 25/- each. This was a wonderful offer but I could not afford it. So I went into partnership with another boy in the house, Michael Stoddart. He managed to extract sufficient money from his father's Post Office Savings book. We bought the converters, commissioned the scrap-yard owner to take them up to Cheltenham and shared the profit. Michael Stoddart went on to be a prominent Investment Trust director in the city.

After taking School Certificate at the end of my first year, I moved up to the Modern Languages side of the Fifth Form and then to the Sixth. This carried with it certain privileges which in retrospect seem odd. For example, we were allowed to go into Marlborough at more extended hours and beyond Hyde Lane, laid down as the frontier for most pupils. We were also allowed to carry an umbrella; I was proud of one I had bought in Spain while on a French exchange with a family who had a summer residence in the Pyrenees; it had two elaborate tassels hanging from the handle. Oddest of all was the privilege to wear trunks in the school's swimming pool; boys in the Lower School swam naked and so, I noticed, did my housemaster, Reginald Jennings. The swimming pool at that time was exceedingly basic. It was built into the former moat of the castle behind the college and was filled direct from the river Kennet which flowed nearby. The water was beautifully clear but being from a chalk stream it was icy cold and took a long time to warm up to a temperature which I could enjoy. By then the water was turning green and thick, for there was no filtration or chlorine treatment. At some point during the summer it was decided that the water was not clean enough for our health, the pool was emptied and we began again with clear, cold Kennet water.

My school reports were positive, although the recurrence of words such as 'immature', 'ebullient', 'effervescent', 'slapdash', 'haphazard', 'lively' suggests that I was not above reproach. I owe much to the masters who had taught me. Dr William Rutland took me for French and English for three years but did not, so far as I can recall, become involved in other activities. During my national service in the Royal Air Force, I was posted to R.A.F. Yatesbury, only a few miles from Marlborough, and he invited me out for a meal, took me to see *Our Man in Havana* at the local cinema and presented me with a jar of honey from his bees. When a year or so later a Beagling Club was formed in the school, he wrote a very strong letter of objection to the local paper. He was essentially an academic with a caring outlook for his pupils and the environment. Some years later he wrote to me with his news and explained that he had been dismissed from London University by a Resolution of the Senate and was campaigning to clear his name. I could not understand the reasons for his disgrace; it had something to do with a book he had written on Swinburne and its publication in New York.

The master who most influenced me was probably the Rev John Bridger. He taught me German for three years; he was a stimulating and entertaining teacher. Beside his lessons he would often invite us to his room in school after lunch for coffee, and I also much enjoyed serving for him in chapel when he took the 8a.m. Holy Communion service on Sunday. I was not alone in my admiration for him. At a Thanksgiving Service in Sherborne Abbey for Michael Coates in 2015 I was interested when Bishop Timothy Dudley-Smith referred to him in his tribute as 'one of the most remarkable schoolmasters of his generation'. Bishop Timothy subsequently told me that John Bridger excelled in five sports at school and university, and left Cambridge with a triple first in French, German and Theology. A few years after I had left Marlborough, he moved on to Uppingham, then to St. Lawrence College in Ramsgate and I lost touch with him.

Another German teacher was George Tarleton, housemaster of B1. He was reserved, almost introvert in outlook, but to him I owe a love of German songs by Schubert, Schumann and Hugo Wolf. From time to time he took us up to his room where he played records on an antiquated gramophone using a bamboo needle of triangular cross-section. From time to time this had to be clipped to ensure a sharp point. In the house, Arthur Titley had been replaced by Reginald Jennings who ran the place firmly but fairly; he made me a 'captain' in my last year and took great trouble to keep in touch with what was going on in the house through evening meetings in his drawing room. In the summer of 1950, he said to me: 'Selby, it is time we thought about university; I will telephone Clare.' And that December, I went up to Clare College, Cambridge, to sit the scholarship exam and was offered a place – but not a scholarship. It was enough, although once again I had not quite made the grade.

The last year, working hard for the scholarship examination to Cambridge, had been a challenge and progress was less manifest than previously. I did well enough to gain a place at Clare College and my future lay in Modern Languages rather than in Science as would have been the case if I had secured a Higher Certificate pass at the end of my second year. I left the school with some sadness in December, 1950. I had enjoyed my time there and had come a long way from that unhappy first term at Upcot to a position of responsibility in a well-run and cheerful house. However, I feel that it did not leave so deep an imprint on my mind as had the years at Rannoch during the war.

National Service then intervened. I had been in the Royal Air Force section of the Combined Cadet Force at school; I had opted to do this because I did not much enjoy the toil and trouble of army field days, even though it was fun to load a pencil into the breech of a .303 rifle, followed by a blank cartridge to fire off at a rabbit. It was therefore natural that for my National Service I should join the R.A.F. Looking back, it has seemed to me odd that the R.A.F. in its wisdom assigned me to radar, although I knew nothing of physics and was hardly qualified to deal with electronics, while others in the service went off on an intensive combined services Russian course for which I might have been as good a candidate as others, if not better. They would not have known of my interest in making wireless sets in earlier years, which at least gave me some idea of what it was all about.

Within three weeks of leaving Marlborough I was on my way to basic training at R.A.F. Padgate. Living in barracks presented no great difficulty for me; it was much the same as a dormitory at school. There were, however, marked differences in routine. Rather than with the ringing of a bell we were woken by a distorted rendering of Reveille over loudspeakers. We did not remake the bed but folded blankets and sheets to a precise size and shape and placed them in a neat pile at the head, with the pillow on top. It was a cold January, and heating was provided from a tall, cylindrical, and very smoky coal-burning stove. We were under the strict control of a corporal who had his own room at one end, and he drilled us indoors and out. He was particular about our appearance, especially our hair which had to be very short. 'Am I hurting you?' he would ask as he stood behind one on the parade ground. To the answer 'No', he would shout: 'I bloody well ought to be, I'm standing on your hair – get it cut!' He was also fussy about our uniform which had just been issued. His own was immaculate, even to the point of placing rings of metal chain in his trousers so that they hung evenly above his gaiters.

It was here that our future direction was decided once we had finished our square-bashing. I was destined for radar supervision and training for this comprised two courses. One was at R.A.F. Yatesbury a few miles down the Bath Road west of Marlborough, the other at Bawdsey Manor in Suffolk where we learnt the principles of radar and the different systems then in use. We slept in a normal barrack hut but our lessons were all in the Manor. There was very little drill and we had free time to swim from the beach below the Manor or to go into Felixstowe on the ferry. After passing out of Spitalgate Officer Training Unit, I was posted to the Fighter Command Group 12 filter room at Watnall near Nottingham, where in-coming reports from radar stations of approaching aircraft were displayed on a large table, with small wooden blocks pushed around by W.A.A.F. members, as seen in any film about the Battle of Britain.

After a couple of months I was sent to R.A.F. West Beckham on a ridge of high ground behind Sheringham on the north Norfolk coast. It was a relatively small station commanded by a Flight Lieutenant and was responsible for running three types of radar. The first, Chain Home, had been developed during the late 1930s and was the mainstay of the early warning system at the beginning of the war. It consisted of four pylons 360 feet high between which hung transmitter curtains sending out pulses of radio energy. Nearby were wooden receiver masts with crossed dipoles. The signals reflected back by an aircraft appeared as a blip on a cathode ray tube. This gave the distance easily enough; direction had to be assessed by comparing the relative strength from the two crossed antennae. This was not that accurate, even less so was the height which had to be guessed from the aircraft's point of entry into the lobe-shaped field of view. The apparatus needed to run the system was huge, tall, iron cupboards filled with immense valves, replicated in case of a breakdown. It now sounds primitive – indeed it was – but it was key to detecting German attacks in the early years of the war and a vital element in eventual victory.

Chain Home could not pick up low-flying aircraft and to remedy this a second system, Chain Home Low, was installed in 1941, shortly after the Battle of Britain. It used a rotating mesh aerial with 360 degree coverage. Images of incoming aircraft up to a range of about 180 miles were displayed on a cathode ray tube with a rotating scan, a system in use for air traffic control. Altitude was determined by a vertical nodding dog aerial which had to rotate to point in the right direction. West Beckham's C.H.L. was at Bard Hill, a few miles to the west. Those manning the unit were taken out by bus while a few responsible for starting up the equipment had temporary accommodation out there.

We worked in shifts. Our task was to detect hostile aircraft coming from the east, specifically from the Soviet Union as the Cold War developed. For some reason it was considered that if they did attack, it would be during the day. We therefore operated the radar from half an hour before sunrise until half an hour after sunset, with four shifts in summer and three in winter. The pattern was to do shifts for three days and then to have the fourth day off. From time to time extensive exercises were held, when we would operate radar twenty-four hours a day. It was exciting to nip outside when aircraft taking part in the exercise flew overhead – Meteors, Vampires and the occasional Canberra bomber. Otherwise, not much happened apart from a regular early-morning flight from Schipol in the Netherlands to Heathrow. Twice, however, an object was seen on the radar travelling at a speed way beyond that of normal aircraft. In both cases, the local press reported sightings of a U.F.O. which matched those we had seen on radar.

We had other duties besides manning radar. Perhaps because of my experience in the school cadets I looked after ground-combat training, organising occasional exercises and rifle shooting at a nearby range. This was overseen by an experienced Flight Sergeant who was himself a good shot. We drew rifles from the station armoury each time we went; these were .303 Lee Enfield and one had to adjust the sights to match one's particular characteristics. The rifles were numbered and I made a point of using the same rifle on consecutive occasions. The Flight Sergeant was surprised and a bit upset when I achieved higher scores than him at 200 and 600 yards.

I was also asked to take charge of hockey and boxing. Our facilities for both sports were limited and matches were usually held at other clubs. I enjoyed taking teams and refereeing from the touchline in a hockey game. For boxing I was manager and spectator and fortunately was never asked to box.

Fishing remained my chief leisure interest. I had bought a second-hand two-stroke motorcycle at Watnall and used this to get around north Norfolk. There was trout fishing in a small river near North Walsham but I was not able to get permission to fish there. Nearer the station at Selbrigg there was a small lake with plenty of pike. I fished this and had one of 19 pounds, the largest I have ever caught, but was soon turned off by the gamekeeper – it was private fishing. He gave me the owner's name and address but my request for permission to fish was politely turned down. Later, I wrote again from Cambridge and this time I was successful. This led to a friendly relationship with the Bainbridges, who invited my brother David and myself to stay with them and fish the lake from their boat.

Dancing and drinking also figured in our lives. There was a village hall at West Runton where we would go of a Saturday evening to dance with local girls. We used station transport to get there because a fellow officer, older than myself, had a driving licence. On one occasion there was a station dance at West Beckham; the girls were invited into camp and much beer was consumed. This was my first experience of over-indulgence. I drank more than I should have done and decided to try smoking; it made me feel very ill and I have never touched a cigarette since.

I had enjoyed my time at West Beckham enormously and would have been happy to stay on longer. I had a place to study languages at Cambridge and it would have been foolish to forego the opportunity. I accordingly sold off the motor-cycle, packed up my belongings, including the pike's head which I had pickled in methylated spirits, and, after a brief stay at home in Broadstairs, went up to college. I joined the Royal Auxiliary Air Force and for three years returned for a fortnight's summer attachment at West Beckham and in the last year at Trimmingham where a more advanced radar system had been installed, largely at the behest of the Americans who were worried about protection for their bases in England. The entrance was camouflaged as an ordinary house, and the operations room was underground.

Barnjet, Broadstairs, the author's birthplace

Archibald Martin

Magdalene Martin

Boys with their gas masks wait at Broadstairs station for
their train to Rannoch (Wellesley House archive)

Moor of Rannoch Hotel with Loch Laidon beyond
(J.B.White, Dundee)

Rannoch Lodge, leased to Wellesley House during the war

Dunan Lodge in 2014 with keeper's cottage behind

Posing for the camera on a fishing trip, August 1940.
The author (left) brothers John (centre) and David (right)

The author fly fishing at a pool near Dunan

A picnic on a high lochan above Rannoch. Such experiences
left many with a life long affection for the beauty and grandeur of
Scotland (Wellesley House archive)

Launching a hot-air balloon in Broadstairs after the war

On a Field Day from Marlborough, about to take a flight in a Tiger Moth

Littlefield House, Marlborough College, on fire in 1962
(Marlborough College archive)

RAF West Beckham.

RAF West Beckham Sports Day advertised with a truck resembling a Chain Home radar station

A nineteen pound pike from a lake near RAF West Beckham

Skating on the frozen Cam, with Clare College behind

Village boys from Fahlegård on the river Driva in Norway

Fishing boat on the Tana river in north Norway

Setting out on the postpath from Utsjoki to Inari in north Finland

Trout, grayling and pike cooking on the hearth at a
Mieraslompolo farm

Church at Hólar i Hjaltadal, formerly centre of the diocese of
north Iceland.

A hut for smoking char

View of Hólar

Communist party meeting in Oulu, 1956

Striking protesters marching through the town

Chapter 4

University and a Scandinavian Tour

My first memory of Cambridge had been my arrival in December, 1950, to sit the scholarship exams. It was a cold, dark evening and I was accommodated in Memorial Court across the river. I sat the exams and had an interview with the then Master, Sir Henry Thirkhill. I was not awarded a scholarship but performed well enough to be admitted to study languages. So in September 1952 I was back in Memorial Court and my immediate neighbour was Allan Last, a science undergraduate. Oddly, for one of my first lectures I went with him to a physics lecture, such was my interest in radar. By the time I resumed study in languages, I had largely forgotten such French and German as I had learnt at school and was the despair of my tutors in both subjects. While I enjoyed German with a Czech émigré philosopher, Paul Roubiczech, French interested me less. The literature syllabus for Part 1 of the Tripos exams seemed unduly narrow. More importantly perhaps, my fellow pupils were predominantly bright young girls straight up from school and against that sort of competition, I felt I was unlikely to come out well.

German was thus my main subject and in the first long vacation, the summer of 1953, I arranged to spend time in Austria; a fortnight on a language course in Mayrhofen, a fortnight in an international youth work camp digging ditches and a fortnight staying with a family in Feldkirch. Among the students on the language course were several girls from Finland, with whom I got on extremely well. I knew nothing of that country, its language, culture or history but was fascinated by it, so much so that on my return to college in October at the beginning of my second year, I told my tutor that I wanted to give up French and take Finnish instead. Unfortunately, Finnish was not on the academic menu; but I could take Swedish – after all, ten per cent of Finns are native Swedish speakers – and this I immediately decided to do.

There were no more than five or six of us on the Swedish course, taught by a charming lady, Brita Mortensen, who sadly was killed in a motor accident in Canada some years later. At this stage, it was a question of learning the grammar and vocabulary well enough to study the works of some twenty 19th century Swedish poets, playwrights and novelists. We had little practice in speaking the language.

I had to stick with French as a subject for part I of the Tripos, normally taken at the end of the first year but in my case postponed a year as the prospects of a decent grade after only one year were poor. I had not abandoned the idea of learning Finnish; also in Clare was a Finnish post-graduate in geology, Joachim Donner, who kindly gave me lessons.

It was not just the pretty girls that inspired me to study the language. I was totally enthused with Finland and twice went with some friends to the Sibelius concert at the Festival Hall to celebrate Finland's National Day on 6 December and the composer's birthday on 8 December, in the presence of the Finnish Ambassador. These were conducted by Sir Thomas Beecham who contributed so much to a knowledge of Sibelius's music in this country; when in later years we visited his home in Ainola, we were told that Sir Thomas would send a telegram to Sibelius to warn him when his works were to be broadcast by the BBC. On our visit we were shown the green tiled stove in which on his instructions his widow burnt all his unpublished manuscripts. It was a tragic loss to the world of music.

For the second part of the Tripos, taken at the end of the third year, a language student at that time had to offer five literary papers as well as a paper on the language and another on history. Three of mine were on German literature of the 19th century and one on Swedish literature of the same period. A fifth subject had to be found. Not wishing at the time to delve deeper into medieval German, I turned to the long list of options available in the faculty guide of the Department of Modern and Medieval Languages. Right at the end of the list was a short section of papers from the Faculty for Anthropology and it included a paper on the language, literature, and religion of Iceland in the 10th and 11th centuries. It would involve a basic knowledge of ancient Icelandic, reading the great Icelandic sagas in English and the history and beliefs of that period. I seized on a subject which covered a wider canvas than the traditional literature papers to which I was already committed.

Icelandic is more difficult than German or Latin, but the fundamental concepts are similar. I pursued these studies with enthusiasm, and as one of only two candidates from the Modern Languages Faculty taking Icelandic, I like to think that this helped me to obtain a Grade 2:1, which I doubt very much I would have done if I had stuck with French.

The summer term of my second year at Cambridge had ended with

46

the usual period of leisurely idleness which comes between the end of exams and the beginning of the long vacation, idleness in the sense that no academic work is done, but a busy time otherwise with visits to friends, coffee-drinking and above all preparations for travel in the long vacation. Tickets and visas have to be obtained, suitable clothing bought and whatever equipment one needs has to be looked over and supplemented where necessary.

I had decided to visit Scandinavia, a part of the world which attracted me, not least by reason of its excellent fishing. A visit there would also be useful for my Swedish studies. I worked out a route that would take me up through Norway to Lapland, down into Finland and back home via Stockholm and Copenhagen. The journey would last three months.

A diary was kept for the whole of this time, with detailed descriptions of the places visited and accounts of various experiences. I sailed from Newcastle on a ferry of the Olsen line and by coincidence met up with Bob Oliver, a keen salmon fisherman who was on his way to Fahlegård for a fortnight's salmon fishing on the river Driva. The fish there run big; we had heard that two salmon of 54 pounds had been caught earlier that year. Bob Oliver kindly invited me to stay for a couple of days and to fish his beat. My diary noted for 15 June. 'After breakfast we went out fishing. Mr Oliver caught one small fish of about 26 pounds.' I had no luck; my tackle was wholly inadequate for so large a river and the gear Bob Oliver lent me was difficult to manage.

I may not have caught any fish in those two days but they certainly made a great impression, as I recorded in my diary:

'I thoroughly enjoyed my stay there, chiefly on account of the delightful atmosphere which surrounded the place. The valley is bounded by steep mountains whose summits were often shrouded in twirling wreaths of mist or, from time to time, glistening in the breaks of sunshine. The air was filled with the incessant murmur of the river and the small streams which plunged down into it. The Fahle farm stood on a hillock of grassland and was furnished in traditional Norwegian style, combining the rustic beauty of old carved chests and birch wood cupboards with cushions and pictures which seemed to come from afar, including some items from England, which had probably been sent as gifts by salmon fishers of the past. The atmosphere of half a century ago still lingered in this quiet Norwegian valley, where the passage of time had left no impression and no remembrance of the German occupation.

'On the second day the weather had cleared and the beauty of the sunlit landscape added greatly to my pleasure of fishing. Even the children here seemed to be happier and although I do not usually have much affection

for small boys, those that came from the surrounding farms to watch us were a delightful collection and it was from them that I had my first lesson in Norwegian. I have not often developed a strong attachment for a place in so short a space of time as two days, but I must confess that my heart was heavy as I bade farewell to Mr Oliver and the Fahles and went down to the road to wait for the bus.'

My next visit was to a remote part of east Norway, around Røros, a town based on the mining of copper ore deposits which had been discovered in 1644 about ten kilometres away. A Swede on his way to Trondheim in search of work had settled in the area to hunt and fish. One day he shot a deer which in its death throes kicked away the moss to reveal an ore stone, which the man took to be of gold. Some years later a German engineer realised its significance and founded the town and mine of Røros. When I was there, one shaft was still being worked with modern machinery, another was a tourist attraction. This takes the visitor down a gradual slope for about three kilometres; it was bitterly cold, with ice on the walls. We also visited the church in Røros which struck me as being also a tourist attraction rather than a place of worship; I was distressed to see that the organ, allegedly the oldest in Norway, was covered in graffiti.

I had set out on this trip with romantic views about the pleasure of living alone in the wild. I accordingly arranged to spend a week in lumberjacks' huts several miles further east, beyond Femunden lake. It was an experience but not an entirely successful one. I had relied on catching trout for my food and had brought with me little more than porridge oats, dried vegetables and soup powder. The going was rough, the distances between huts great and I easily got lost although I had map and compass. Occasionally I was given coffee and cake or biscuits by friendly forestry workers. It rained a great deal and the mosquitoes tormented me. Halfway through the week, I noted: 'the worst part of this week's holiday is the utter loneliness of it all'. I had romantic ideas of being alone in the wild, fostered by the French philosopher Rousseau and German 19th-century poetry but had not realised how important is the company of other people to one's enjoyment of life. I was about to abandon the project when two boats appeared on the lake where I was staying. It cheered me up, I stayed on after all and caught a fish for my supper.

A further burden was the weight of my rucksack. I had tried to keep the contents to a minimum – just one change of clothes, waterproofs and a sleeping bag; but also the necessary fishing tackle – four rods, four reels, several tins of flies, casts, spinning baits, lead weights, landing net, gaff hook, spring balances and preserved minnows and prawns. When I left England I had looked forward to wandering about freely and again had been influenced by reading certain German works of the Romantic period where the idea of 'Wanderlust' is attractively portrayed. Besides this, the top of the hit parade at the time was a song called 'The Happy Wanderer'. This was a translation of the song 'Mein Vater war ein Wandersmann', and I liked to sing the German original as I walked along. It is typical romanticism; the last verse:

> 'D'rum trag ich Ränzlein und den Stab
> Weit in die Welt hinein,
> Und werde bis an's kühlen Grab
> Ein Wanderbursche sein!'

> 'So I carry a little knapsack and
> Staff far into the world,
> And until the cool grave
> Will be a wandering lad!'

I found my rucksack unbearably heavy as I walked through the Norwegian forest and the ideal of the happy wanderer was soon dispelled. In fairness, however, a few weeks later I was walking long distances across Lapland without too much trouble. I was just that much fitter by then.

It is easy to overlook just how long Norway is and how great are the distances between different places. The journey from Røros to Oslo by train took all day and was tiring. The purpose of travelling south before setting out for the Arctic was not only to visit the city's museums but to take advantage of a rare opportunity to witness a total solar eclipse. This was due to take place around lunchtime on Wednesday, 30 June, 1954.

The path of totality, only a mile or so wide, was to pass over Telemark, south of Oslo and I joined a coach party to the village of Bolkesjø where we were to be based at the Tourist Hotel, a journey of several hours. There was an air of considerable excitement on the hotel terrace where a reporter from *Morgenbladet* was haranguing the crowd on the subject of eclipses in general. At that moment the sun was partially obscured by cloud but there was hope that this would clear; the sky was already turning dark.

I helped myself to some hotel writing paper on which I recorded the event:

> 'I had turned away from the crowds who were swarming on the
> terrace and went uphill over the road and after climbing through scrub

and bush, I arrived on a small promontory of rock, from where I had a clear view out over the treetops and away into the distant landscape of mountains and lakes. There I positioned myself with my camera and waited. The sky grew darker gradually as the moon obscured more and more of the sun's disc, and when there remained only a second or two before totality, the corona and protuberances became clearly visible on the opposite side of the disc. Then the last ray of light was blotted out. The clouds, which had threatened to spoil the view and which stretched around the horizon, shone with a lurid red and orange light, getting brighter towards the horizon. There was still some light about. I could see easily the trees around in silhouette but since there was some light coming from the lower part of the sky all around, there were no shadows. The lake below reflected the weird pallor from the cloudless sky above. The sun itself was a fantastic object to look at. The middle, where the moon was, was completely black. Around this was a ring of gentle light and stretching out on either side, the beautifully soft and delicate corona.

'The wind seemed to blow slightly cooler, but it did not become colder than if a cloud had obscured the sun. The stars were not visible, for the sky was still faintly luminous. The planet Venus, however, shone brightly to the left of the sun. I had hoped to observe Mercury, but there was too much stray cloud about.

'This eerie night seemed to pass all too quickly. The dawn came with a rush. The sun's light is so intense that as soon as the smallest part of the orb is revealed, the light seemed to flood out. There was most cloud about towards the east, and this changed immediately from the dark steely grey it had been to bright white and it was possible to perceive the shadow moving away across it. The lurid orange that had belted the horizon vanished in a few seconds; the world seemed to come to life again. I heard a cock crow from the farm down below me and the cuckoos seemed to cry more than other birds. As I write now, still seated on my rock, the sun is regaining its warmth and life returns to normal.'

I had planned to spend a week fishing on the Tana river, which borders Norway and Finland in the far north. To get there, I took the overnight train from Oslo to Trondheim and boarded a small mail boat bound for the far north. The other passengers were mainly local people; five noisy Norwegians who drank vast quantities of beer but looked distinctly seedy when we reached rough water, and a family who looked very poor but whose ten-year old son played an expensive looking accordion with amazing confidence and skill.

I left the ship at Ifjord at around 2 a.m. and filled in time fishing in the river before the hotel opened. I made the mistake of going to sleep in the open; although I had anointed hands and face with oil, mosquitoes bit my ankles through the socks. We then travelled up the Tana river by boat as far as Storfossen where, to avoid rapids, we transferred to an open lorry for a most uncomfortable ride and then for another hour by boat to Sirma, where I was booked to spend a week salmon fishing.

The Tana had the reputation of holding Norway's biggest salmon. It is a big river, not unlike the Tay in its nature, wide and evenly flowing. The usual method was harling, that is, to be rowed in the current by a Lapp ghillie with lures trailing out behind. It is not exciting but holds the prospect of hooking vast fish. At that time of the year, one needs to fish at night when the midnight sun is at its lowest. I arranged to have one of four bunks in the attic of the Sirma Fjellstue, since these would be less noisy in the daytime, and engaged a Lapp ghillie, John, and his boat. The Tana boats are long and narrow, with thick, short, heavy oars. John's boat was old and leaky; it had to be bailed out every ten or fifteen minutes. To move back upstream a pole is used to punt the boat along the quieter edge of the river. This is much more difficult than punting on the Cam as I found out when I tried; if the bow is allowed to turn to one side of the current, the boat is skewed round and swept back.

Fishing in this way is very hard work for the ghillie and understandably, John would declare every couple of hours: 'Vi ska gå til stranden og koke kaffe'. He lit a fire and hung over it on a green stick a small copper kettle filled with water and coffee grounds. The brewing of coffee by one Lapp ghillie was a signal for others to come ashore to join in, resulting in a cheerful party; they seemed to me a very friendly collection of people. The local schoolmaster, a Norwegian from southern Norway, told me that they seldom quarrel; they are all related to one another in the village and by force of circumstance intermarry quite freely. They are also deeply religious, being diligent in Bible reading and prayer. The biggest reindeer owner in the district at that time, Ole Per Utsi, had only two occupations, looking after his herd of 5000 reindeer and reading his Bible; on this he was very knowledgeable and enjoyed discussing Old Testament problems with clergymen. Fishing was not allowed on Sunday and when I suggested that I might then wash my clothes, I was firmly told by Einar that that was not on.

During the week I caught the odd small salmon and lost a very large one which John estimated at around forty pounds. By then it was getting intensely hot, even at night, with the temperature one day at 88°F; it was time for me to move on into Finland. Before leaving Sirma, some of the guests at the inn went up to say good-bye to Einar the schoolmaster for a final coffee-drinking session; he kindly gave me a book on the

Lappish language, which seemed to have no similarities to either Finnish or Norwegian.

Today there are roads on both sides of the Tana and on into Finland. The whole area is popular with holidaymakers, especially for those enjoying outdoor life, with huts, shops, petrol stations and all the paraphernalia of a tourist destination. It was not like that then. When I left Sirma to continue my journey into Finland, it was a bright, sunny day with a gentle breeze as the post boat carried me on the two hour journey up the Tana river to Utsjoki. This was the main centre for those parts and after stocking up with food I set out for Inari. Six kilometres on the way south is the fine Utsjoki church. I had admired its spires from a distance, rising up above the birch trees. It had been built in 1845 and escaped destruction during the war because of its isolation. It was the centre of a vast parish and the Lapps came in twice a month for services, staying in huts down the slope nearby. The church had no heating so that, in winter, services were held in the parsonage. The minister showed us round the church, took us up into the bell tower and generously gave us refreshments in the parsonage afterwards.

The post path from Utsjoki to Inari was just over 100 kilometres in length. The countryside is undulating with low hills and many lakes, predominantly open moorland, birch scrub and, further on, pine and fir trees. After a while the path left the hills and ran straight ahead for a long way, a part of the journey which was rather depressing. I would spend the night either at a farm which provided hospitality on a bed & breakfast basis, or at a post hut. The walk took just over four days and at all the stops I was made welcome and given food and somewhere to sleep – not always comfortably. It was still too hot to use a sleeping bag and mosquitoes were everywhere. At Mieraslompolo farm I was shown to a barn and slept on reindeer skins, while at Palomaa farm the Lapps gave me a comfortable bed and there were no mosquitoes in the room. The Finnish Sámi seemed to be ahead of the Norwegians in fitting wire gauze over the windows.

For food I ate biscuits with butter, rusks, and odd sundries during the day, with frequent stops for brewing coffee. I was of course very hungry by supper time and much enjoyed the food provided at the farms where I stayed. Finnish food was less influenced by the Smørgåsbord system of a range of meats and fish which is common in Scandinavia. I had certainly eaten well in Sirma Fjellstue with salmon or meat and fruit, while breakfast was coffee, a boiled egg, cheese, sausage etc. In Finland, porridge was normal. At Mieraslompolo, dinner was porridge with sugar and milk, followed by smoked Grayling, bread and butter, and yoghurt.

Nowhere was there alcohol of any kind.

There also seemed to be differences in the families, with a greater number of children in Finnish families. There were nine children in the Utsjoki parsonage and seven at Meiraslompolo, with more on the way. They looked different from Norwegian children as I noted in my diary:

> *'There are also differences in the features of the children. The hair is long in a dishevelled sort of way like a kind of thatch, hanging down all the way round the head. The eyes of all these children were dark and luminous, and large, and I began to feel quite uncomfortable when a five-year old fixed her stare on me for five minutes at a stretch.'*

At the post hut where I spent one night, there was a hearth and fuel; one just had to cook up one's own meal from what one carried. While I was preparing my supper, the postman came in, so I gave him some soup and he kindly agreed to post a letter for me and ring up the hotel in Inari to book me a room for a couple of nights later.

It was quite late when I reached Kaamanen, the last settlement in my walk. Having two hours to wait for the bus to Inari I went into the house of a Lapp for coffee and pancakes. He had a visitors' book which included many entries by Germans who had returned to see the country they had been forced to leave when Finland signed a peace agreement with the Soviet Union. Among the pages of the book was a letter in which a soldier described his experiences. He had been very happy in Lapland for two years and they had run a small farm with cows and a hayfield. In 1944 the Russians had come and the Germans had fought with two divisions against the Russians' ten. Out of a company of 120 men, only eight had been able to escape into Norway. The burning of the houses and villages was done to prevent the Russians from using them and so to hold up their advance. Nowadays it is always the Russians who are blamed for inflicting the greatest damage. After the capitulation, his group of people had been told by the English that they would be sent back home, but they were in fact handed over to the Americans, who gave them to the French. After his eventual release, he had settled down as a baker. The author of this letter may have confused the nationality of the troops attacking at the end of the war; they were Finns, not Russians.

At Kuusamo I enjoyed the delights of staying in a hotel, where I was honoured by the Union Jack flying outside and another on my table at dinner. I was also able to arrange for the bath water to be heated – a real luxury. Before moving south to Kuopio I spent a week in the far east of the country, near the Russian frontier. This is now the Oulanka National Park, a popular destination for holidaymakers who appreciate wild country and enjoy staying in remote cabins. At Käylä there were five other people staying in the same hut. While this meant more fishermen on the water, it was very pleasant to have other people staying with me. Here and elsewhere I would fish at any time of the day or night; if, for example, I was not sleeping well because of the heat, I would go out to fish for a couple of hours. The sun no longer shone at night as it was south of the Arctic Circle, but there was plenty of light. The fishing was good and it all worked out better than the similar trip in Norway. I wrote in my diary: 'So I have come to the end of another fishing stay and it has, I think, been the best so far, both for the fishing and the living conditions. Also, it was an interesting terrain geographically with the deep gorge and the vast forests all around.'

The uncle of my Finnish teacher in Cambridge, Gabriel von Bonsdorff, had invited me to stay in the central Finnish town of Kuopio. They lived in a wonderful, single-storey, wooden house, beautifully furnished with fine paintings and furniture. He and his son Johan took me on a number of outings to hardboard, softboard and plywood factories, and to logging sites. We also fished in the lake and streams running into Kuopio lake.

In Kuopio there was also some social life and I went to a dance with Johan. The conventions of the dance floor in Finland were strange to me. I had already been to a dance in the village of Ämänsaari. There I had hoped to be able to hear some Finnish country dance music but no – they played gramophone records of the usual American sort. The hall was quite large with benches all around and down one side of it sat all the men, down the opposite side, all the girls. When a dance began the men got up and drifted over to select a partner from the 'stock' across the way and soon quite a number of couples were on the floor. At the end of the first piece of music, everyone stopped and stood still, waiting for the next record. Immediately this was finished, the men led their partners back to the female side of the hall and then returned to their own side. As there was a shortage of seating and a surplus of people, there was always a mad scramble at the end of each set of two records. The girls never came to sit with the men, nor vice versa.

The same conventions were observed in Kuopio. There was an open air dance floor on an island in the lake. A band was playing but once again I was disappointed not to hear Finnish folk music. I noticed a fair number of attractive girls but meeting up with them was not easy. They congregated on one side of the floor, while the men stood around forming a barrier. As soon as the dance began, the men surged forward to get their favourite partners: in the general mêlée, those trying to dance could only do so with difficulty. I met up with a girl who spoke a little

English – Ritva. We had a few dances and I met her again the next day to see a film. At our next rendez-vous, she brought a chaperone whom I did not like much. In the end, when I rang Ritva as arranged to take her out, she told me her mother had forbidden her to go with me. I was not pleased but met her several times again later in my stay.

By coincidence I was in Kuopio for the all-Finland finals of the women's 'pesäpallo', literally 'nest ball'. It is similar to rounders but very much for adults. There are eight in a team, and one team bats while the other fields. A batsman has three chances to hit the ball and then run to the first of three nests on the edge of a pitch some sixty or seventy yards long. The ball is thrown with surprising speed and accuracy between the fielders who wear leather gloves. This being the national championship final, the game was taken very seriously. Each team had a male team leader who shouted advice from the edge of the field but did not take part. In addition there was an umpire at each nest and at base, a table with two scorers and a large scoreboard. The final was between Kuopio and Vaasa; Kuopio won 13-3.

On my last day in Kuopio we set out for an evening at Haminalähti, headquarters of the Kuopio Shooting Club, where we enjoyed the sauna, the pleasantest I had experienced. The club was right on the lakeside, with windows looking out across the water. It was a beautiful sunny afternoon, the sauna was hot and the lake a delight to swim in; surprisingly it did not feel cold although the difference in temperature was from 90°C to 17°C.

The next morning before I left for the station, Mrs von Bonsdorff told me of her experiences in Finland, which I noted in my diary:

> 'When she was young she had been taken prisoner by the Red Finns in Viipuri because her father was fighting for the White Finns in 1918, and had been thrown into a cellar with many others. They were sentenced to death and told that the whole prison would be blown up with dynamite. After half an hour the guards came back and told them they had not enough dynamite to blow the walls but would shoot the prisoners as they came out. She and her sister, the only girls, were spared and told that they would be sent to the Russian barracks. Many were shot, others turned loose and then the White Finns arrived.'

I also heard about the evacuation from Karelia in 1940:

> 'Herr von Bonsdorff was commander of the frontier guard at Sortavala and their family was one of the last to go. There was no time to pack things. The Russians allowed one week for the whole area to be evacuated, the distance between the old and new frontiers being at that

point about seventy kilometres, and they advanced ten kilometres a day, relentlessly. All the Finns smashed up their houses and furniture and everything that could not be taken with them was destroyed or burnt. The evacuation took place in late autumn and there was much suffering. Herr von Bonsdorff had also been one of 2000 young Finns who had slipped out of the country in 1916 for training in Germany.'

She also gave me an interesting account of relations between Finnish and Swedish speaking Finns:

'In times of crisis, the hatred between Swedish and Finnish speaking Finns disappeared completely. This hatred had been very real 50 years ago [1900s] for all the educated and wealthy Finns spoke Swedish and were in the minority. Today there still lingers a certain amount of estrangement between the two races. The Swedes keep to themselves and the Finns feel themselves slightly lost among the refinements of the Swedes, although they will not admit it very readily. The industrial wealth and ability lies with the Swedes, and the artistic talent with the Finns, and the strength of Finland lies in a blend of these two races.'

These differences owe their origin to Finland's history. It had been part of Sweden until 1809 when the Russians took it over as a Grand Duchy in the Tsarist empire. It was a predominantly agricultural country and only from about the middle of the 19th century did Finnish nationalism emerge, as was happening in so many European countries. I doubt whether any feeling of 'estrangement' now remains between the two cultures.

In an ironic transition between technologies, I travelled from the Bonsdorff's house to Kuopio bus station in a horse-drawn carriage, then to the airport to fly to Helsinki. Here I spent a week staying with Marja, one of the girls I had met the year before in Austria. I was generously entertained and taken round the sights of Helsinki with her friends. I wrote in my diary: 'It is sad to be leaving Finland. A beautiful country, with the kindest and most hospitable people I have met anywhere, even in Norway.'

The change from Finland to Sweden did not come easily. I found Stockholm crowded and noisy. I had been awarded a bursary by the Swedish Institute to study Swedish, staying with a Swedish family in the suburbs of the city. The father was a retired archivist and an agreeable personality; his wife was much engaged in running the household and looking after their three daughters, one of whom, Birgit, came with me on visits to the city and helped me with folk dances. I was anxious to learn as much Swedish as possible and worked at it in the stuffy town library.

My Swedish teacher in Cambridge, Brita Mortensen, got in touch and we met up; she was surprised that I did not like Stockholm and suggested I should get out into the countryside. She also advised me to remove the flag of Finland from my button-hole, which a girl in Rakatunturi had given me as a keepsake. It was not long, however, before I settled in and enjoyed all that Stockholm offers – Drottningsholm theatre for opera and Skansen for folk music and dancing with Birgit, and much more.

A few days were spent staying at a hotel in Mörrum in south Sweden to fish in the river. It was good to get away from the city, even better to land an eighteen pound salmon. Then to Denmark for a night in the Copenhagen Youth Hostel, in a none too pleasant dormitory with thirty beds and no ventilation. The ferry to Harwich had been delayed because of a storm and I moved into the cheapest hotel I could find, the Annex to the Mission Hotel near the main square, where breakfast was accompanied with a reading from Scripture. And so back to Broadstairs.

It was not long before I returned to Cambridge and I now feel guilty that I had not spent more of the long vacation at home with the family. I think the time away was justified. I had visited all the Scandinavian countries and met with great kindness and generous hospitality wherever I had been. I had learnt a lot of their history and culture and had some remarkable experiences, not least in fishing. All this was a help in my last year of studies at university, which included Swedish.

On leaving university I attempted to put my basic knowledge of Icelandic to good use by taking a holiday job in an agricultural college at Hólar í Hjaltadal in north Iceland; the language had evolved little since Viking times on account of Iceland's isolation from continental influences. Nevertheless, it was a struggle, as was the agriculture. With the long summer days we were expected to labour in the fields until between 10 and 11 o'clock at night if the weather was fine. My diary records that I went to one or two dances in the village. At one, I danced with an Icelandic girl who kept saying something to me, a word which I did not understand. I asked my next partner what it meant; it meant 'Stop!' I have never been much of a dancer.

After a month at the agricultural college, I set off to fish and by chance was given a lift by a minister who had been attending a conference at Hólar, which is the Episcopal centre for northern Iceland. I ended up at a farm beside a famous salmon river where I would have liked to fish. It was, however, strictly private and I was not allowed to cast a line there. The farmer was helpful and suggested that I fish a small tributary nearby and here I had good sport. When I came to go at the end of the week, he charged me £7 in Icelandic money for the fishing but gave me credit for the same amount in respect of a salmon I had handed to him. He was, I suspect, a religious man for he had noticed with approval that I had in my room a copy of the Bible and notes from the Bible Reading Fellowship which I had taken with me on my travels.

My last week in Iceland was spent with a minister near lake Myvatn. He kindly lent me a bicycle so that I could fish a river where the trout were exceptionally large and keen to take the flies I offered them; I landed several of around 6 pounds in weight. It was not comfortable fishing; the landscape was barren and strong winds would blow along clouds of fine volcanic dust. In Reykjavik I was able to visit Thingvellir, the site of the first democratic Parliament and places of geological interest. Iceland is a remarkable country.

Three years at a university like Cambridge were a wonderful experience and obviously offered much more than just the opportunity to indulge in travel during the long vacation, as described above. For my first year I was accommodated in Memorial Court, near the main college building and quickly settled into the student way of life, even if I had problems with my studies after National Service. In the second year students were expected to move into registered lodgings around the town. In these one's conduct was subject to certain regulations, for example the need to be in by a certain time. Alan Last, my neighbour in my first year, and I were fortunate to be assigned to a private home in Newnham. It was the Old Oast House in Malting Lane belonging to Sybil Drew, a fencing instructor of some standing since she had trained the British Olympic team shortly after the war. She was often away and Alan and I came and went as we pleased. On Sundays she invited us to join her for coffee and a piano recital in her large drawing room given by a mathematics professor, David Popplewell. Not long after I left, she moved to Notting Hill in London and was again my landlady when I moved there on joining the Foreign Office. For our last year at Clare we had rooms in the Old Court overlooking the river.

We enjoyed the normal social life as well as attending lectures and tutorials. I thought I would have another go at playing rugby and signed up for a team. It was still not to my taste – I was viciously tackled and did not try it again. I did not row but enjoyed punting on the river with friends and one winter skating on it. More to my taste was a dining club – the Clarence Society – probably named after Lionel, Duke of Clarence, a son of Edward III. Membership was a combination of undergraduates and fellows of the college. Once a term, we met to dine together on a menu designed by one of the undergraduates as president. He would plan both food and drink on a particular theme, for example French,

Italian or Scottish dishes. For my turn I arranged a Swedish meal with Smörgåsbord and roast goose accompanied by schnapps and Carlsberg lager, generously given to us by the UK distributors. The college kitchen nearby prepared and served the meal for us.

At that time, attendance at dinner in hall was virtually compulsory, a formal affair at which every one wore a gown over a jacket and tie. A lengthy grace in Latin was read before we sat down. Our food was served by waiters who also took orders for beer which was brought in pewter tankards. Former college members receive an invitation every ten years to a reunion dinner where similar formality is observed, but I believe that arrangements nowadays are much more casual.

Much was made at the time of the May Ball and I believe still is. I am not keen on dancing, nor on staying up all night to take part. A friend with similar views in another college owned a car – unusual for an undergraduate in those days – and arranged for us to go away for the week-end to fish at Blagdon reservoir near Bristol. It was wonderful to get away. I also fished for pike in waters near Cambridge within cycling distance.

I had of course worked hard at my studies during those three years and had overcome my earlier shortcomings. The Tripos part II exams had been taken and I was pleased to achieve Grade 2.1 in the result. Modern Languages on their own are not the gateway to a career unless accompanied by other qualifications; I needed to explore possibilities and seek employment for the years ahead.

Chapter 5

Looking for a Job

On returning from Iceland after six weeks spent partly working on a farm, partly fishing minor rivers, it was necessary to start looking for a job – or rather determining a career, for it was more usual at that time to decide on a lifelong occupation and then to seek employment within that framework.

Correspondence from family members during my last term at Cambridge made plain that I was already worried about this; letters from my mother and elder brother David exhorted me not to worry about it, but rather to concentrate on my studies to ensure the best possible result in the final exams. Once these were over, I had to face up to reality. I liked the idea of some kind of career in trees and forests but of course I was totally unqualified for this. Teaching was another option but I was anxious to go abroad, preferably to Scandinavia, rather than settle into a job at home. One thing was certain: I did not want to work in London. I wrote in my diary: 'I made a firm resolution that I would never take a permanent job in London. It is such a foul city, so dirty, noisy and crowded: I have had many opportunities of watching the masses of people crowding like sardines into the Underground and struggling for standing room in the suburban trains. It seems an abnegation of life itself to commit oneself to this sort of existence, every day of the year, and every year of one's working life. Acute discomfort and an appalling waste of time.'

Such rantings were of course unrealistic and impractical. Since Scandinavia was the source of most of the timber imported into the United Kingdom, I made inquiries about timber-importing firms and had been given an introduction by John Boyce, headmaster of Wellesley House, to Brandt & Co, a firm with offices in the City and lots of connections with timber suppliers. I was interviewed by the Managing Director of the Wallboard and Plywood Department, who wanted me to deal in these wares, especially with regard to Germany. He told me that in my career

I would finally arrive at *his* position. This did not impress me and I told him so. According to my diary, 'he insisted upon the necessity for the keen commercial spirit of competition and reiterated the importance of being able to 'do down' other people.' I objected that I would be far happier to let everyone have a fair and equal share of trade and do away with this vicious kind of business. I also objected to having only a fortnight's holiday a year, which seemed to me to be quite preposterous. I would need at least four weeks to allow me to ski in winter and fish in the summer.

'May I enquire what your hobbies are,' I then asked, 'and how do you spend your spare time?'

'Well,' he replied, 'I only play bridge, and that takes my mind off business schemes. My work in any case allows me no free time for anything else.'

I was not encouraged by this but nevertheless offered to give the job a trial run for a few months, an offer which, not surprisingly, was refused.

In October, 1955 my tutor Dr A. H. McDonald, who had served in intelligence during the war, suggested that there might be opportunities in the Foreign Office and kindly gave me an introduction to a member of the Personnel Department. Not long afterwards I was summoned to interview with an invitation to lunch at a club in Pall Mall. It was a pleasant and relaxed occasion, although I had unwisely mentioned that I had been in Finland and tried to learn the language at university. I was asked to answer the telephone when it rang and respond. The call was in Finnish and I could manage no more than the most elementary greetings.

My host had indicated that he was from MI6 and at the end of our lunch-time conversation, told me that he did not think that a job in his department would suit me; he pointed out that my interests were in the countryside and his organisation was town-based. He also pointed out, in the nicest way, that I was inexperienced; if I was still interested in two years time, I should come back. Meanwhile, he suggested, why not try for the straight diplomatic service? It was 30 November, the last day for applications for the Senior Civil Service; I could cross the road to Savile Row where the Civil Service Commissioners had their offices.

I had already considered this course of action the year before but had done nothing about it, partly from sheer indecision, partly from reluctance to get involved and the heavy odds against success. Besides, I had already booked to go on a skiing party to Austria that January. Now the circumstances were different and I duly filled in the forms just in time before the office closed.

To quote again from my diary:

'I shall not easily forget those January exams, which took place immediately after the New Year. All previous exams I have taken have been at the height of summer, when we could relax in the shade of trees or go swimming. Now London was at its worst, with a thick layer of smog enveloping the capital. I stayed at the Ashley Court Hotel in Queen's Gate, Kensington. The exams took place at the Town Hall, Kensington, and when I arrived there in the fog on the Monday morning, I found several friends whom I knew from Marlborough and Cambridge – people I had always considered to be the most intelligent. There were over a hundred candidates; many were dressed up in city clothes and some behaved with disgusting precociousness and affectation, as if they were the cream of the aristocracy and sure to get through.'

The exams were intended to assess the knowledge and competence of the candidate of any academic speciality. There were five papers; Essay, English, two General Papers and General Intelligence. I did my best.

I must have been feeling quite despondent for on the second evening in the hotel, I telephoned the agents for the Finnish Steamship Company and made a provisional booking for a passage on the next available sailing to Finland; I was determined to go back to the country of my dreams, even at the risk of not being able to get a job there. I was fed up with life in England which I found boring; although I was doing some quantity surveyor work for my father in his office, I did not really enjoy it; my future did not lie in that direction.

One possible option was to apply to the British Council for a post in Finland, teaching English to adults; I had been reading a book *Journey to Finland* by Diana Ashcroft and I felt this was something I would enjoy. I went to the British Council offices off Oxford Street and was firmly but politely told that the posts were for one year from September, with recruitment taking place in July.

Then things began to look up. A day or so later, returning home from London, I was told by my mother that the British Council had rung up to say they had found something for me and wanted to see me as soon as possible. It transpired that the Teacher Secretary in Oulu, North Finland, had been obliged to come home at short notice and the English Club wanted a replacement. I was offered the job more or less as a foregone conclusion and on 18 January, 1956 I sailed from Hull on the cargo ship *s/s Clio*. And to my delight I was informed by the Civil Service Commissioners that I had passed the exams and would be required to attend the next stage in the spring.

It was a magnificent crossing. There were only eight passengers on board so we got to know each other and the captain was very friendly. The journey had been advertised as bound for Helsinki but at the last moment this was changed to Turku in south-west Finland. No reason was given but the freezing-over of the Gulf of Finland was a likely explanation. Crossing the North Sea was rough in the wake of a gale the previous day and there was little or no cargo on board to stabilise the ship. The gale returned with the ferocity of force 11 as we sailed up the Baltic. As I wrote in a letter home:

> 'The sea was a remarkable sight, with enormous waves passing by and spray being blown along so that from the upper deck, it looked like a desert of shifting sand. Towards evening, we had to turn north so that the wind was coming from the side. It became somewhat uncomfortable at this stage and I could not eat much dinner, although I was not ill'.

On the final morning, just as it was getting light, we entered Turku harbour. It was very cold, the sea was frozen and the landscape covered in snow. I had arrived.

Finland has an interesting history as a country between East and West. Until 1809 it was a province of the Swedish empire and Swedish influence is still much in evidence. Roughly ten per cent of Finns speak Swedish as their first language, living predominantly along the west coast on the Gulf of Bothnia. During the 19th century, the professional and land-owning families were from the Swedish speaking aristocracy; administration and education were likewise in the hands of Swedish speakers. There was little scope for higher education and training, and artists, for example, went abroad to study, mostly to Düsseldorf in the first half of the 19th century. Russia invaded Finland in 1808 and Sweden could do little to protect its eastern territory. At a ceremony in Porvoo cathedral in March, 1809, Finland formally became a grand duchy of Russia, enjoying a considerable measure of autocracy. The tsar Alexander II was widely respected for his liberal policies. His statue stands in the main square in Helsinki. In 1899, after Nicholas II had made plain his determination to bring Finland under more central control, wreaths were laid at the foot of Alexander II's statue as an expression of Finnish admiration for a former and more liberal Tsar.

During the 19th century, as in Germany and other European countries, there was a general awakening of Finnish nationalism, typified by the Kalevala, a lengthy epic by Elias Lönnrot which inspired artists like Gallen-Kallela and Sibelius, whose compositions Finlandia and the Karelia suite enjoyed great popularity in Finland and abroad. Finland, as a Russian grand-duchy, became involved in the First World War. When the Russian revolution in 1917 brought an end to Russian participation in hostilities, the revolution spread to Finland and a civil war broke out between the communists and White forces. The leader of the latter was Marshall Mannerheim who succeeded in establishing a democracy and became Finland's first president.

In World War II, Finland fought against the Russians in two conflicts. The first was the Winter War in 1939-40. Under the secret protocol of the Molotov-Ribbentrop Agreement Karelia was assigned to the Soviet Union's sphere of interest. The Soviet government considered that the Finnish frontier now came uncomfortably close to Leningrad and demanded the cession of the Karelian Isthmus bordering Lake Ladoga and military bases. Finland refused and the Russians invaded prompting the Winter War. Finnish forces fought bravely and with some success. They had received international support. Britain supplied 120 fighters, twenty four bombers, and also anti-aircraft guns and a range of other equipment. In the end, Soviet numbers overwhelmed Finnish defences and a large area of Karelia was handed over.

When Germany invaded the Soviet Union in 1941, it wanted to attack Leningrad through Finland. If the Finns had not allowed them to do so, they would almost certainly have been occupied. Thus Finland found itself engaged in a Continuation War. Territory lost in the Winter War was recaptured along with other areas, only to be lost again in 1944. Some 400,000 people crossed into Finland in that year. Under the peace agreement with the Soviet Union, Finland was obliged to drive out the remaining German forces from the north of the country. Finland also lost the Petsamo province with its access to the North Atlantic and in addition to extensive reparations was obliged to cede the Porkkala peninsula west of Helsinki to the Soviet Union as a military base for ten years.

It had seemed possible that Finland would share the fate of the Baltic States, Poland and other East European countries to become a 'Democratic Republic' under Soviet control if it had not complied with Soviet demands. Fortunately this did not happen but Finland had to steer a narrow course between East and West, ever conscious that too close a relationship with West Europe and NATO countries could trigger Soviet intervention, for example if they accepted Marshall aid. Equally, there were commercial and economic reasons for Finland to trade with the west. The country's president in these years was Urho Kekkonen, who maintained a policy of strict neutrality for which he was criticised in western circles for cosying up to the Russians. The year I arrived in Oulu, reparations had been completed and Porkkala was returned to Finnish sovereignty in January, 1956. This position was maintained during the Cold War, with Helsinki from a position of neutrality becoming a force in attempts to improve east-west relations. For many years, the Helsinki Protocol, establishing rules of conduct in human rights matters, was often quoted by western governments as justification for criticising Soviet behaviour.

On arrival in Oulu, I was provided with a bed-sit in a block of flats overlooking the main square; it had the pretentious name of 'Valkea Linna' or 'White Castle'. The British consul, Mr Douglas, and his wife were my mentors; they looked after me most hospitably and helped me to settle into my work with the English club. For my first event there we began with a Quiz, which went well and was followed by tennis and a sauna. The club's junior section met soon afterwards and to my surprise was attended by forty young people, thirty girls and ten boys.

The job entailed much more than just teaching English. I was in effect the English Society's secretary, responsible for administering its various activities. Members were mainly middle-aged and from business and professional backgrounds. Lessons took place either in my room or in the students' homes, in the latter case invariably with coffee and cakes. In fact, I almost lived off coffee and cakes as I had little money and there was not much food available. Fresh vegetables were not to be found; the nearest one got to vegetables was pickled gherkins.

The teaching was fun, less so the secretarial work. This involved organising activities such as quiz nights and expeditions. In one case we had a visit to Virpiniemi, a village some twenty-five kilometres from Oulu, for skiing, a sauna and a talk on English folksongs by a lecturer from Helsinki. Part of my duties was to arrange transport for those going on the trip, a task made more difficult by the inability of many to commit themselves one way or the other; it seems they preferred to wait and see how they felt on the day and then decide.

Cross-country skiing was my favourite relaxation. The countryside around Oulu is undulating and covered by extensive forests. The only constraint was the temperature as it was often too cold to go out. One morning I was surprised to see people in the street walking backwards; the thermometer had dropped to -40°C, bringing a risk of frostbite if one's face was not properly covered. In practice, any temperature above about -27°C was bearable for skiing and I would take advantage of what little daylight there was to ski off into the countryside. There were well-defined tracks in the snow which one could follow leading to a hut offering hot drinks, very welcome in the cold. One day the ground was covered with fresh powder snow; I took a wrong turning following fresh tracks and to my embarrassment found myself joining up with an army patrol on a training exercise. On a few occasions, I went out at night by moonlight onto the frozen sea. The northern lights were in full array, with curtains flickering across the sky in red, yellow and green, a sight I shall never forget.

In March 1955, there was a general strike which closed down the railways and the post for three weeks. The reasons were partly political, partly economic; Finland had just completed its programme of war reparations to the Soviet Union and for many life was difficult. I had written home to say that I did not feel threatened despite unrest but a few days later I was attacked on my way home late one evening by a drunken youth. He shouted at me with words which I could not understand except for 'Saksalainen'; he thought I was German. His dislike of Germans was no doubt fuelled by memories of the last stage of the Continuation War, when at Russian insistence Finland fought to remove German forces. Receiving no reply to his tirade, he gave me a black eye which took a few days to mend.

As my time in Oulu came to a close, I was sorry to leave. By now the weather had improved with cold, frosty nights and warm sunshine by day – perfect conditions for skiing and each day was noticeably longer than the one before. After staying in Kuopio with Kim's uncle's family, the von Bonsdorffs, I flew back to England in time for the next stage of my Foreign Office application. It had been a most enjoyable and rewarding time. The unhappy encounter with the yob in no way diminished my love for a beautiful country and its friendly people.

After returning home from Finland, the next stage in the Foreign Office's selection process was a two-day session for a limited number of applicants. This comprised interviews, discussion groups with each candidate taking a turn in the chair and giving a ten-minute talk on a topic of one's choice. The chairman was an official, Paul Holmer, whom I was to come across later in Moscow. This must have gone well as a few days later I was invited to report to Carlton House Terrace for a final interview.

In the centre of the room was a large ring-shaped table. On one side of the ring sat seven officers. I was not informed who they were but as chairman in the middle was the Head of Personnel, John Henniker-Major. I sat opposite. I remember only two of the questions put to me. If successful, would I be prepared to learn Arabic as a hard language? This was awkward. I knew that HM Government attached great importance to our relations in the Middle East, but I did not want to learn that language with the consequent commitment to postings in the hot dry lands of the

Arabic-speaking world. To reply 'No' would almost certainly result in rejection. I therefore tried to get round it by explaining that in principle I would enjoy learning a hard language but would prefer Persian. John Henniker-Major then asked me:

'Martin, what do you consider to be the most significant recent event in Anglo-Danish relations?'

I hadn't a clue and said so. 'It would be the Anglo-Danish Bacon Agreement' explained John Henniker-Major. Maybe, I thought, but how was I expected to know about bacon? Perhaps the question was intended to be a difficult one to see how I reacted.

Not long afterwards I received a letter informing me that I had been accepted. There were only eight of us to join the service that year. The person at the top of the list had been assessed at 300 points. I was one of four on 240 points. On the written exams in Kensington Town Hall, I had scored a few marks less than my future colleagues. I was fortunate to get in.

We began in September with an introductory course attended also by young diplomats from a range of Commonwealth countries. We had a series of talks, some good, others less so. One of the latter was so long-winded and boring that I think the Malayan group suddenly started vigorous applause to bring the talk to an end.

Those of us who were to study a hard language were being asked for our preferences. The choice lay between a one-year course in less difficult languages, of which Russian was one, the slightly more difficult such as Persian or Amharic for two years and the really hard ones – Chinese and Japanese for example, which required three years. I had put in for Russian, but with Persian still a possibility. During a lunch break, another entrant, Leslie Fielding, and I were taking a stroll in St James's Park when he raised the matter.

'I have been asked to choose between Persian and Russian', he told me 'and I cannot decide which to go for. I will toss up for it – heads for Russian, tails for Persian.'

'That can't be right', I interrupted as he dipped into his pocket for a coin, 'heads should be for the royal Shah of Persia, tails for the communists.'

'OK,' he replied, 'heads for Persian, tails for Russian'. He launched the coin spinning into the air.... and it came down heads.

It has always amazed me that the course of my life from that moment on should have been determined by the spin of a coin, even more so my part in it by reversing Leslie's suggestion. He went on to Iran to learn Persian, was later posted to Pnom Penh at the time of the Khmer Rouge, an event described in his book *The Killing Fields*. Later he moved to Brussels as the UK's representative on foreign affairs with the European Union. Since retirement he has published *Kindly Call Me God*, an interesting and entertaining set of memoirs, and *Mentioned in Despatches* recalling his despatches from posts abroad in the past and contemplating the role of diplomacy in the future.

There were four of us on the Russian course, Alan Urwick, John Ure and myself in Branch A and Norman Flower in administrative Branch B. Lessons took place in a small room in Carlton House Terrace and were given by a Russian émigré, Mr Esterkin (We never knew his first name and called him 'Gospodin Esterkin'). He was good company, but a sad little man who once said that he had no object in life. It transpired that his wife had been a Belgian racing driver and died in a crash; he had no children. Lessons went on all morning with a coffee break at a café in the Haymarket, while in the afternoon we had homework, mostly learning vocabulary. For a change I would often go ice-skating and take skating lessons at the rink in Queensway, having skated a lot in Finland.

It was a grind and looking back on that year, I perceive two short-comings. We did little, if any, oral work and, secondly, the Russian we learnt was not the Russian of the post-revolution Soviet Union. In the Easter break, John Ure and I spent a delightful fortnight staying with a Russian family, the Tolstoys, near Drogheda in Ireland, who grew mushrooms. We spoke some Russian by then but for much of the time we indulged in our hobbies, riding for John and salmon fishing for me. The lack of oral practice in the nine months of study in London was to some extent made up for by a stay of three months with White Russian émigrés in Paris and by taking further lessons. Although Paris had much to offer, it was unfortunate that I fell ill and had to have an appendix operation at the British Military Hospital shortly before returning home to join the family on a salmon-fishing holiday on the river Dee in Scotland.

It was felt appropriate for me to gain experience in the office in London before going abroad and I was given a desk in the American Department with responsibility for the Falkland Islands and Antarctica. This was at a time when there was some tension between those countries claiming sovereignty over Antarctic territory. The basis of the claims was in theory a country's width of latitude extended in a cone to the South Pole. Claims inevitably overlapped and Argentina in particular was resentful of the U.K.'s claim based on a cone extension from South Georgia and the Falklands which they in any case regarded as Argentine territory.

From time to time, Argentina would set up a base on British Antarctic territory and in order to protect our legal position, we were obliged to deliver a note to the base objecting to it having been established at that spot without our permission and reasserting our sovereignty. Failure to do so would give Argentina some measure of right by default. The Admiralty were involved in the mechanics of delivery; I would meet my opposite number in the Admiralty at a pub at the top of Whitehall where we would discuss over a pint the best way of getting the note handed over.

It was an unsatisfactory state of affairs and fortunately it was later resolved with the conclusion of the Antarctic Treaty, signed in 1959. This followed on from the International Geophysical Year of 1957-58 and entered into force in 1961. It provided that all claims to Antarctica should be held in abeyance (i.e. put on ice) for twenty-five years, with an undertaking to co-operate in exploration and scientific research. My head of department, Henry Hankey, was responsible for much of the preparation.

These first months in the Foreign Office were difficult, mainly because I was not tuned in to the conventions of office conduct. On one occasion, I had sent some papers first to the Legal Adviser and then to an Assistant Under-Secretary when I heard that the matter was to be the subject of a Parliamentary Question the following week. This demanded immediate action so I rang up the Assistant Under-Secretary's office and had a note put on the file asking for its prompt return. The Assistant Under-Secretary was annoyed at 'receiving orders from below' and rang up my head of department to say so. My assessment of the need was correct, but perhaps not the way I had handled it.

Drafting letters also caused much difficulty. Drafts were written in long hand on a blue-tinted paper with a wide margin and submitted to the assistant head of department for approval. This was Toby Hildyard, a brilliant diplomat who demanded high standards. My drafts were returned to me mauled about and needing a complete rewrite. This was very depressing, but I learnt much from him which has served me well, not only in the Foreign Office but in later years writing reports on my pupils at Shrewsbury School and also on retirement working for CPRE and the Shrewsbury Civic Society.

The diary I kept at the time recorded a certain unhappiness with what I was doing. One day, after seeing a Swedish film *The Great Adventure* about forests and the creatures that inhabited them, I wrote:

> *'Whenever I see a film like this and at other times too, I long for a life
> in the country, away from wretched towns, with their dirt, bustle and*

noise and at such times I often wish I was a farmer or someone always in the country, and regret having joined the Diplomatic Service 'What shall it profit a man if he gain the whole world, but lose his own soul?' But then I ought not to complain, for a diplomatic career must surely be one of the most interesting and varied and I am very lucky to be where I am.'

And so for the time being I stayed there.

PART 2

Chapter 6

First posting in Moscow

My first year working in the Foreign Office had not been easy but at the end of it, it was time to prepare for departure to Moscow. The Cold War had emerged quietly at the end of The Second World War once the victory celebrations had died down. There were many reasons for this including tensions between the Soviet Union and the Western allies over the spheres of influence agreed by the allied leaders at Yalta in 1945, fundamental political differences between capitalism and communism and the innate Russian suspicions of foreign powers. Diplomatic staff serving in Moscow and Soviet representatives in London were in effect in the front line, accepted as necessary by the host country but regarded as the enemy in an ideological struggle.

Russian distrust, even fear, of foreigners has deep roots going back to the emergence of a Russian state in the 11th to 13th centuries, first in Kiev with links to Byzantium, later in Muscovy. Of great significance in the formation of the Russian state was the Mongol invasion in 1237. Genghis Khan had died in 1227 having created an empire stretching from China to the frontiers of Europe. This was split up between his seven sons and the eldest Juji inherited responsibility for the conquest of the western part. A reconnaissance expedition in 1221 provided intelligence for his son Batu to launch an offensive; within six years Russia, Poland, Silesia, Hungary, Serbia and Bulgaria had been conquered by the Golden Horde, forced to submit to Tartar rule and pay tribute for the next two centuries.

While Tartar domination had delayed the emergence of a Russian state, it bequeathed a positive if unpalatable legacy. The Mongol empire was based on meticulous administration, an efficient communications system covering the vast area of the empire and utter ruthlessness in enforcing Mongol rule. Moscow, which had been stormed by Batu in 1238, became the centre for Tartar administration. Conscription enforced by Genghis Khan on every male of any nationality within the empire

71

led to the creation of military strength, while the Tartar system for gathering tribute was the basis for a system of taxation. The Tartars were driven out in 1462, with Ivan the Great establishing the independent state of Muscovy. Tartar cruelty and ruthlessness were also inherited as evidenced by Ivan the Terrible, who reigned from 1533 to 1584 with oppression and terror – he even murdered his own son. The Romanov dynasty of tsars was founded by Mikhail Romanov in 1613 and lasted until the 1917 Revolution.

Russia lacked clearly defined and defensible frontiers and was engaged at various times in wars with its western neighbours, notably Poland, Lithuania, Sweden and Austro-Hungary. At the same time it was realised that successful development required western trade and technology. In 1554 Richard Chancellor had led an expedition to the White Sea and opened up trade with Russia via Archangel, while Peter the Great founded St Petersburg in 1703 bringing in mostly Italian architects and craftsmen to create a new capital city. He also established a demanding bureaucratic administration. His flirtation with the West was much resented by Moscow traditionalists.

Distrust of foreign powers had been fostered by invasion from the west both by Napoleon in 1812 and Hitler in 1941 (despite the Molotov-Ribbentrop Non-aggression Pact of 1939). These two invasions have left their mark on the Russian psyche. So has the Anglo-French intervention in the 1919 Civil War on the side of the Whites. The contribution by western countries to the Soviet Union during World War II through the Arctic convoys was never given the recognition it deserved during the communist years. In fact, it was rarely mentioned, although the Russians had offered an award to crews involved in the convoys, an offer which our government was unable to accept. An ambivalent attitude towards the west, a desire to protect Russian traditions from foreign influence on one hand and the need for trade and Western technology on the other persist to this day.

This was the setting into which I entered as Private Secretary to the Ambassador, Sir Patrick Reilly, and his wife Rachel. Sir Patrick was one of our most distinguished diplomats of the time. He had been a scholar at Winchester and fellow of All Souls, Oxford. He had served in Tehran, Athens and as Minister in Paris before being appointed as Ambassador in Moscow in 1957. This was a difficult time in Anglo-Soviet relations, indeed in relations between the Communist East and NATO countries in the West at the height of the Cold War. It was to prove a very challenging post for the Reillys.

The Embassy was located in a former sugar baron's residence in a prime position on Sofiiskaya Naberezhnya, overlooking the Moskva river and, beyond that, the Kremlin with the golden domes of the churches standing high above the fortifications; one could not have found a more spectacular place for our Embassy. In contrast to the Kremlin's resplendent domes, the Moscow streets were drab and dreary and both men's and women's attire lacked style, colour and interest. In winter, the scene was particularly gloomy. However, large red banners exhorting the population with messages such as 'Forward to the Victory of Communism' and 'Workers of the World Unite' brightened the streets and Red Square. Here too were large portraits of Lenin and Stalin, whose bodies lay on display in the Mausoleum – that is, until Khrushchev's demotion of Stalin in the historical hierarchy led to the removal of his body and the replacement of his portrait by his own. There were impressive military parades on the national festivals of May Day and the anniversary of the Revolution on November 7, with the Politburo members lined up on the Mausoleum.

Processions with banners and portraits of the communist hierarchy have their origin in Tsarist times, when icons would be paraded on religious feast-days. Also inherited from the Tsars was the cult of the personality, with pictures of communist leaders replacing the icons. This tended to disappear after the collapse of communism in the Soviet Union. It is however, an ingrained characteristic of Russian leaders. In 2014, when Vladimir Putin celebrated his sixty-second birthday, it was reported that artists in Moscow unveiled portraits of Mr Putin as Hercules carrying out the twelve legendary tasks with a contemporary twist; instead of battling the Hydra, he was seen in hand-to-hand combat with the many-headed monster of Western sanctions, imposed after Russia's actions in the Ukraine. Elsewhere, children dressed in white sang 'Happy Birthday, President of Russia' in a video shot in St Petersburg.

The Embassy housed both the Ambassador's residence and offices. The central building was on two floors, with an attic above for the servants' quarters and a basement below with kitchen, larder and storage area. The main offices were on the ground floor, while above was a large drawing room in French empire style suitable for receptions; also on this floor were a dining room, the Ambassador's private quarters which included a luxurious Gothick bathroom, and the pantry with a lift to bring food up from the kitchen below. Two separate wings, one on each side of the main entrances, housed research, consular and administrative offices, and the doctor's surgery.

At the back of the house were two further buildings, formerly stables, which had been converted into flats for members of the embassy staff.

It was one of these flats that I was to share with John Ure, my colleague on the Russian language course in London, who had come out to Moscow a year before as my predecessor and as a Chancery Officer concerned with political matters. The flat consisted of a long corridor, with rooms off it, all on the same side overlooking the embassy yard with a bedroom each, a sitting room, dining room and kitchen. It was furnished by the Ministry of Works and we brought with us our own additional furnishings such as pictures, lamps, rugs, crockery, cutlery, etc. I had also brought a piano with me as I was taking lessons at the time and wanted to keep these going.

We also imported all our drink and a lot of the food we needed since little was available in Russian shops. Day-to-day groceries, meat, fish etcetera were provided by Moscow's Bureau for Servicing the Diplomatic Corps 'Burobin'. Weekly deliveries would consist almost always of caviar, smoked salmon, meat of various kinds, chicken, and game such as partridges or duck, and vegetables. These were the staple of diplomatic dinners and not available in Moscow shops for the general public.

An essential link with home was the Diplomatic Bag. Once a week two Queen's Messengers would bring out all mail, both official and private, under strict security supervision. My mother and I exchanged letters every week; I usually covered between four and ten sides of paper recounting all that had been going on. My mother meticulously filed all these letters and they have been an invaluable source of information.

The Diplomatic Bag also brought parcels from home. There were strict regulations on the size and content of parcels – nothing to be included that might leak out and damage other contents. I was surprised to find that shoes would be sent home for repair and clothes to be mended and cleaned. The bag would also bring out food, again subject to regulations regarding size and weight. My mother sailed close to the wind with some of her parcels for me, which might contain fruit from the garden and were most welcome. So we had little need to go shopping in Moscow, which in itself was difficult; there was little to be had in the shops and one was put off by the bureaucratic system whereby one had to queue up three times, first to find out the availability and price of what one needed, secondly, to pay for it at a till and finally to return to the counter with the receipt to collect the goods, the receipt hand-written in purple ink.

Burobin also supplied domestic staff. John Ure and I had a cook, Tonia, an elderly woman whose cooking was variable in quality, sometimes indifferent but on special occasions, if we had guests, she would produce good meals for us. The kitchen was not as clean as we would have wished and it was infested with cockroaches. These came out at night to scout around for food. To begin with I would suddenly switch on the light and hit as many as I could with a slipper before they sought refuge in dark corners. I saw off many but there were always more and in the end we had to have the kitchen disinfected with chemical insecticide to get rid of them.

As Private Secretary to the Ambassador my first responsibility was to make sure that he received all the papers he needed in his office and to keep track of his movements as set out in each day's diary. He travelled in a Rolls Royce limousine and I was required to ensure that his chauffeur was available when needed and that the car awaited him outside the front door. Often I would accompany him, and on occasions Lady Reilly, to functions such as national-day receptions at other embassies. Detailed guidance on how this was to be managed was provided in *Guidance on foreign usages and ceremony, and other matters, for a Member of His Majesty's Foreign Service on his first appointment to a Post Abroad* by Sir Marcus Cheke, Vice-Marshal of the Diplomatic Corps (January, 1949) This book was criticised and made fun of at the time for being out-of-date, for example in its detailed instructions on how and when visiting cards were to be sent to colleagues in other missions to inform them of one's arrival and it was later replaced with other guidance. For my part, I found its advice on the role of a Private Secretary in accompanying an Ambassador and his wife to receptions extremely helpful. I had to ensure that Lady Reilly sat on the Ambassador's right, while I perched on a tip-up seat immediately in front. If it was just Sir Patrick and myself, he sat on my right. If invited, I would attend the reception and summon the car as soon as he indicated that he wanted to leave; this was done through loudspeakers overlooking the parking area. If for some reason I got out on the way home, I would wait until the car had moved off before turning away (again as instructed by Marcus Cheke).

Another responsibility was that of making the appropriate arrangements for both receptions and meals at the embassy. Guest lists would be drawn up by the Ambassador and myself in consultation with staff members involved in the event, often numbering several hundred in the case of receptions including Soviet officials from the Ministry for Foreign Affairs and government departments where appropriate, colleagues from other embassies, representatives of the press and so on. I would meet guests by the front door, help them with their coats and point the way upstairs; if the visitors were important I would go with them and introduce them to the Ambassador and Lady Reilly. Towards the end of the party I would accompany such people down again and see them off.

For meals there was the problem of placement. Marcus Cheke explained the usual convention of the first lady guest sitting on the host's right, the chief male on the hostesses' right and so on. This seemed straightforward but there were complications. The first was the need to evaluate the order of precedence among disparate groups such as government ministers, heads of mission and officials from both missions and government departments. The second problem arose if, at the last minute, one or more of the guests cried off and one had to make the necessary adjustments without upsetting any one as some diplomats are unduly sensitive to their position in society and make a fuss if not satisfied. Marcus Cheke warns: 'In England, it often happens that the hostess says vaguely: 'Oh, let's sit down anywhere....'. If she does this abroad, the results are disastrous; every foreigner feels acutely embarrassed, and even if they manage to scramble into their correct places they are bound to feel offended.' Sir Patrick was always very anxious that all should be sitting next to the right people and for me at least, this took up a great deal of time to make sure that he was satisfied with my suggestions.

All this was put to the test a few months after my arrival with the visit of the Prime Minister Harold MacMillan and the Foreign Secretary Selwyn Lloyd in February 1959. The purpose of the visit was to achieve a better relationship with the Soviet Union and ease tensions in east-west relations at a time when these were distinctly sour, with the possibility of a summit meeting later. It would last ten days and involve talks with Soviet leaders and visits to Kiev and Leningrad. All this meant a great deal of work for the Ambassador and members of the staff. John Ure was to be concerned with arrangements at Third Secretary level while I was responsible for events in the Embassy. Another colleague, Derek Thomas, had to listen to a Russian band rehearsing the National Anthem to make sure they got it right.

Sir Patrick flew to England to spend the week-end at Chequers to brief Harold MacMillan before the visit. Meanwhile both John and I worked hard on preparations; he had to organise the distribution of presents worth £7,000 and draft speeches for the Prime Minister to deliver on various occasions during his stay, while I organised the reception for some five hundred guests, the despatch of invitations and a table plan for the dinner at the embassy.

The Prime Minister's party arrived at around midday to a formal ceremony in front of the airport building. It was relatively warm for the time of year (-2°C) but windy and damp and for those of us waiting on the tarmac, it felt a lot colder than it was. Nikita Khrushchev arrived shortly before the plane touched down and walked down the line of diplomatic and embassy staff shaking hands with everyone; he struck me as a small man of ugly porcine appearance. The plane was on time and Harold MacMillan and Selwyn Lloyd inspected a guard of honour while national anthems were played and then came down the line of waiting diplomats. Speeches were exchanged while we all stood around in the cold. The party then set off for their residence in the middle of Moscow.

This was not the end of their day. Once MacMillan and Lloyd had settled in, they called on Khrushchev and the Foreign Minister Andrei Gromyko and were entertained to a large dinner at the Kremlin, which went on until 8 p.m. They then had a two-hour drive to Khrushchev's dacha in the countryside where another large dinner awaited them. They had had to get up at 6 a.m. in London and did not get to bed that evening until very late; they were absolutely exhausted.

The main event on the following Monday was a visit to Moscow University on the Lenin Hills. I accompanied the Ambassador to the residence to join the convoy of cars which travelled with motor-cycle outriders down the centre of closed-off streets. The arrangements at the university were chaotic; no effort had been made to control the large number of journalists and members of the public and wherever we went we had to fight our way through the mob. Furthermore, the lifts were not large enough to accommodate all of us; every time we changed floors (and there were many of them) the party was split up. I stayed with the Ambassador as best I could during visits to several laboratories, a geological museum, a lecture room where MacMillan gave a short speech to assembled students, then on to an assembly hall for further speeches.

The dinner which Sir Patrick gave for the Prime Minister and Foreign Secretary went well. The Soviet leaders were there in force and clearly in a good mood; the talks earlier in the day had been going well. Neither John nor I attended but there was much laughter, toasting, speech-making and pranking. Both Khrushchev and Mikoyan, First Deputy Premier with responsibility for foreign relations and a close supporter of Khrushchev, were enjoying themselves although I heard later that the former did not much appreciate somebody's joke about hunting wild pigs and he left soon afterwards.

The following day we had the embassy reception. I had been largely responsible for this and can best describe it with an extract from a letter home:

'The intention had been to keep the reception as small as possible; in fact the final guest list amounted to about 570 to 580 people and I think fully 500 people came. They consisted of about 350 Russians, 100

or more press representatives, 40 Embassy people and about 25 in the delegation. In the Embassy White Room a large table had been set at right angles across the room, leaving a gap of about 4 feet. This formed a barrier, behind which were placed the Prime Minister, the Foreign Secretary, Ambassadors and the main Russian leaders with interpreters. My job was to stand in the gap and let through only those people who were entitled to be there and to hold back journalists who were of course very keen indeed to get in. The party began at 7.30p.m. and for a quarter of an hour all was well. Then the journalists began to gather and push and for three quarters of an hour it was like a rugger scrum. I was on my own and just could not hold back the crowd. One man said he was a Russian but I did not know the name and so I assumed he was a journalist pulling my leg. I kept him out for half an hour, until he became really indignant and it transpired that he was an official interpreter from the Ministry for Foreign Affairs. By about 8.30p.m. I could hold back the crowd no longer, and they all flooded past me – they were in any case already infiltrating under the table. The Prime Minister and Foreign Secretary were promptly led out through the pantry and round a back way to the Ambassador's drawing room where they locked themselves in – the Prime Minister was not feeling very well after an exhausting day.'

Further difficulties arose the following day when, after a day of talks, the party were to go to a performance of Romeo and Juliet at the Bolshoi Theatre. I had been rushing around all day taking flowers to the theatre and attending to other details. I had changed and was about to set out when Lady Reilly phoned up to say she had no ticket. I had not managed ticket distribution and assumed she would be in the central box. In fact she was not and there ensued a frightful scene in which the Ambassador angrily wanted to know why she had not been given a ticket, this being a question I was in no position to answer. When we got to the theatre I gave her mine and sat in a spare seat at the back of another box. For me this was unsatisfactory, as I could not see well and I did not really enjoy the performance after a tiring day, but at least the Reillys were happy.

Documents in the Foreign Office archives make clear that up to this point, the visit had gone well. Discussions had ranged from an ultimatum over Berlin, which the Russians regarded as provocative, to problems of noise from the prestigious Soviet aeroplane TU-104. Allowing for the need to heed Khrushchev's sensitivity, the atmosphere had been friendly. Talks the following day broke down. Khrushchev had publicly spoken about discussions in an aggressive way calling for an Anti-Aggression Pact, in effect attacking the United Kingdom. He announced that he could not accompany the Prime Minister to Kiev because of toothache, and Mikoyan had another commitment. The British party discussed how to handle this new situation, even considering breaking off the visit, and they had to do this in the garden in freezing cold and snow as there was evidence that their dacha was bugged. Visits to Kiev and Leningrad proceeded as planned and as the visit approached its end, relations improved with a magnificent reception at the Kremlin on the eve of their departure.

The visit had resulted in a better appreciation by each side of the other's policies. It had been dominated by Khrushchev's sensitivity and outspokenness and a proposal for a later meeting of east-west Foreign Ministers in Paris. In the event, nothing came of this. Relations between the Soviet Union and NATO countries worsened with the shooting down of the American U2 spy plane over Siberia. The U2 was a reconnaissance aircraft capable of flying at great altitudes; unfortunately the Americans had underestimated the range of Russian anti-aircraft missiles. The Soviet press made a great deal of this event and laid on an exhibition in Gorky Park. The pilot Gary Powers had survived and the display of his equipment, camera and the photographs he had taken were indeed impressive.

Receptions at the Embassy always involved a lot of work. The largest was the Queen's Birthday Reception held at embassies all over the world in honour of her Majesty's official birthday at the beginning of June (her actual birthday is April 21). The Moscow QBR of 1960 was held on June 9. For the preceding few days Kay Rawson, the Ambassador's secretary, and I were working hard trying to make sure that all had received invitations who should have done and keeping track of all the British visitors who applied for invitations at the last moment, some of whom had to be asked and others refused. The number was 1,500. The party was a shambles. It was to be held in the garden but at 3.30p.m. it began to pour with rain and we had to hold it in the Embassy. All the rooms were choked with guests; about 670 came in addition to the 130 or so Embassy people who were there already. Luckily the sun came out and we were able to move the party out into the garden where it went on until about 9 p.m., having started shortly after 5 o'clock. It was an exhausting day; members of the staff are required to turn up before the beginning and to stay on until after the last guest has gone.

As Private Secretary I was also involved in the Reillys' domestic affairs, paying the locally engaged staff who worked in their household and occasionally fetching wine for meals from the cellar. Food was even more of a problem for them than wine as they did not want to rely on Burobin to provide the necessary supplies for the extensive entertainment which they offered. This was the beginning of the era of deep freeze and one of my most memorable expeditions took me to Leningrad to meet Lady Reilly, two footmen and 1,000 pounds of frozen meat for the embassy. I had travelled to Leningrad by train with the Reillys' cook, Freddy Whittaker. Again, my letters home gave a full account:

'I had ordered the lorry to be available at 4 p.m. (to catch the train at 11.50p.m. with the meat) and arranged to pick up a representative of Intourist whom I understood to say that he would help me at the station. The lorry was not, however, going to be available until 5 p.m. and so I sent on Whittaker and the footmen by taxi to get all the meat and luggage off the ship, while I had a quiet tea and then came on with the lorry.

'One of our chief troubles was actually getting into the port area, which was defended like a military camp and where it took 10 or 15 minutes and several telephone calls before one could get in. When I finally got to the ship, the time now being about 5.30p.m., I found none of the stuff unloaded except a few trunks, and the captain drunk and still drinking in his cabin, being kept company by Whittaker. There were then countless delays and in the falling gloom and fog, there began a nightmare the like of which I have never experienced. First the dockers refused to unload the stuff. Then the man from Intourist arrived in a furious temper, because I had left him behind and he was so offensive that I had to turn my back and walk away. However, once he had cooled down he was remorselessly efficient and got us over a lot of hurdles, during the course of which I signed my name about fifteen times for customs formalities, port formalities, certificates from port doctors and goodness knows what else – all in a great hurry and fighting against bureaucratic idiots.

'Having done all this, we returned to the ship to sort out the dockers (who had also agreed to do the work for 100 roubles each). I asked the Chief Officer (the Captain was by now honked!) to get his crew onto the task. This he could not do as the law demanded that the cargo must be unloaded by dockers. The dockers meanwhile had been working like blacks to get the main cargo unloaded, so the Chief Officer ordered the ship to be closed up and work stopped. By the time we had struck a bargain with a Soviet representative, it was found that the Russians had gone off for their dinner. At last, however, we got them back and they unloaded. The Intourist man then threw another fit as he had been throwing fits all afternoon, the meat which I had understood to be well packed in wooden boxes was loosely done up in pappy cardboard boxes which were wet and coming to pieces. One box containing pheasants had *disintegrated and the birds were dropping out. Well might the man have a fit, for the passenger trains will only take personal luggage. All forty-five articles were loaded onto the lorry and we went off to the station. We got porters to look after the stuff and in fact had no row with the railway authorities. It was now 9 p.m. and we had a good dinner at the hotel to celebrate our final victory – caviare, wine and the lot. How glad I was to be on that train rolling back to Moscow complete with meat and luggage!'*

The Reillys were pleased with the outcome of this trip and kindly presented me with a brace of pheasants as a token of their gratitude. The two footmen, Aubrey Younger and Michael Edwards, were from the army. They were smart, bright and pleasant young men; they had put up with a frightful day in Leningrad with great patience and cheerfulness. Aubrey played and sang well, albeit (as I pompously noted in my letter home) 'not in a genre of music that I find attractive.'

Another memorable encounter with Soviet officials took place in May, 1959, when Field Marshall Montgomery of Alamein paid a visit to Moscow. I went out to meet him along with other embassy staff such as the minister and military attaché. I quote from my letter home:

'When we got there we found a large assembly of military personalities and a vast number of press reporters and photographers who had spilled out onto the tarmac, much to the Russians' annoyance and anxiety. When the plane came in, and Monty came down the gangway, there was absolute pandemonium with Marshall Sokolovsky in the middle of it all. Monty said a few words to the press and the Russian generals assembled there, with a great deal of photography going on. At this stage an agitated customs official came up and asked me to get hold of the Field Marshall's passport for stamping. When he was moving off to the car, I accordingly asked him for it, which seemed to annoy him and I was given a fairly rude answer by Marshal Sokolovsky to the effect that passports were all nonsense and quite unnecessary. Monty therefore got into the Rolls with the passport in his pocket. When the customs officer heard that I had been unable to secure the passport there was a fearful shindig and an angry little man told me that I would have to get hold of it and bring it out to the airport at once. I had told the officials what Marshall Sokolovsky had said; one man replied that the Marshall had no right to waive regulations and the other denied that he had ever said anything of the sort. After a great deal of bother I agreed to send it out next day after they had threatened that there might be difficulties when Monty left if this were not done. The story was picked up by the press

and a number of correspondents filed it. The censors cut it out altogether except that one man got it through and there was something in the Daily Mail about it.'

The rest of the visit went off very well. I was looking after him and found him an energetic little man with fierce blue eyes and typically military in all his arrangements. He organised his life carefully; I sensed that he would hate nothing more than for his arrangements to go wrong as a result of inefficiency. He was forthright and took decisions immediately after a rapid assessment of any problem. He argued that if things were not right, there was no harm in telling the truth. In this way he made remarks about the state of health of American leaders which appeared in the press with unfavourable criticism. It seemed to me that he lacked an understanding of the importance of tact and diplomacy; it was rich when he said that soldiers should keep out of politics because they did not understand what they were up to.

When time allowed, Sir Patrick would undertake official visits to other parts of the Soviet Union. The Ambassador was travelling as Her Britannic Majesty's representative and a programme would be worked out beforehand to include meetings with local ministers and senior officials. The aim was twofold – for the Ambassador to learn more about the country he was serving in and to explain H.M. Government's views on any issue that might arise. As Private Secretary I would accompany him and Lady Reilly to interpret at meetings with local dignitaries as well as to help out with day-to-day arrangements. I was included in two visits of this kind, the first being to Central Asia in June, 1959.

Central Asia, particularly the cities of Tashkent, Samarkand and Bukhara, appeal to the visitor because of their colourful history and the very different cultures encountered there. Their incorporation into Russia and subsequently the Soviet Union took place in the 19th century as a result of Tsar Nicholas I's expansionist policies, gradually absorbing successive khanates and eventually threatening British India. Rivalry between the two powers never came to open war but the numerous adventures by representatives of one sort or another have come to be called 'The Great Game' and many books have been written about it. Among the best are works by Peter Hopkirk and my colleague John Ure, who had from the outset been fascinated by Central Asian history and the stories of those involved in it.

There were five us, Sir Patrick and Lady Reilly, Lady Reillys brother, Mr Sykes and his wife and myself. Mr Sykes was one of the United Kingdom's leading agricultural experts, owning several large farms himself and acting as consultant to many others including the Queen's farm at Windsor. The emphasis of our visit would therefore be on agriculture in Central Asia. Unfortunately the visit got off to a bad start. After a three and a half hour flight from Moscow, we arrived in Tashkent hot and tired, to find that there was nobody there to meet us; there had been some misunderstanding between the Embassy's Russian Administration Section and Intourist, who were responsible for our itinerary. I felt at the time that it was hardly my fault but I suppose I should have checked all details before leaving. We were picked up after half-an-hour's wait in the hot and dusty airport, difficulties were resolved and thankfully there were no further misunderstandings.

The next day began with an interview with the chairman of the local Council for Economic Affairs, a challenge for me as interpreter as the chairman's explanation of the local economy included the numerous statistics so loved by Soviet officials. Of more interest was a visit to inspect a collective farm just outside Tashkent. Collectivisation of agriculture was arguably the worst aspect of Stalin's policies in the 1930s, when prosperous farmers were forced out of their land, many being sent to concentration camps or executed in a reign of terror. Their farms were brought together to form collectives under strict party control, resulting in a disastrous loss of production and, for many, starvation.

The countryside around Tashkent is dry and dusty with an annual rainfall of around thirteen inches and agriculture heavily dependent on irrigation. The main product is cotton, but fruit, vines, vegetables and corn are also grown. The deputy president of the farm told us that it had earlier consisted of many small individual holdings before being combined into a collective in the 1930s. He explained that the workers still have a large interest in food production and are paid extra money according to the amount of the harvest. They also have their own land-holding of a quarter of an acre, and are allowed to own one cow, two calves, five sheep and as much poultry and bees as they wish; they are permitted to sell their produce in the local market. One had the impression that they did not have too bad a time, although it was impossible to make an informed assessment on so short a visit and without talking to the workers themselves. We were shown a cowshed where milking was going on by hand and then went to the farm's boarding school where the farm workers' children are educated. There were about 250 children boarding there and provision seemed adequate from what we could see. We were also shown a kindergarten where babies and young children were cared for while their mothers were at work.

Our visit to Tashkent ended with an opera performance by an Uzbek composer Ashfari. I noted at the time that the opera combined an eastern storyline, eastern music and style of singing with a distinctly western style of production reminiscent of Verdi or Tchaikovsky. I met the composer in an interval (he was also conducting) and he told me that it had taken five years to compose the work. Under Soviet rule, local Uzbek music was banned from radio and Ashfari would have had the difficult task of portraying elements of Uzbek music in a way which complied with the strict parameters laid down by the communist system. We much enjoyed the performance and felt that in this respect he had succeeded.

An early flight the next day took us to Samarkand, a fabled city which in the 14th century had been Tamerlane's capital; he was an adventurer who had fought in the Khan's army before murdering him and seizing power for himself. He set out to turn Samarkand into one of the most fabulous cities in the world, building several mosques notable for their architecture, fine decoration and light blue tiles. The largest is the mosque of Bibi Khanym, which had fallen into ruin and we were shown also other mosques and mausolea erected for his various wives, friends and court officials. The Registan comprises three madrassahs, one from the 14th century and two from the 15th, all then in the process of restoration. We were also taken to the observatory built in 1489 by Tamerlane's grandson, Uleg Bek, a man of exceptional learning. Calculations made by him as to the length of the year have been found to be only two minutes out. All that remained of the observatory was a huge sextant for measuring the elevation of stars. Samarkand is a remarkable city and has since been designated as a UNESCO World Heritage site.

During our stay we saw all these interesting monuments and paid a number of official calls on local dignitaries. We also went for a little excursion into the countryside in the direction of the mountains. On this trip, we passed through a lot of attractive Uzbek villages, where the local inhabitants seem to spend their time sitting cross-legged on rug-covered tables drinking tea out of exquisite bowls and talking in the shade of the trees. The countryside looked very dry where there was no irrigation. It must be difficult to grow anything in those parts. This may be so, but I also noted that one of the pleasures of visiting that part of the world was being able to eat an unlimited quantity of fresh strawberries, raspberries and cherries, as well as tomatoes, none of which could be had in Moscow.

Our next visit was to Bukhara, another yet more ancient city of Central Asia, with many remarkable buildings in it. It struck us as a sharp contrast with Samarkand in both history and culture. The buildings, although remarkable, were of drab brown sun-baked clay bricks. The Khan of Bukhara's palace is perhaps the most interesting from a historical point of view, with its notorious prisons and torture chambers, including a pit where people perceived to be enemies were thrown down to keep company, with very little food and water, with poisonous snakes, vermin, large ticks and general filth including the bones of previous victims. Several English adventurers involved in the Great Game met an unpleasant end in Bukhara; their stories are well described in John Ure's book *'Sabres on the Steppes'* amongst others. Such barbarities were going on into the beginning of the 20th century. I wrote more cheerfully:

> *'But most attractive of all is the fact that this is one of the few towns in the Soviet Union which has retained its very oriental atmosphere. There are no straight streets with modern buildings – all is made of clay bricks and there are still markets under domes at the intersection of streets. Storks build their nests on the top of minarets and domes, which gives the place a fairytale atmosphere.'*

Unfortunately we did not have much time there. Perhaps as well. At the time the main hotel was very primitive, there being no lavatory except for a really filthy-smelling hole in the ground in a kind of shed in the yard, dirty and full of flies, and the rooms had five beds in each. So we returned to Tashkent. I must have overindulged in the strawberries, raspberries and cherries in Samarkand, for I had been unwell and Lady Reilly that evening would not let me eat more than Marmite soup for supper.

Our final visit was to Alma Ata, a yet more striking contrast with what we had seen before. So enthusiastic was I about it that I began my letter home in Alma Ata on June 3rd:

> *'We left Tashkent, the capital of the Uzbek Republic of the Soviet Union this morning at 11 a.m. after a very hurried packing together of our luggage and half an hour's interview with the Uzbek Deputy Minister of Agriculture. We flew in an IL-12, an old Russian plane, but none the less a safe and pleasant one; the journey went very well until we actually reached Alma Ata where a thunderstorm was in progress and we weaved about for nearly five minutes before coming in to land. Here the atmosphere and vegetation is entirely different from that of Tashkent, Samarkand and Bukhara. Whereas in the latter towns the weather tends to be hot and oppressive, with high temperatures (although fortunately we struck a cool period and it wasn't too bad) Alma Ata is cool, leafy and agreeable. Instead of being surrounded by deserts or at best dusty cotton fields, it lies at an altitude of about 3000 feet in the foothills of a vast range of mountains which rise immediately behind the town to an altitude of 17,000 feet. The jagged peaks are permanently capped with snow and glaciers, and the view from the town is simply magnificent – a*

long range of snow-clad peaks, with wooded foothills beginning on the outskirts of the town.

'We were met at the airport by a representative of the Intourist travel agency, who informed us that the Kazakh Government had put at our disposal, as their honoured guests, a villa on its own. At the other towns we had always been put up at hotels. The villa is a very large two-storey country house, standing in a large garden with apple orchards and summer houses dotted about and a fast-flowing (but I fear fishless) stream flowing through it, near the house. We each had a suite of rooms. My own suite consists of my bedroom, which is luxuriously furnished with hideous Soviet candelabra, bathroom, lavatory and a semi-circular covered balcony, with pillars supporting a flat roof.....In brief, it is a simply delightful spot, comparable to some of the finest scenery in the Alps. It is so pleasant to be here, first after the really appalling time I and the Ambassador have had recently in Moscow, and secondly after the rather tiring journey to the other places where I have had to do quite a lot of hard work making arrangements and being interpreter at official meetings with ministers and other officials.*

'When we had settled in, we had lunch and split up; Sir Patrick, Mr Sykes and I went to call on the Minister of Agriculture and the ladies went to the Zoo. My enthusiasm for the landscape was shared by the others and that evening we went off by car into the mountains as far as we could and for about half an hour on foot up a track. The scenery was reminiscent and very characteristic of the Alps. A fast stream flowed through the valley, which was grassy and abounding in wild flowers of many strange as well as familiar varieties, while at the end of the valley the vast peaks rose up into the clouds. We reached a Soviet touring base, similar but less orderly than an Austrian one, and after collecting some wild flowers, including a wild tulip, we turned round and came back to our villa for a dinner of caviare and chicken.*

'On our last day we visited a state farm about thirty kilometres from Alma Ata, where we were received by the president and learnt how it was run. It is an enormous concern with lands stretching out towards the desert only recently brought under cultivation. The main crops were barley, milk, meat, poultry and vegetables for the town of Alma Ata, and in addition pigs, rabbits and silver foxes for their fur. We then set off into the virgin land area for some distance on a very rough road. The ground consists of small hillocks, is very dry, although fertile and rainfall is only twelve to fifteen inches annually. Here barley was grown mostly for feeding to cattle and poultry; in some seasons the crop is good, in others, the rains fail and it is poor. We also saw tomatoes and* *cucumbers being grown but these were poor in appearance. In fact, the general impression we received from visiting this farm was one of bad management and slip-shod methods, with inadequate equipment and storage space. Also, the employees seemed to be unhappy; for example, when we met a lorry load of workers, the president of the farm was greeted with catcalls and whistles and the workers on their own seemed very sullen. We had presumably been taken to visit what was considered to be a model state farm; the performance of other farms must have been even less impressive.*

'Our flight back to Moscow the next day took six hours in a turbo-prop IL-18 seating around 100 passengers. Among these was a ladies' basket ball team. They were a presentable lot and I spent some time talking to them. Once we had got over the unfortunate arrival problem in Tashkent, all had gone well and the Ambassador said how pleased he had been with the expedition. We all returned to Moscow very much refreshed mentally, if perhaps a little weary physically.'

The Reillys took me on a further official trip in July, 1960, this time to Siberia. I wrote home about this in two letters from which the following account is taken:

'We got away on Thursday morning at 9 a.m. and took off in a TU-104 for Irkutsk at about 11 o'clock. The usual airport at Omsk was shut by side winds and so we put down at Sverdlovsk instead after only two hours flying. We were told that we should have to wait there for about four hours – it was sunny and bright and apart from the mosquitoes quite pleasant. After an hour only we were summoned to the aircraft and flew on to Novosibirsk, arriving there at 5.15p.m. Moscow time (9.15p.m. local time) On landing, we damaged a wheel and slewed off the side of the runway; we had expected to stay only an hour, but this held us up and by the time they had finished changing the wheel, the weather in Irkutsk had deteriorated and closed the airport there. Fog and thunderstorms. We had some food in the restaurant and waited for Irkutsk airport to be opened. The airport at Novosibirsk has no facilities at all. It was a miserable little airport building filled with miscellaneous would-be travellers with their luggage and babies.

'Since we were important persons, we were let back into the V.I.P.'s restaurant, which was otherwise empty and here from about 8.30p.m. we dossed down on sofas to get as much sleep as we could. It was all rather hideous and I must say that the Ambassador took it very well, without a lot of fuss. Of course, there is absolutely nothing one can do except put up with the discomfort. We finally left Novosibirsk at 4 a.m. (Moscow

time) 8 a.m. local time. When we reached Irkutsk the difference was five hours and it was 11.30 local time.

'Irkutsk is quite a large town of about 300,000 inhabitants stretching out over a considerable area. The surroundings consist of thickly wooded hills, and the most important feature is the Angara River which flows out of Lake Baikal, 60 kilometres to the south-east. It is a big river with a strong current and absolutely crystal clear water because it comes form a large lake. The river in Irkutsk must be about three-quarters of a mile wide and bigger than any British river. In character it is like a larger version of the river Tay; gravel, sand, and a broad even flow.*

'Irkutsk is a green town, there being a lot of parks and gardens surrounding houses and trees along the main roads. It had been spruced up in expectation of Eisenhower's visit which was to have taken place in June but was cancelled. Away from the principal streets, the roads are very rough. There were a lot of wooden houses there, many of them very fine indeed, decorated with carved woodwork. They looked more solid than the usual wooden houses around Moscow.*

'The town has an interesting history. It was founded in 1670 by a party of Russians who arrived there on an expedition up the Yenisei and Angara rivers. It was established as an outpost of the Tsarist Empire and a fort was built there against the local Buryat tribes. It was then used as a place of exile for those who incurred the Tsar's disapproval and many revolutionaries were sent there. Among the most famous were the Decembrists, officers and members of the aristocracy who rebelled against the Tsar in December, 1825, including Trubetskoy and Muravev. At the beginning of this [20th] century a number of revolutionaries such as Lenin, Trotsky and others were sent to this part of the world. Subsequently, this part of Siberia was the scene of some of the worst excesses of Communist slave labour – the railway from Taishet to Lena being only one example.*

'We were met at the airport by two representatives from Intourist and a man from the regional executive committee of the Irkutsk area. We were taken by car to a small house in the town, with the explanation that the hotel was being repaired and that this house was an annex to the hotel for distinguished visitors. It was certainly a government guest house. We had a generous number of attendants laid on to look after us; we ordered whatever meals we wanted and they were produced for us. They were very good.*

'We began our tour of the town after lunch and a rest, both of which we sorely needed after our bad journey from Moscow. We went to the Irkutsk hydro-electric station. This is a large dam above the town which* *has had the effect of flooding the river valley up as far as Lake Baikal, and of even raising the level of the lake by three feet. It was an interesting station, with the power house built into the dam and fed by openings in the wall of the dam; there are no connecting pipes. At this point the dam is made of concrete; elsewhere it is of sand with a concrete waterproof core. The director of the station told us that there were a number of features which were peculiar to Siberia and planned to cope with the extreme cold. These included a special wall upstream of the dam, roofed in to prevent floating ice from being washed against the dam and drawn down into the turbines. Any bits of ice which get under the wall inside are melted because in winter, hot air from the cooling system is blown into the roofed-over cavity between the dam and the wall. Another peculiarity of the Siberian winter is the formation of ice blocks, or rather crystals which are heavier than water and sink to the bottom or else swim along in the water. This occurs if the water is supercooled below freezing at a time when there is a storm blowing which prevents the formation of ordinary surface ice. To prevent this 'sluga' from blocking up the grilles, they fit them with powerful electric heaters.*

'We also looked over the workers' settlement which was near the dam. The houses were quite good and better than the equivalent in Moscow. I noticed one row of houses which looked most un-Russian and I think they must have been built by Baltic exiles of one kind or another. But the man showing us round professed ignorance of the architecture. On our return journey we came through what is shortly to be the new 'university town' where they are rebuilding a number of technical colleges and hostels for students; a rather dreary looking part of the town.

'After this we visited the museum. This was one of the best that I have seen from the point of view of the contents. At one time, prehistoric societies must have attained a very high standard of craftsmanship, for the flints, bone carvings, bronze and iron were beautifully executed. There were one or two interesting exhibits from the time of the Decembrists, an ancient spinette with the strings arranged vertically, and a Swiss music box which had several operatic airs on it. The music box was not in working order but could have been made to work if it was looked after and done up. Although I knew that Trotsky had been in Irkutsk, I asked the museum people whether he had. They said he hadn't. As you may recall, Trotsky was forced to flee from Russia and was finally murdered by hired assassins in Mexico.

'We had dinner in the evening at our residence and went for a short walk round the town before retiring to bed. We saw some interesting churches; there are two which work and several that don't. One of the

latter is of most unusual gothic design and we discovered eventually that it had been built by Roman Catholic Poles after the Polish insurrection in 1863.

'*The next day, 23 July, we left fairly early by car to go to Shelekhov. This is a new town; there was nothing there four years ago except forest and an old farm. They are in the process of building an industrial town of 110,000 inhabitants [in 2010 47,963], the main industry being aluminium and electrodes; they use the power from the Irkutsk station. We saw a factory producing building materials. Most of them are made of concrete reinforced with iron bars. The roof joists for the factory are made of concrete with steel rods under tension within them. The products did not look to be of very good quality and I suspect that before long the reinforcing bars will start to rust and the concrete to drop off. In winter they use steam drying; the panels for housing are dry in a day; the joists are allowed a week. The aluminium factory is a long way from being ready but when complete it will produce 50,000 tons of aluminium a year.*

'*The town did not look very attractive. The shop that we looked into was poorly stocked without fresh fruit or vegetables, and we were met at the door (at 11 a.m.) by a couple of drunks who were coming out singing. The dining room we looked at was also a very grim place. I should not like to live in Shelekhov at all.*

'*After lunch we looked at an experimental agricultural station; it was a poor shoddy affair with poor organisation and the nine separate departments were scattered about over a vast area without any proper communication between them. We looked at the cattle sheds which seemed to be in fairly good order and the chicken sheds where there were a lot of birds but the equipment was very ancient and backward, without automatic feeding and so on. They had a variety of breeds which produced cocks with badger hackles but I was not able to get hold of any feathers. On our way home we visited a local church where a service was about to begin. Our Intourist guide was visibly embarrassed by our wanting to go in and did her best to dissuade us. They are odd people. However, we went in. The church was quite an interesting one of the late 18th century, but the icons were not of any great interest.*

'*After dinner I decided to fish in the Angara and set off for a place not far from where we were staying. I tried spinning but was told repeatedly by a very drunk local that this was no good at all, as there were no fish there that take a spinner. Most of the local anglers were fishing with wet fly, not as we do, but by using spinning tackle with a revolving drum reel, a thick nylon line and a hefty rod, and a block of wood which* has the cast attached to it. They cast out the wooden block (with flies behind) and slowly wind it in. The fish they can catch with this tackle are grayling; usually of a pound to two pounds in weight. Another local angler said he would show me how to catch fish and we went off to his home to collect his gear and then walked to another part of the river. He was also rather drunk. By the time we started fishing it was already nearly dark, and we only got eaten by the mosquitoes. Afterwards he insisted on my coming back to his flat for vodka and beer and something to eat. His flat consisted of one room where he and his wife and two children lived (one son was away in the army). The place seemed to me to be in a fearful pickle. There was no proper kitchen or cooking facilities apart from a primus stove and a single cold water tap. The host produced vodka and from under a trap door in the floor some beer, stale bread and slices of revolting jellied brawn and pickled cabbage which I had to make a pretence of enjoying.

'The next day we had to get up early and leave our residence at 8.30 a.m. to go to Lake Baikal for the day, 60 kilometres from Irkutsk. We left from a jetty above the dam in a new kind of Soviet boat; a diesel vessel, taking about 150 passengers; which, after a certain speed, rises out of the water and goes along on water skis. This boat was brought out to Irkutsk especially for President Eisenhower to ride in but the visit was cancelled at the time of the summit; Irkutsk was left with this boat to their credit. By this method it can cruise along at 40mph or more without effort, but it is only suitable for very flat rivers. It took us just an hour to get up to the lake. On arriving we found that the Limnological Museum was still shut and so we began by looking round a curious tourist base. This is a luxury affair, consisting of six beautifully made wooden houses, with a restaurant in one of them, on a hill overlooking the lake. It is for foreign tourists and government officials only, the ordinary Russian tourist will not be able to stay there (some in this Marxist paradise are more equal than others).

'Lake Baikal is the most extraordinary and interesting lake in the world. It is about 400 miles long and 40 miles wide and at its deepest point 4,700 feet deep. It is the biggest freshwater lake in the world (in volume of water) and the deepest lake of any description. Whereas most other lakes (except in Tanganyika) e.g. the Caspian, the Aral Sea, are salt or semi-salt, the water of Lake Baikal is almost as pure as distilled water. Because of its great depth and size, the water is always at the same temperature, apart from in the shallows around the edge. Here it is at +3º C to + 5ºC (very cold in summer) but it does result in it freezing much less hard than other lakes in winter.

'On arriving at the Limnological Museum, we were shown round by the director, a Ukrainian born in Siberia, G. I. Galazy. It was a most interesting place. There is a small historical section showing the various people who had worked there. Among the first were some Polish scientists who were exiled here after the insurrection of 1863. There were the various sections showing the different sorts of fish found in and around the lake. One very interesting aspect of their research is the study of earthquakes and floods from the trees that grow on the shore. Since the level of the water never changes except as a result of earthquakes or very exceptional floods, it is possible by cutting down trees growing near the water's edge, to see in which years (by counting the rings) there were floods. The scientists are at present very concerned on account of the hydro-electric dam in Irkutsk. They say that if this raises the water more than three feet, it will extinguish certain plants which are only to be found on the shores of the lake.

'Of fish there are about fifty different varieties, twenty-four of which are only to be found in Lake Baikal. Of the kinds familiar in England there are grayling (two varieties, one found in the lake itself and the other in rivers), perch, which attain a maximum weight of four or five pounds and are usually under two pounds in weight. These lurk about at the mouths of streams eating small fish. Then there are pike which occasionally grow to a vast size reaching seventy to eighty pounds weight. But most important is the omul which is a cross between a trout and a dace in appearance, and grows up to only four pounds or so. They are quite plentiful and spawn in one particular river, the Selenga. When they move up to spawn, they form a living wall of fish. Each hen lays about 10,000 eggs out of which only three reach maturity, since so many other things eat the fry and the eggs. As a result of the value of omul for industry, they have built a fish farm. Study on how to rear omul continues but it is difficult because fish that live in Lake Baikal don't survive if taken elsewhere because of the peculiar properties of the water. Out of 100 fish fry released from the farm only two are expected to reach maturity. Other sorts of peculiar fish found only in Baikal are a series of ten or so varieties of bullheads which live at a great depth on the bottom. One variety, the golomyanka, is a very fatty fish and alters its depth by the amount of fat which it has on it. It does not lay eggs but young fish are carried about inside it until it swims to the surface to let them free. If caught and left in the sun, it melts away until only a skeleton is left. Finally there are sturgeon. These were nearly exterminated at the time of the civil war when there was no control on fishing and there are still very few of them. It is said that in 1917-1918, live sturgeon were taken out of the spawning streams and sold in Irkutsk that were ten feet long and weighing over 300 pounds. Then there are taimen, a variety of sturgeon which resembles salmon in that it lives in fast water and can be caught on a spinner. These grow up to about 90 pounds in weight. Another trout-like fish is the linok, which can also be caught on spinner or fly, but only attains a weight of four or five pounds.

'Apart from all the fur-bearing animals that live around Lake Baikal such as sable, mink, fox, Siberian squirrel and so on, Lake Baikal has its own variety of seal which originally came from the Arctic by swimming up the Yenisei and the Angara. The shooting of seals in winter, when they come up through holes in the ice, is confined to 2000 to 3000 animals a year. I also asked Galazy about fly life; he said that there were three or four types of Ephemerida, quite large varieties and a few other sorts but I gathered that in general the fly life was not rich. The coldness of the water would account for this.

'We had lunch at a restaurant on Baikal at which Galazy spoke most interestingly about fish and animals, although I think the Ambassador was rather bored by it. After lunch we took one of the station's research vessels, the size of a small fishing boat, and went up the lakeside to call at a biological research station run by Professor M. M. Kozhov. He spends six months each year at this remote station, with a number of teachers and students. When we arrived, there was considerable excitement and the population came down onto the jetty to welcome us. They seemed very interested to see us and were most friendly. I hoped to do some fishing here, but the weather was coming up rough (twelve days a month are stormy on Baikal) and we had to return almost as soon as we had looked over the museum and the aquarium where they are growing omul and other sorts of fish.

'Unfortunately we did not have time to go over and look at a steamer which we saw anchored in a harbour with smoke coming out of its two very tall funnels. This was the Angara; it was built by Armstrong on Tyneside in the 1890s at the order of the Tsarist government. It sailed along the North coast of Russia, up the Yenisei and then the Angara river. There are rapids at several places on the Angara; at these it was dragged up on rails which it had brought with it for this purpose. Apparently it is still in working order and in use for carrying cargo and passengers up and down the lake. It was bought in the first place (together with an ice-breaker called the Baikal) to ferry passengers and goods across the lake on the Trans-Siberian railway before the line round the lake had been completed. The Baikal, which took three tracks inside, was sunk during the civil war.

'That evening, although it meant offending our Russian hosts, we went out to the town restaurant for our meal so that we could see how the natives of Irkutsk spend their evenings out. It was a very miserable place, with all the windows shut and dirty table cloths and slatternly waitresses, and a mean band in open-necked shirts playing out-of-date songs. The food was unappetising, but our forbearance was rewarded by our having a strange looking man come to join us at our table. He turned out to be a Yakut diamond prospector on leave from North Siberia. He could scarcely speak any Russian, but kept on talking about American aircraft, Cuba and the Congo, quoting from the Soviet press. He disbelieved anything that we told him, and like other people one meets, thought that there might be war. A most discouraging encounter.'

The last visit on this journey was to the Bratsk hydro-electric station on the Angara about 500 kilometres to the North-West. At the time it was to be the largest such installation in the world, creating a lake over 250 miles long and generating 4½ million kilowatts. It did not seem to us a pleasant place to live and work because of the extremes of temperature, ranging from 40°C in summer to -55°C in winter. For three months, clouds of ferocious flies attack any one outside and account for a twenty five per cent fall in production. We were told that Bratsk would eventually have a population of 100,000, based on employment associated with the dam. According to the Lonely Planet guide, it is now 246,310.

While waiting at Novosibirsk for the onward flight to Irkutsk, I had noticed Mig fighter aircraft taking off and landing. Embassy staff had been asked to report anything of military significance they noticed on their travels and these Soviet fighters were impressive. We had time to spare and by standing on the seat in the Gents' toilet, I was able to obtain a very good view of them; I made as good a pencil sketch as I could and proudly handed it in on our return to Moscow. It was of great interest to the Air Attaché, who forwarded it as a secret document to London. A few months later when I was home on leave, I saw my mother opening a packet of tea and out fell a cigarette packet style card; on it was a picture of a Mig fighter identical to the one I had tried to sketch, so nothing secret in that.

The Kremlin from the British Embassy Moscow (Kathleen Berton Murrell)

Moscow Embassy Staff in 1959. Sir Patrick and Lady Reilly centre, author top left in a Russian hat. Derek Thomas just below him on his right

Harold MacMillan arrives at Moscow airport and is greeted by the
Soviet leader Nikita Khrushchev (author's archive)

MacMillan and Khrushchev at the British Embassy in Moscow,
when the bureau was presented as a gift
(author's archive)

Sir Patrick and Lady Reilly at a reception in Moscow. Their Private Secretary stands respectfully to one side

Visiting the Bratsk hydro-electric scheme on the Angara river (author's archive)

The Bratsk dam under construction

Lake Baikal (David E. Martin)

On the way to Yaroslavl. Foreign visitors quickly attracted the attention of local residents

Michael Duncan at Pereslavl Zalesky

Tallinn under snow, March 1960

A lone figure waits at the end of the street. Perhaps he was watching us

Chapter 7

The Moscow Cage

Life for diplomats in western embassies in Moscow and other communist countries was dominated by restrictions of all kinds and in addition, was subject to our own considerations of security. We were all considered to be enemies of the Soviet state, even spies. The Soviet attitude was defensive, in that every effort was made to keep us away from ordinary Russians lest we should infect them with western ideas of democracy, undermine the principles of communism in those we met or engage them in espionage.

It was also aggressive. First, every method was exploited to penetrate the embassy to find out what we were reporting back to London and what London was telling us on important issues in Anglo-Soviet affairs. Secondly, and more seriously, attempts were made to subvert us and if possible compromise members of staff in order to recruit them as spies to provide information over a wide area – political, economic, technical and military. It was as if we were living in a cage of glass bars, bars put up by our own side in an effort to hinder penetration and protect staff and by the Russians to keep us operating within our own tight community. We could see out clearly enough but activity was largely confined within.

The use of hidden microphones has often been publicised. Perhaps the most famous case was the discovery of a microphone hidden in the eagle decorating the American Ambassador's study. We would occasionally have microphone sweeps in our offices; I was amazed to see one hanging out from the panelling in the office registry. Our technicians could seek out a certain number of microphones but there always remained the possibility or indeed certainty that others had remained undiscovered. Discussions in the Embassy on any confidential matters would therefore take place in a specially designed room within a room. This was made of copper standing on vibration-proof stilts to prevent both audio and electronic penetration from outside, with a recording of a babble of voices as from a cocktail party to conceal whatever was being said

95

within. It was even feared that the KGB would find a way of 'reading' letters being typed on a typewriter through the sound emitted by the keys and so confidential letters were also typed out in the copper box.

The weekly Diplomatic Bag was mentioned in the previous chapter as a means of bringing in staff requirements – occasional items of food, clothing and so on. Its essential purpose was of course to convey official correspondence both in and out of the embassy. There would be several bags each week and these were escorted by two Queen's Messengers who would never let them out of their sight. Uncertainties and delays in flights meant that they often experienced a great deal of hardship especially when the weather was bad. They displayed remarkable dedication and their vital work has not in my view been adequately recognised.

Telegrams were also a vital chain in our communications with London and here again, security was paramount. For most of my time, the one-time pad system was used for confidential material. A message would be encoded into sets of numbers for the interpretation of which a dictionary was necessary. These were then added line by line to the random numbers in a pad, of which a unique identical copy was held in the embassy safe. A reversal of the sums in the message and reference to the dictionary revealed the contents of the message. Most telegrams were decoded by registry clerks who were expert. Occasionally one would arrive with the prefix 'Dedip' which meant that a diplomat was required to decode it. If a dedip telegram arrived in the night also marked 'immediate', I would have to go into the office to work on it, which I did not much enjoy; it was a slow business and I often found that the message was not really immediate at all.

It went without saying that our homes were also bugged and we were all briefed not to say anything of a sensitive nature. There were two ways to circumvent this difficulty. The first was to go outside to carry on a discussion, always on the move lest a directional microphone was aimed at a particular spot. The second was to write things down on a piece of paper which was then burnt and the ashes broken up. Disposing of the paper down the lavatory was not good enough lest the KGB had some system of sorting out paper on its way down the drain. This seems far-fetched, but so did many of the precautions that we were obliged to take.

Russian-speaking members of staff were usually followed by KGB officers to keep an eye on what we were doing. There were two reasons for this. Most important perhaps was the need to ensure that we were not engaged in spying, either by looking at or photographing sensitive sites, or meeting people whom we may have recruited to pass on intelligence. Secondly they would wish to ensure that we did not engage with ordinary people to undermine official propaganda. In Moscow the followers, 'goons' as we called them, were discreet; in my first year when I didn't have a car and got round on a bicycle, I was not aware of being followed at all, but in my second year I certainly was. This sort of surveillance was normally quite discreet but outside Moscow, the goons were less skilled at keeping out of sight. Once, on a visit to Leningrad with a colleague, Nicko Henderson, we were followed by six goons in two cars, which gave rise to a game of hide-and-seek; we were amused to catch three of them in the telegraph office of a railway station busy changing their coats. They saw the joke and returned our smiles. On another trip to Riga with a colleague, we were enjoying a picnic lunch in the countryside and were surprised to see our goon crawling through the undergrowth to have a look at us. I only heard of one case when the goons turned nasty. This was when the French military attaché and a companion travelling in a car had provoked them in some way and were forced off the road.

The need for caution in one's dealings with Russians was extremely frustrating. Russians are in general friendly and hospitable in their attitude towards foreigners. Whatever their attitude, they were nevertheless under pressure to conform to Soviet policy and to carry out their responsibilities as required by the state. Soviet society was riddled with KGB informers (although less systematically than in the German Democratic Republic). Any one tempted to depart from communist precepts in their conversation or actions would need to bear in mind the probability that their behaviour would be reported back to the 'competent organs' as the Soviet authorities liked to describe their security service. Martin Nicholson, an exchange student in Moscow University in 1961, notes that his Russian fellow students trusted foreigners more than their own compatriots who might be informers. *(On the Fringes of Europe: Student Years 1956-1963)*

For embassy staff this situation raised serious barriers in any relationship with local Russians. If we came into contact with a Russian who was friendly and inclined to pursue the contact, there were good reasons not to take it further. Either that person was naive and ignorant of the dangers of association with a western diplomat, or he/she was a KGB stooge. Some were well aware of the dangers, for example a Red Army officer who hitched a lift with me and then asked to be dropped off at the first opportunity when he discovered who I was.

For myself, having spent a year learning the language and liking the country I was living in, it was very annoying not to be able to make friends with people I met and who were clearly friendly and anxious to talk. One particular incident remains in my memory, which I described at length in a letter home:

'As you know, 1 May is a great festival in this country, being the day on which the workers celebrate their solidarity, i.e. Labour Day. It is a whole holiday, also the day following. It is the main festival of the year when there is a gay atmosphere about the place. On Friday evening, therefore, I went out with a man from British European Airways to look round the town. We decided to take a river boat so as to watch the fireworks from the water, and when we were queuing up for our ticket and were near the head of the queue, a Russian lad came up and asked us to get him a ticket to save him queuing. This I did and he came down to Gorky Park with us, where there is a kind of fairground on a small scale for general amusements. He was a nice chap and during the course of the evening he showed us round the place, bought tickets for us (by jumping the queues as above). He was intelligent and amusing, aged fourteen, by the name of Pauli. The final thing he wanted to do was to play chess in the chess hall, and when I told him that I did not play, he offered to teach me. But it was then 11 o'clock and the chess hall was just closing down. We therefore arranged to meet the next day at the boat jetty at 4 p.m. and this we did. We played chess and he explained the moves to me and also corrected me on moves, and proved to be extraordinarily intelligent. I finally left him playing with someone else and he asked me to meet him the next day to play again.

'As I was going away, we left it arranged provisionally for a fortnight's time, that is, to-day. I should explain that he insisted on buying me fruit juice. In short, it was a most enjoyable afternoon and a real pleasure to meet and talk to a Russian in Russian, in the same way as one would in the West without any political considerations to mar the conversation. However, people to whom I mentioned this in the Embassy strongly advised against seeing the child again as it would do him harm to have associations with Western diplomats, and there was always the possibility that the Soviet authorities, who watch us pretty constantly, might frame up some sort of incident with unpleasant consequences.

'I have therefore just had the unpleasant task of seeing him and explaining that I could not play chess with him any more which was a thing he just could not understand, leaving him with a bad impression of myself and of England. I am prepared to put up with most of the inconveniences of living in this country, but this business of not having anything to do with the locals (who are often so very pleasant) is the one thing which I really do find hard to accept. But it would be foolish to take any risks which could result in unpleasantness and my being expelled from the Soviet Union, how sickening it is.'

Whether this was a put-up KGB job or not, it was probably wise not to pursue the contact with Pauli, much as I wished to have done so. A more direct incident occurred not long afterwards, when our cook Tanya was about to go on holiday:

'Our cook is going on leave this month. Today despite the fact that other people have been waiting weeks for one, Burobin sent us along a temporary replacement and she should start work tomorrow. She is nineteen, dark blonde, attractive and has the aptitude of showing off to the utmost the characteristics which the Creator has bestowed and in this case generously on the female sex. Clearly a plant by the KGB.'

This opinion seemed to be confirmed when shortly after her arrival, she asked me: 'Shall we go fishing this week-end, Mr Martin?'

Any deviation from British or Soviet law on sexuality could also offer the KGB opportunities for recruitment. At the time, homosexuality was illegal in both countries and its practice could be used as a means to blackmail. The most notable case was that of John Vassal. He had been appointed in 1952 as a clerk in the Naval Attaché's office in Moscow. He was introduced to the homosexual underworld and invited to a party where he became drunk and was photographed in a compromising position with other men. He was blackmailed, being threatened with serious consequences under Soviet law if he did not co-operate. Initially he was asked for relatively harmless information about members of the Embassy staff. With time, the pressure on him increased and until his arrest in 1962 he supplied the Russians with copies of thousands of secret documents.

Another approach would be to get a Russian to befriend a member of staff and invite him back home to his flat. Once there, he would apologise that he had to nip out to buy something and as soon as he had gone, his wife would tear off her clothes and scream for help. A Soviet militiaman who happened to be around would burst in and arrest the staff member on grounds of abuse and he would then be threatened with prosecution unless he was prepared to help by answering a few questions. These would be quite harmless to start with but as the person concerned became increasingly compromised, more serious matters would be raised.

A diplomat could claim immunity from prosecution but would have to leave immediately. A member of staff without diplomatic immunity was faced with possible prosecution. I heard tell of a case some time previously when a Chancery guard had a sleazy film sent out through the bag. He invited some friends in to see it and by way of a screen, hung a white sheet over the curtain rail in his flat. Unfortunately he omitted to draw the curtains and as his flat was on the ground floor facing out onto the street, a large crowd of people assembled to watch the film which was visible through the sheet. The indignant Soviet authorities were so incensed with this that they threatened to arrest the person if he should put a foot outside the embassy. So he was obliged to stay in the embassy compound for a year or so until a visiting minister agreed an exchange with a Russian being held in London.

Life in Moscow at this time could be stressful and certainly I found it so in my duties as Private Secretary. There were compensations, however. We were a tight-knit community both within the embassy and the wider NATO countries. We exchanged parties, lunches and dinners over and above the official receptions at the embassies of countries with whom we had diplomatic relations. As bachelors, John Ure and I were generously entertained by married colleagues as well as by unmarried staff; dinner parties, private receptions and outings into the countryside to ski in winter and to picnic and swim in summer were numerous. The Moscow countryside was beautiful and largely unspoilt. To go further than forty kilometres from Moscow required at least forty-eight hours notice to the Ministry for Foreign Affairs, but many delightful destinations were available within that range and such outings were frequent. Within the forty kilometre radius, there were few restrictions, although certain areas were off-bounds as I discovered when I went pike-fishing in a part of the countryside containing the dachas of important Russians and was politely asked to go elsewhere.

Travel beyond the forty kilometre limit was more problematic. Any journey away from Moscow required specific permission from the Ministry for Foreign Affairs and all travel bookings and hotel reservations had to be made through the embassy's local office, with a note to the Ministry. It seems unbelievable that the economy provided no travel agents but you could not just walk into a shop and buy a ticket. I was reminded of this when I was shown the copy of a note sent to order an airline ticket for Paul Holmer, a chancery colleague:

> *'The Embassy of Great Britain presents its compliments to the office for servicing the Diplomatic Corps and has the honour to ask it to reserve a place to London on the aircraft flight BE489, leaving on the 29 June of this year for the First Secretary of the Embassy, Mr Holmer.'*
>
> *British Embassy*
> *Moscow, 3 June 1959.*

Music and theatre also provided opportunities for relaxation and in consequence a way through the glass bars of the cage. In my case I was trying to learn the piano and in response to my request for a teacher, Burobin sent me a delightful man, Leonid Belkin. He came to our flat each week and when I had time, I would practise. Few things are more annoying than a student practising and it was much to John Ure's credit that he put up with my efforts without complaint. Although I did not make much progress, Belkin invited me to concerts and private parties. He took me to the school where he taught music; we played some Mozart together and then he and his own teacher sat down to play Rachmaninov's Third Piano Concerto. Not long afterwards we went to a convivial party given by some friends of his. In this way I came to meet Russians informally and without anxiety over their genuineness. Obviously they had security approval to meet Western diplomats and for me it was a great pleasure.

Within the Embassy Derek Thomas had organised a choir to sing carols at Christmas, with a service of Nine Lessons and Carols taking place in the drawing room. We also went round blocks of flats where acquaintants lived to sing; the fact that we were doing so in a country where Christianity was suppressed by the government added further pleasure and satisfaction. Sunday services were held each week in the Ambassador's study and since there was no resident chaplain in Moscow, it fell to me to take them. Later, an English theological student, Michael Bourdeaux, on a year's exchange, kindly took over. Another student on the exchanges arranged through the British Council was Gerald Brooke; he was musical and played the hymns on the embassy's ancient pedal organ. Both these two achieved notoriety after leaving Moscow. Michael, who had been appalled by the persecution of Christians in the Soviet Union, set up Keston College in Bromley to study the position of Christians in communist countries and to publicise their predicament; little was known about this at the time, when many in the west still looked to communism and the Soviet Union through rose-tinted spectacles. Gerald joined an organisation which aimed to smuggle anti-Soviet literature into Russia. Unfortunately it had been penetrated by the KGB; he was arrested on arrival in Moscow in 1969, put on trial and sentenced to five years hard labour.

Our most productive escape from the glass cage was through travel to other parts of the Soviet Union. These were private and recreational rather than official visits such as the Ambassador's to Central Asia and Siberia. Private visits were usually short, perhaps just for a week-end if one could get away from Moscow and were essentially recreational. You still had to make all travel and accommodation arrangements through the authorities but once you had arrived, the programme was up to you. In practice we often called on local authorities as a courtesy and also to seek introductions to places and people of interest.

My first such trip was to Yaroslavl in March 1959 with Sir Patrick and Lady Reilly and Lady Reillys sister and brother-in-law. We set out after the Sunday morning service in the Rolls Royce with the Ambassador's chauffeur at the wheel, taking with us material for picnic lunches and other essentials. After lunch we spent an hour at the monastery of Zagorsk. The scenery was most attractive, with small hills and thick forests of birch and pine. Our next stop was at Pereslavl-Zalesky with an unusual monastery on a hill. The town itself was dreary and by then the weather had worsened; it was beginning to rain. After Rostov, we had the last forty miles to travel over dead flat country with endless vistas of wet snow and puddles all around; I had rarely experienced so strong a feeling of depression and desolation as we travelled, albeit in Rolls Royce comfort, over the Rostov marshes on a wet evening in late winter. Stiff whiskies and soda in the Ambassador's bedroom restored our spirits and dinner was excellent; caviar with vodka followed by partridges and vegetables. I doubt whether this was standard fare as the hotel knew of our coming. The next morning we had breakfast in the Ambassador's room including Nescafé, with bread and marmalade we had brought with us and, after washing up, we set out at 8.30 on the return journey. By now it was snowing and the Rostov marshes were not as depressing since they were covered in snow; more falling snow reduced visibility to about a mile and cut out the endless vista of waste land.

A further week-end visit to Yaroslavl was undertaken in February 1960, with Michael Duncan (who had replaced John Ure in the flat), an embassy secretary, Gwyneth Ellis, an Australian, Barbara Manning, and myself. We travelled in more modest transport, namely Michael Duncan's Hillman Minx convertible. It was bitterly cold and a convertible is not ideal for such conditions. After stops in Pereslavl Zalesky and Rostov to visit museums and churches, we reached Yaroslavl as it was getting dark after a scary journey over roads covered in ice. After moving into our rooms we went for a walk along the bank of the frozen Volga. It was now even colder, at least -20°C, and a bitter wind was blowing off the river. We had to wrap ourselves up all over the face to prevent frostbite. On returning to the hotel we enjoyed a good dinner celebrating the passing of my probation which had come through a few days earlier.

The next day we looked round Yaroslavl. Little remains from the earliest period of its history. It was founded in the 11th century by Yaroslavl the Wise, son of Vladimir Monomach of Kiev. The most interesting features of the town date from the 17th century, when Yaroslavl was on the trade route with Western Europe via the White Sea, before the foundation of St Petersburg. Foremost is the church of St John the Baptist (1671-1687), which has many gilded domes and some beautiful 17th century frescoes. We visited this church with the man in charge of the restoration of old buildings in Kiev, Mr Mitrofanov, a man with a pleasant disposition and interesting to listen to. We also saw the church of the prophet Elias, a similar one built in 1647 and also adorned with fine frescoes. In both churches, inside and outside, it was unbelievably cold and at least -25°C, still with a fresh wind off the Volga.

As we were loading the car to leave, a mournful funeral procession went past consisting of a brass band playing dirges, people carrying wreaths and in front of it all, a man carrying a coffin lid on his head. The coffin, with the corpse uncovered and visible to passers-by, was in a lorry; behind that came a procession of old women wrapped up in scarves and shawls, trudging along in the cold in felt boots. It threw me into a sombre mood, which only dispersed after we had driven away from Yaroslavl, across the flat snow-plains where one had visibility of at least twenty-five miles in the clear sunlight. We stopped off for a night at Pereslavl Zalesky in a gloomy and dreary hotel. It was on the first floor of a building and had no name. There was no running hot water, just a cold tap, and no flushing apparatus for the toilet. Despite this we enjoyed ourselves, with dinner at the town's only restaurant. The food was not too good and served cold by a slatternly and slovenly waitress who annoyed us by constantly fiddling with a wireless set. The place was empty except for four people at a table who might well have been our goons, for we had been followed all the way to and from Yaroslavl. The next morning it was still so cold that Michael's car would not start. We tried in vain to find a taxi to give it a tow but were finally rescued by another guest in the hotel, probably a senior official in the fire service, who had his Jeep sent round and got the car started. (Not all hotels in the Soviet Union were that bad; one was prepared to accept certain discomfort and most were quite reasonable. As I noted in a letter home: 'Unlike our flat which crawls with cockroaches and mice, they are usually free of vermin.')

It was not long before a friend in the American Embassy, George Winters, and I were off to a little visited area of the Soviet Union called Ufa, capital of the Bashkirian ASSR (Autonomous Soviet Socialist Republic) at the south-western end of the Ural Mountains and Syktyvkar, capital of the Komi ASSR, north-east of Moscow. We had permission to visit both places but the day before we were due to leave, I had a telegram to say that the airfield at Syktyvkar was closed because of melting snow. We enjoyed the train journey to Gorky (now renamed Nizhny Novgorod) arriving in the early morning to go out to the airfield, where we were given a room in the airport building and breakfast. From Gorky, we continued by air to Kazan, which we were going to visit instead, and then to Ufa. Arrangements at the airport were relaxed. Passengers just scrambled on board and without further ado, the pilot pressed the starter and off we went.

This was a private visit, but my American friend (a member of the CIA) and I were keen to meet local officials in Ufa and find out more about life in the places where we were staying. Immediately after lunch we called on various organisations to seek interviews. We were well received by the Council of Ministers where an official promised to arrange something for us the next day and at the Economic Committee we were told that the chairman would receive us at 10 a.m. He spent the whole day showing us round the town, with visits to the House of the Pioneers, the Medical Institute, a ride in a speedboat on the Belaya River, a children's polyclinic and the museum. In the evening we went to the theatre as the director's guests.

We had free time next day:

> *'To pass the time we wandered into a secondary school, an unthinkable thing to do in Moscow, and asked to be received by the Director. This turned out to be a portly woman in her fifties, a bit of a battleaxe, who seemed surprised and then pleased to see us, and she arranged for us to be shown round the school by one of the assistant masters. It was an old school and not one that would have been shown to foreigners in normal circumstances. There were a lot of dingy and not very clean passages, and the whole place was in a bad state of repair. All the pupils, of which there were 1,200 from the ages of seven to seventeen of both sexes, were day attendants. They remain in this school for the whole of their education and the first seven years are devoted to normal subjects. In their eighth year they begin to specialise in mechanical training, and we saw rooms where the children are taught the mechanics of cars and lorries, with engines cut in half and working models of different parts of machinery. We also saw a metal workshop where the standard of craftsmanship did not look to me very high, but probably the instruction was good.'*

> *We had seen a lot in Ufa and the warmth of our reception was outstanding. We did not approve of the communist system but could appreciate that here at least, rapid progress was being made in housing, education and health. Our next stop, Kazan, was much less rewarding. It was a dusty, noisy town of 800,000 inhabitants; we were not successful in making official contacts and the hotel was uncomfortable.*

I think it may have been on this trip, or it could have been elsewhere, that I was asked by my colleague Derek Thomas to take a small portable radio with which to monitor the BBC's Russian service. The broadcasts were invariably jammed by Soviet transmitters in the larger cities but could be better picked up in smaller settlements and in the countryside. Short-wave transmissions are reflected off the Kennelly-Heaviside layer in the upper atmosphere, while the range of jamming stations at that time was limited to little more than the horizon around them; it was clearly impossible for the Russians to cover the entire country with jammers. The Kennelly-Heaviside rises higher in the ionosphere at night when short-waves were better reflected and able to reach further than during the day. The BBC were anxious that we should monitor their transmissions around midnight so that an assessment of their effectiveness could be made. It was a bizarre thing to have to do late at night, but one which we nevertheless enjoyed.

A few weeks later, two Embassy secretaries, Jennifer Couch and Gwyneth Ellis, and I joined up for a week-end in Kiev. It is the most ancient Russian city and the capital of the Ukraine, often regarded as the cradle of Russian civilisation. In the 10th century, it existed as a principality under the Vikings. Then under Yaroslavl the Wise and Vladimir Monomakh, it became a centre of great learning; Yaroslavl brought artists and priests from Greece and had churches built in the early 11th century. Thereafter the power of Kiev declined owing to internal strife, the Mongol invasion in 1240 and that of the Crimean Tartars in the 14th and 15th centuries. It belonged to Poland for a considerable time and was only united to the principality of Moscow in about 1640. It was for long the centre of religion and among the most sacred relics left in Russia are the catacombs of St. Anthony and St. Theodesius.

'We went down the first set of catacombs having bought ourselves each a small wax candle which we lit to see the way. The catacombs are very extensive and were lived in by the monks, some of whom carried their asceticism to such extremes that they immured themselves into their cells and had water and food passed into them through a small hole. When they died, the hole was closed up and their name and picture in the form of an icon hung up over the aperture. One man is said to have buried himself in the ground up to his neck, and lived like that for thirty years, and he too was left there after he died. His head was visible in 1914 when Baedeker wrote his book, but we did not find him there. There were about seventy saints there altogether, some immured as described above, others in glass-topped coffins fully clad in their vestments, mummified with only their brown and wizened hands visible. It was all rather macabre, as is so much of the Orthodox religion, which, at any rate in Russia, seems so preoccupied with death.

'Some of those who were with us were believers, nearly all very old women who kissed the glass above the head and the feet of the mummified saints and mumbled prayers and repeatedly crossed themselves. The atmosphere of the macabre and grotesque was further heightened by the fact that from time to time we heard the chanting of Orthodox prayers without being able to say where the sound came from; we thought probably through ventilation shafts from the church above us.'

We had been struck by the number of elderly women, evidently very poor and in some cases disabled, who had nevertheless made the pilgrimage from far away to worship at the holy shrines in Kiev. The second set of catacombs, of St. Theodosius, was similar although less extensive. The churches too were unique, particularly the cathedral of St. Sophia, founded and built by Yaroslavl the Wise in 1037 to mark his victory over the Pecherengi, a wild Asiatic tribe. The mosaics in the apse are original and represent one of the greatest examples of Middle Byzantine art. We were told that it has never had to be restored. We also visited St. Vladimir and St. Andrew's churches. That evening we returned to Moscow by TU-104 tired and hot after a busy week-end of great experiences.

Karelia is an ill-defined area of land lying between Finland and northern Russia. In 1812, after Russia's defeat of Sweden, it was subsumed as part of the Grand Duchy of Finland, simply because the Karelians spoke a dialect of Finnish rather than Russian. That there were no distinct boundaries mattered little as it was all part of the Tsarist Empire. With the establishment of a separate independent Finland following the Russian revolution, a frontier between the two was established which recognised Karelia's ethnic links with Finland. Demographically the frontier did not alter the fact that there were Russians living in the area designated as part of Finland and vice-versa. While some people may have moved one way or the other, there was no ethnic cleansing as was to occur in later years.

I was keen to visit the area, the history of which I outlined in chapter 5, and to see what conditions were like. In March 1960, an Embassy colleague, Cynlais James (First Secretary in Culture), and I had intended to visit two towns in what was then the Karelian Autonomous Soviet Socialist Republic, Petrozavodsk and Sortavala, and had sought permission from the Ministry for Foreign Affairs to do so. Petrozavodsk had been founded by Peter the Great in 1703 and was essentially Russian in character and religion, as were areas of Karelia further north. Sortavala, on the other hand, was a town on Lake Ladoga which even as a part of the Grand Duchy from 1812, had been predominantly Finnish in character and Lutheran in religion until subsumed into the Soviet Union after World War II. Maybe for cultural reasons, or maybe for military, we were refused permission to go there and decided instead to go to Tallinn, the capital of the Estonian Soviet Socialist Republic and formerly an independent country.

We found Petrozavodsk to be a bleak place and at that time very cold. At the theatre on our first evening, I fell in with a Finnish lady, originally from Oulu. She was reluctant to say anything about the war but was nevertheless glad to speak to a foreigner, to the extent of getting hold of some brandy from under the counter during the interval.

Next day we started on a round of official calls, beginning with the Ministry of Culture, then the University and finally an Internat Boarding School. The University was not of great interest but the boarding school was. I quote from my letter home:

'We were received by the Director, who explained to us that his school had about 700 children, who boarded there and it was in many respects like a public school in England. The children go home at week-ends. We looked round the classrooms and workshops which were all well equipped (indeed better equipped than the University). A most striking feature was the cleanness everywhere and the good manners of the children, who greeted us with politeness and deference. We also looked over the living quarters where the children live in dormitories of eight to twelve in a room, and the spacious and airy dining room and kitchens, where supper was being prepared. The food seemed quite good. Oranges were also available [most unusual in Soviet Russia at that time]. An odd feature was that all the cooking was done on a long kitchen range fuelled with logs of wood. We learnt that the children organise themselves as far as discipline is concerned; they have a council of elected representatives and a commission, appointed by the council, which goes round inspecting rooms and tables. They award points and the children with the highest score get free visits to the theatre. Much use is also made of incentives; in work, points being similarly awarded for diligence and study. These Internat Schools are quite a new thing, being introduced as a result of a ruling by Khrushchev. They are certainly very remarkable and I hope that in time they will result in a higher level of education and manners among ordinary Russians.

'At the library we found a huge collection of books in Russian but not many in Finnish. Our final call was on the deputy chairman of the Karelian Council of National Economy, who arranged for us to see a saw mill just outside the town. We were not impressed. It was a small enterprise, badly run and generally rather down at heel. No attempt was

made at proper organisation and efficiency. The director was a woman who wanted to argue politics with us.'

We travelled to Tallinn by train with a sleeper to Leningrad and a change of train for the onward journey to Tallinn. On arrival we were immediately struck by the totally different appearance of the town from anything we had experienced in the Soviet Union. The centre is in the form of a figure of 8, with the smaller half consisting of a fortified hill with ramparts, walls and turrets, a Lutheran and a Greek Orthodox church, while the larger loop is the main part of the old town, again surrounded by walls and towers and containing many old buildings of the 16th and 17th centuries. These are in a typical Baltic style, a cross between German and Danish, with tall rather narrow gables and two rows of attics in the roof. For the first two days of our stay, it snowed incessantly. This gave the town a very picturesque aspect and there brooded over it a snowy silence and sense of forgottenness which made one think that we were in the Middle Ages and not in the Soviet Union in the 20th century. Walking through narrow cobbled streets past ancient buildings was a very different experience. Nearly all the people we came across were Estonians, who distinguished themselves with their good manners and sense of dress style. The town was full of delightful coffee bars, serving good coffee and delicious cakes patronised by crowds of local people of very bourgeois appearance. We found an excellent restaurant, where the food was good, and a German-style beer-cellar. This was well-filled with young people of working class appearance, many very young but again, well-mannered and, as I wrote home at the time, there was none of the vulgarity, such as spitting on the floor, which we might have experienced in the Soviet Union.

Diplomatically speaking, we were treading on delicate ground. Estonia had been an independent country from the end of the First World War. It had then been overrun by Germany and later the Soviet Union to become the Estonian Soviet Socialist Republic under communist rule. Western governments objected to this and there were many Estonian refugees living in the United Kingdom. It would not have been appropriate to call on senior officials in the puppet government lest we as members of the British Embassy, should appear to be condoning the status quo. We accordingly paid a low level courtesy call on an official in the Ministry for Foreign Affairs.

A particularly interesting meeting was with the Rector of the Estonian Pedagogical Institute. We were told that this institute trained all teachers for primary school and the junior classes of secondary schools. Instruction was in Estonian only with no Russian taught. The Estonians have a high reputation for their music and they are extremely proud of it. In order to maintain this standard, they insisted that all junior class teachers must be able to teach singing and music and act as choirmaster wherever they may be. Everyone had to learn to play the piano and one other instrument, and must be able to sing. In order to qualify for entry, you had to pass an examination in music, consisting of tests for the ear (tone), rhythm and you also had to sing a song. If you could not do all these things, you could not become a junior class teacher in Estonia.

Our general impression was that the Estonians, who have only once in their history been an independent country (1918-1940), were doing quite well, despite their membership of the Soviet Union, and showed every sign of maintaining their national character. The standard of living, although lower than before the war, was appreciably higher than in other parts of the Soviet Union. People appeared to be happy. Although there was probably still some hardship, there was no atmosphere of repression which must have existed in Stalin's time.

Our last day in Tallinn was clear, sunny and warm and we spent the morning walking round the town which looked so beautiful with snow on the roofs. Our journey both to and from Tallinn had been difficult as we had far too much luggage, more than we could manage on our own, and Kenneth's suitcase was really a trunk. At the ticket barrier in Leningrad, the woman on duty remarked to Kenneth 'I spit on you, comrade, for having such a load of luggage.' Was this intended as a joke? I think not; we were back in the Soviet Union.

Three months later, I returned to Tallinn with Michael Duncan, with whom I shared the Embassy flat, and two secretaries. My letter home after the visit rang with enthusiasm:

'We left the Embassy after supper on Friday and took off for Leningrad at 9 p.m. There we just had time to collect tickets before catching the midnight train to Tallinn where we arrived, after twenty-seven stops during the night, at 9.17 a.m. I had to try to trace a consignment of wines ordered by the Ambassador which for some reason had been held up in Tallinn. We had lunch at a restaurant (pike in tomato sauce) and swam in the sea as the weather was fine and the water quite warm. I was again enchanted by the architecture, with ancient stone walls, towers and fortifications, the attractive winding streets and ancient buildings with courtyards and red-tiled roofs. It was also refreshing to hear the organ playing in the cathedral and in another church we passed, the main religion being Lutheran and not Orthodox.

'Once again in the beer cellar, we sat at a table with drunken labourers who, on discovering that we were English, began to speak very forthrightly about the Soviets and the Russians. One of them proposed Estonia's toast and declared that one day there would be a real celebration when the Reds had been driven out. It was a Hogarthian scene indeed.

'The Gloria restaurant, as good as ever, was filled with Estonians celebrating mid-summer, a national festival in Estonia, with much singing of nationalistic songs. We were sitting next to a party of Estonians, one of whom was in charge of yachting. They had drunk quite a lot of vodka and after inviting us to go yachting the next day, insisted on ordering up a bottle of liqueur and coffee for all of us. The next morning we duly arrived at the yacht club at 10 a.m. as arranged but none of the party turned up. Either they were still recovering from the night before or had had second thoughts about the wisdom of taking western diplomats sailing, or they had been warned off by the secret police, probably the latter. While waiting we watched one or two yachts setting off with their attractive and well-dressed crews. Each person had to present their documents for inspection to a Russian customs officer before leaving and their times in and out were noted down. It would have been difficult, probably impossible, for us to have gone out in any case.

'Back in town, we attended part of a service at the cathedral, which was followed by Holy Communion and a baptism. An old lady showed us round the church, which contains the graves of a lot of the old Swedish and German nobility. They are also cleaning the heraldic shields of the noble families and hanging them up on the walls of the church. One of the graves belongs to an old Scottish warrior who came out in the late 16th century and was killed in battle against the English. A great deal of restoration work is also being carried out.

'The beer hall was again full of students, drunk to various degrees, who were celebrating the end of term. They were again embarrassingly outspoken about their dislike of the Russians and the Communists and declared how much they liked England and the free West and how much they wanted to belong to it.

'For our journey back to Moscow, we took the train to Leningrad where we changed onto the Red Arrow train to Moscow, arriving at 9 a.m. in time to start work at the office. It may seem fantastic that we should have travelled so far in order to spend about thirty hours in Tallinn, a journey in inconvenience, distance and expense equivalent to going to the north of Scotland for a day from London, with a complicated change in the middle. It had been a wonderful experience. Tallinn is so fantastic a place, both historically and architecturally, also politically. Our enjoyment had been heightened by an atmosphere of conspiracy; for the whole time that we were there, we were followed on foot or in cars by large numbers of secret police watching our every movement.'

Looking back on this outing, it seems surprising that the Soviet authorities were prepared to let us visit a part of the Soviet Union where anti-Soviet feeling was so rife and vocal. This was at the height of the Cold War and the close surveillance of our movements reflected their concerns at our presence there. One wonders whether there had been some kind of reciprocal agreement under which Russians at the Soviet Embassy in London were allowed by our own security people to visit outlying parts of the United Kingdom in exchange for similar facilities for us in Moscow. So far as I know, this was the first time that western diplomats were permitted to visit the Baltic States. We were fortunate to have been there, not just because of the contrast with drab life in Moscow but also to enjoy the beauty of the town before Estonia became independent again in 1991 and Tallinn a honey-pot for foreign tourists flooding in on cruise ships.

Shortly after returning from a holiday at home I had a spare week-end before the arrival of the new Ambassador and his wife, Sir Frank and Lady Roberts, and took advantage of it to visit Riga. At that time, the city was the capital of the Latvian Soviet Socialist Republic. Formerly it had been an important town in Livonia and then the capital of Kurzeme or Courland. James, Duke of Courland, became famous in the 17th century; he had two or three colonies in the West Indies and Africa and entered into treaties with Charles II among others. In 1710, Peter the Great conquered Latvia and incorporated it into the Russian Empire. In 1919 after the Civil War, Latvia became an independent country. It was overrun by the Russians in 1940 and the Germans in 1941. Before the war about three quarters of the population were Latvian and fifteen per cent German, with various other nationalities also present. The Germans controlled most of the commerce and from earliest times were responsible for building up the town with its many fine buildings. The Germans were mostly driven out at the end of the war, but many still remained working in restaurants and similar occupations.

In our wanderings round the town we admired many of the old buildings that remained after the war; sadly some of the finest had been destroyed. Generally, the buildings were in poor repair. We visited the war cemetery, the original part of which had been built before the war in memory of those who had died for Latvian independence and, ironically, next door was a similar memorial to those who were killed during the 'War of Liberation' by the Red Army.

My companion, Tom Haining, was an enthusiast for trams, so we visited the tram depôt. We were told that the first trams had appeared in 1891 drawn by horses. Most of the trams had been built by a Belgian company who had bought the concession for operating trams in Riga; some of these were very old but about thirty new trams were being manufactured each year.

We had particular trouble with the goons in Riga, who followed us everywhere obtrusively. We could tell they were worried when we spoke to the waiter at the Astoria restaurant in German. For our second night, we had booked a table at the same place and on arriving found that every table had also been booked for well-known customers. Our goon followed us in to be told that there was no room for him; he was finally obliged to take the manager aside to show him his goon's identification card, and was then given a seat. By then we were fed up with being followed so closely and determined to shake the goons off. Having warned the waiter that we would be back shortly, we both got up to go, Tom returning to the hotel for cigars and myself to the toilet where I chatted with the German attendant. When we reassembled, the goon had gone and we then met various Latvians with whom we drank brandy and coffee. Again, there was outspoken criticism of the Russians. An enjoyable evening and at about 1 a.m. we staggered back to the hotel.

The security officers made up for it the next day, following me round museums and several churches which I visited. These varied in character and level of attendance. The two Lutheran churches each had about eighty worshippers; the priests were youngish but as they preached in Latvian I could not understand them. The first Catholic church was packed solid with around five hundred people of all ages, both men and women. The music was of a very high standard, with an excellent choir, including soloists who would have done justice to a cathedral. The goons followed us on a visit to the seaside, by foot with cars waiting on the road and when we sat down on a bench they came crawling at us through the undergrowth. The next day we left by air for Moscow, seen off at the airport by further members of the local authorities. We were sorry to be leaving Riga but glad to leave behind 'the odious lackeys of the police state' as I described them in my letter home. It was probably because of their attentions that I felt that Riga was less relaxed and not so inclined to western culture in its atmosphere as Tallinn had been.

A few weeks later another colleague and I took advantage of the Whitsun week-end to visit Vilnius, the capital of Lithuania. Like Latvia and Estonia, it had experienced a troubled history, with Sweden, Russia and Poland occupying its territory at different times. At the end of World War I in 1918, independence had been declared, but Poland seized the Vilnius region in 1920 and formally annexed the area in 1922; Kaunas became the temporary capital of Lithuania for nineteen years, until the Soviet Union, acting in accordance with the Secret Protocol of the Molotov-Ribbentrop Agreement of 1939, invaded in June 1940, and returned Vilnius to Lithuania. The country was occupied by Germany in 1941 with Jews being executed in the holocaust. Lithuania was the first Soviet People's Republic to declare independence in 1990, a year before the dissolution of the Soviet Union. In the following year Soviet troops attacked the TV tower and a Lithuanian border post, with some loss of life.

It was not surprising that we should find strong echoes of Polish influence in the Baroque buildings as well as in the religion and culture of the town. There were many churches, about half of them Roman Catholic but strongly influenced by practices of the Orthodox church, for example the use of icons. The other half were orthodox. At the Ausros gate, we noticed a shrine containing a wonder-working image of the Virgin Mary. A service was in progress and there were people crowding into the staircase and passage which led up to the chapel containing the shrine. There were even worshippers kneeling in he street.

Unlike on previous visits to Tallinn and Riga, we did not come across Lithuanians in beer cellars or bars. Our only local contact was with a Lithuanian writer whom we had met in a rather poor restaurant and who accompanied us on a tour of the town the following day. That afternoon, we took a taxi out to a bathing beach on the local river, a pleasant spot and a relief from the scorching heat of the day. I swam to the other side to look at what used to be a church but was now a tourist base. A man there was most offensive because I had only a bathing costume on. When I got down to the river again, I saw a Russian deliberately throw a bottle onto the stones at the edge of the water, showering broken glass everywhere. I gave him a ticking off, but it was of course no good. Oddly, we did not appear to be closely followed by the secret police, but I had left my camera unattended for a while and as I suspected, the film in it had been exposed. They were surely keeping an eye on us, but more discreetly than in the other two Baltic towns.

One of the best-known souvenirs of a visit to Russia comes from the village of Palekh, where artists produce a small black papier-maché box beautifully decorated with paintings of Russian folk tales. Four of us decided to visit it to find out more. Although not far from Moscow, the village is not easily accessible. We took the overnight train to Ivanovo, a town renowned for its textile industry and then travelled the remaining sixty kilometres in two cars, arranged by Intourist. The road was rough, consisting in some places of no more than a dusty track across the endless steppe, and it was an exhausting hour and a half's ride.

Palekh was like any other Russian village, with a prominent church, rows of low wooden buildings, a few larger ones in brick and over all reigned the soft and restful atmosphere of the Russian countryside.

In the 13th century, Palekh had been a sanctuary from Tartar invasion for the inhabitants of Vladimir and Suzdal who had brought with them their most valuable icons, but it was only in the 17th century that icon painting became a local art. By the mid-19th century, the industry flourished with roughly half a million icons being produced and quality was giving way to quantity. Our guide told us that this was due to 'Capitalisation' in the interests of greater profits; the painting of an icon would be divided up into a number of separate operations by different artists rather than the whole work being completed by one master.

After the Revolution icon painting was no longer possible and so the artists diverted their talents to the decoration of papier-maché boxes and other objects. The boxes are made from strips of thin cardboard, rolled and pressed, with the addition of flour and water paste onto a former to give it the desired shape. When dry it is treated with linseed oil and planed to give it its final form. It is then painted black and lacquered and, when dry, rubbed lightly with fine stone to give it a matt surface which will take the colours. The subject is sketched on; the principle lines are picked out in white paint, also lighter areas to impart a translucent brightness. The materials employed are the same as those in use since the art of icon painting began; powdered tempera colours mixed with a solution of egg white and vinegar, applied with a sable brush. After the addition of gold leaf and aluminium and a rubbing down with a dog's tooth, several more coats of lacquer are applied.

At the time some 150 artists were working at Palekh and production was running at between two hundred and three hundred boxes a fortnight. An Art Council then graded the products into three categories according to artistic quality and this determined their price when sold. We were told that there is also a school with about fifty students, some from traditional Palekh families and some from other parts of the Soviet Union; they train for five years before beginning work professionally.

We were the first tourists that year and the first foreign visitors since before the war. The authorities clearly hoped to increase tourist numbers by building a hotel and also a new road between Ivanovo and Palekh. In recent years Palekh boxes have been appearing much more widely and at lower prices wherever tourists visit. It would seem that since the fall of communism, 'capitalisation' may well have returned to Palekh. Whether there has been a decline in quality is debatable. One would also like to know whether the painting of icons has returned to Palekh as it has elsewhere in Russia, for example at the Solovetsky Monastery in the White Sea.

In August 1960, the Reillys finally left for home at the end of their time in Moscow before a well-earned leave and their next posting to Paris. The weeks before their departure had been extremely busy, with numerous farewell calls and dinners out every night. A few days before their departure, Sir Patrick's secretary, Kay Rawson, left Moscow and many went to the station to see her off. She had been an excellent secretary, a delightful person to work with and she had made my task a lot easier.

There had been some difficult moments in my relationship with the Reilly family, particularly at times of exceptional pressure with visits. Sir Patrick was an outstanding diplomat, with a comprehensive understanding of the issues in Anglo-Soviet relations and a determination to work for improvements at a particularly critical stage of the Cold War. As a person, I did not always find him easy to work for; he tended to worry and fret before taking decisions and I can appreciate that my own shortcomings as his Private Secretary in my first year would have been most frustrating. Nevertheless, we enjoyed some good times, especially on our travels. My experience as Sir Patrick's Private Secretary was echoed in the Guardian's obituary in 1999, written by Cynlais James, one of my colleagues at the embassy: 'A man of high and generous quality, lacking perhaps in the hard-edge of decisiveness and self confidence'. I was sorry to see them leave. They had looked after me with friendliness, patience and understanding.

Shortly after their departure, I too went home for a family holiday in Ireland returning to Moscow towards the end of September. A change of Ambassador also involves a fresh lot of domestic staff and it fell to me to see them settled in. They were all of military background. Their chef was a marine warrant officer who was to come with his wife; their butler was also military as were the two footmen who were a lance-corporal in the Irish Guards and a private in the Scots Guards. They clearly had no experience of diplomatic life at an embassy abroad and faced a difficult task in acquiring the necessary skills for running the household. From time to time I was summoned to help out. In fact I had anticipated this before the Roberts arrived and had put on my own dinner party in the residence. I provided the food and drink, the object being to teach the British staff how to serve at an Ambassador's table.

Sir Frank Roberts presented his credentials at the Kremlin soon after arrival. It was a very formal affair, with him and the Minister in uniform, the rest of us in morning tails as if for a wedding, and we had driven there in a procession. Life was easier with the Roberts as they were new to Moscow and I had been there for two years, whereas with the Reillys I was new and very much learning how to do things. Sir Frank was a small, energetic but extremely agreeable man really most intelligent and 'quite a handful to work for as Private Secretary' as I put it in my letter home. Lady Roberts struck me as a small, bird-like lady, whose native language was French. She was from Beirut and I found her extremely kind and pleasant. She had very high standards of taste and had been appalled by the mixture of dreariness, indifference and modern-style additions to the décor by her predecessors. She was used to living in one of the best-run houses in Paris with numerous servants.

Problems of bringing in frozen meat were to be repeated. Sir Frank brought in fifteen hundredweight of frozen meat, fruit and vegetables and there was simply not enough space for it in the freezer. This time I did not have to go to Leningrad to collect it and the problem of storage was resolved by putting some of it into a Russian ice house. My job was to supervise the unloading of seventeen sacks of meat and poultry.

In February 1960, I had received a letter from John Henniker-Major, Head of Personnel Department, informing me that I had passed my three years' probation, an event which we had celebrated at dinner in Yaroslavl when we were on a week-end trip there, but the letter had included some reservations. The Probation Board had had some difficulty in reaching a decision due to shortcomings including being erratic in judgement, unreliable on detail, weak in written work in the Foreign Office as well as in Moscow, but much improved during the last year. I was advised that I should not set my sights too high for my future career in the diplomatic service.

I was delighted when I was told at the end of October of my next posting to La Paz in Bolivia as Commercial Secretary. We had been asked to fill in a Post Preference form on 1 January each year and I had put down a preference for any post in the Andes, a part of the world I was keen to visit. It was pleasing that my stated preference had perhaps influenced the Foreign Office's decision. And so, in January 1961, I set out for home. I took the train to Helsinki securing diplomatic clearance for my luggage which included two grandfather clocks which I had bought in Commission shops. I was to have a month's leave followed by a month's training in commercial matters.

Chapter 8

In the High Andes

I had left Moscow on posting to Bolivia with mixed feelings. I was glad to leave behind the constraints of living in a communist country and the pressures of working as the Ambassador's Private Secretary in a busy political and social environment. On the other hand I had enjoyed the fellowship of colleagues in the embassy and other friendly diplomatic missions as well as travel throughout the Soviet Union. The contrast between Moscow and La Paz in almost every respect could not have been greater. The Embassy was of course much smaller. The Ambassador was Gilbert Holliday, formerly Ambassador in Laos, and there was a staff of some fifteen or so UK based members; diplomatic staff were limited in number so that, when one of us was away, others took over his duties.

Bolivia lies in the tropics, 16° south of the Equator. It is divided geographically into two distinct regions. Roughly a third lies high up in the Andes and two thirds to the east are in the upper reaches of the Amazon bordering Peru, Brazil, Paraguay and Argentina. La Paz, or to give it its full title La Ciudad de Nuestra Señora de la Paz, stretches up a steep valley from Obrajes at around 10,000 feet (3,048 metres) to the Altiplano at 13,000 feet (3,963m). In most countries the wealthier parts of a city are on higher ground while more humble dwellings lie down below. Because of the extreme altitude, the reverse is the case in La Paz. The embassy residences and staff accommodation are in the lower parts, while the offices are about half way up, nearer the town centre. It is a long climb up from these areas to El Alto, but once there the barren plain of the Altiplano plateau stretches away towards Lake Titicaca, while along its eastern border rises the magnificent chain of the snow-capped mountains of the Cordillera Real, with several peaks exceeding 20,000 feet (6,096m).

The country has a turbulent history. Modern Bolivia dates from the Spanish conquest of the 16th century. Before the arrival of the Spanish conquistadors, the area had been dominated by a number of Aymara

Indian kingdoms until the emergence of the Inca empire in the late 14th century. Francisco Pizarro moved down the Pacific Coast to Peru where he vanquished the Incas and founded the town of Lima, which became the Vice-Royalty responsible for governing the country on behalf of the Spanish monarchs. His two brothers Hernando and Gonzalo took control of Upper Peru (now roughly Bolivia) and pushed south into Chile, establishing the town of Chuquisaca, later the capital of Upper Peru.

During the 19th century the emergence of nationalism in Latin America, as in European countries, encouraged the movement for independence. Upper Peru in effect became a buffer state between Peru and Argentina. Simón Bolívar, Venezuelan leader of the Latin American independence campaign, had hoped for a confederation of Pacific states but had agreed to separate independent countries and Upper Peru was renamed Bolivia after him, with the Declaration of Independence signed on 6 August, 1825.

Turbulence has characterised the country's history over much of its time. When I arrived in La Paz, I was told that coups had occurred on an average of one every year and a half; in one or two cases, the president had been executed by hanging from a lamp-post in the main square. More stable government ensued after a revolution in 1952 by the Movimiento Nacionalista Revolucionario (MNR) with Victor Paz Estenssoro as president. Nevertheless, in my first letter home after my arrival in March, 1961, I related that there was a curfew in force after 12.30 at night, following disturbances in December. I wrote: 'Any car or person out after 12.30 is liable to be put in jail or more usually, shot at. The police wear no uniform but carry guns' or so I had been told.

A few days later, I attended a reception at a hotel in the town centre.

'Shortly after I had arrived, there was a student demonstration outside the hotel, which was broken up by tear gas, so that some of the guests who arrived after me came with tears in their eyes. On the same day there was rioting in other parts of the town. There seems to be a feud between the municipality and the students; the students wanted the right to use the municipal workers' tennis and badminton courts, but the latter refused. So the students demonstrated and broke every single window in the town hall with stones and bricks, so that it now looks like a ruin; they also treated in a similar way the Ministry of Peasant Affairs and two of the left-wing newspapers. One British tourist was arrested and put in jail for taking photographs of the proceedings.'

Similar incidents occurred from time to time. In October 1961 a doubling in the price of petrol led to three nights of disturbance, with areas of the city cordoned off and a certain amount of shooting. Apart from incidents such as this, the period of my residence in La Paz was relatively stable with the MNR of Victor Paz Estenssoro enforcing law and order. However there was much dissatisfaction with the poor economy and on a visit to Potosí on commercial affairs, I was depressed by what I found. I called on the Rector of the University and spoke to him of my concern over the strength of communism, only to discover later that he was one of the principal communist bosses in the country. The Vice-Rector was also a prominent communist. I felt that the country could not continue much longer in its state of hopeless bankruptcy and inefficiency. If the government in La Paz fell, I thought that the communists would have taken over by the time I came to the end of my posting. There was in fact a coup in 1964 shortly after the end of my tour, when Victor Paz Estenssoro was replaced by General René Barrientos. My friend Alasdair MacKenzie wrote to me that the houses of Barrientos and the miners' leader Lechin had been bombed, while shots had been fired at the house next to his. A couple of stray bullets ended up in his living room and he moved out to the security of the Embassy flat.

The communist threat had not escaped the attention of the British government. Fear that Bolivia could become a second Cuba prompted the appointment of two further members of staff. One was an Information Officer, Dick Sturgess, whose main job was to develop contacts with the local media; this included feeding to the media Spanish translations of any article critical of the Soviet Union and communism, which had been published elsewhere in the world; they were provided by the Foreign Office's Information Research Department. The other appointment was a Labour Attaché, Fred Sharples, to establish contacts with the influential miners' union and other labour organisations. The significance of the communist threat was underlined a few years later when Che Guevara, a colleague of Fidel Castro, fomented the communist cause among Indians in the eastern jungle; he was hunted down by the army and executed. Both the Sturgess and Sharples families became good friends, particularly the Sturgesses; they were a delightful family and keen anglers. We went on many expeditions together.

The embassy offices are located on the main avenue up from Obrajes and had probably been built as a private residence rather than an office. A flight of steps led up to the front door. On entering, to the right of the door was a reception area with a telephone operator sitting behind a panel with wires to plug into the sockets linking to various members of the office staff. The commercial secretary's office was immediately to the left. Upstairs were the offices of the Ambassador, the Head of

Chancery, the Information Officer, the Administrator, Accountant and several typists, all UK based. On the floor above that was a large flat which I was to occupy, with two bedrooms, living room, dining room and kitchen. It had a separate entrance to one side near the garage. I had a cook/housekeeper who looked after me well. When my main luggage eventually arrived I was able to settle in comfortably. The only problem had been moving my piano up the spiral staircase, but it got there after I had unscrewed the keyboard and taken out some of the mechanism, to be replaced once the main part of the piano had reached my flat.

In a yard behind the Embassy building was an outside WC which was never used by staff. It was an ideal place for smoking trout and with the necessary permission I set about using it for that purpose; it was reassuring to look down from the balcony of my flat to see wisps of smoke filtering out under the eaves. To smoke a fish, you need to fillet it and cover with salt. After twenty-four hours, surplus salt is scraped off and the fillets are hung high up in a confined space, in this case the lavatory ceiling. Below you light sawdust spread out so that it smoulders for a further forty-eight hours. In this case I had obtained a supply of good quality sawdust from a furniture workshop in the town. I had seen this process in Iceland where Atlantic char are treated in this way and I was reasonably confident. The result with the large rainbow trout we caught was delicious and I served it frequently as a starter at dinner. It only went wrong once when I tried it on a trout I had bought in the market; the fish has to be absolutely fresh and that one wasn't.

To start with, however, I had stayed a few days with the Head of Chancery, Michael Wenner, followed by a couple of weeks at a hotel in the middle of town. The altitude affects people in different ways because of the lack of oxygen in the air; some even pass out if arriving by plane at the El Alto airport, high up above the town, and need to be brought round with oxygen. For me, breathlessness was the main problem, but also I experienced vivid dreams, almost as if I was in a cinema. Even after several weeks of acclimatisation, I occasionally felt depressed and tired. One is also likely to be more irritable. At one stage I needed more rest and determined that I would not go out more than two nights a week and insisted on going to bed early. However, I must have got over this difficulty for later letters home recount numerous dinner parties ending in the early hours.

My job as Commercial Secretary covered a wide field with the overall aim of promoting British interests. At the end of each month a review of the Bolivian economy was sent in to the Board of Trade for publication in their journal. The situation did not change much from month to month and concocting a monthly report was difficult. The main British interest was in the Bolivian tin-mining industry. There had been numerous small tin mines taking over from the exploitation of silver in Potosí. Many of the main tin mines were owned by Simón Patiño, who bought up Bolivian mines and in addition had a controlling interest in the smelting firm Williams Harvey in England. The larger mines were nationalised in the 1952 revolution and apart from one or two small ones privately owned, the Bolivian tin industry was controlled by the Corporación Minera de Bolivia (COMIBOL). I had frequent occasion to call on them in the fourth floor of an office block as the smelting of Bolivian tin ores was a major British interest. Higher quality ore was shipped to Williams Harvey in Bootle, while mixed ores or those with lower tin content went to Capper Pass near Hull. At that time, our imports from Bolivia were around £10 million in value, while we sold only £1 million of exports.

Promotion of UK exports was of paramount importance world-wide, not just in Bolivia. North Sea oil had not yet been developed and the national trade deficit was rising. Most of my time was devoted to dealing with enquiries from British exporters. Relatively few representatives came to visit La Paz and we certainly did not have to accommodate high-power delegations such as had taken so much time and effort in Moscow. It was rather a matter of providing details of several importers whom we considered to be potential agents for a company's products. We also had to advise on the creditworthiness of those we recommended, all of which was not easy in a country with severe financial difficulties and many firms of dubious integrity.

Trade was not straightforward. There was a flourishing black market in goods smuggled across Bolivia's porous frontiers. British Leyland had an agency in La Paz with a well set-up servicing garage and they also sold Land Rovers. But by then they were already facing determined competition from Japanese Toyotas and were not finding it easy to maintain their market, partly because of labour problems at home affecting quality and delivery. It was dispiriting to follow a car with a large notice on the back stating 'Mi próximo coche será un Toyota'. (My next car will be a Toyota.) It may well have been true.

One representative who did take the trouble to visit La Paz came from Guinness. He brought with him bottles of Guinness with a detailed medical analysis of the product's health value and we were to submit this to the appropriate Bolivian department in an attempt to have it classified as medicine rather than beer and as such carrying a much lower rate of duty. I sent this in with little conviction, even if there was some truth in his assertion; I recalled a boy at my prep school during the war who was prescribed a daily dose of Guinness – maybe he was anaemic and needed the stimulus of that excellent brew. The Bolivian authorities carried out the necessary analysis but sadly and not unexpectedly came to the conclusion that from a medical point of view it was not different from any other beer and classified it as such. The Guinness representative may have left me a sample to try and in another respect it was no different from other beers. When at an altitude of over 10,000 feet you take the lid off a bottle brewed at sea level, it is explosive and much of the beer is lost unless you are quick with the glass.

Bolivia at this time was an undeveloped country with many people suffering deprivation and hardship and it was in our interests to provide aid to help the economy. There are various ways in which aid can be provided: direct relief by donating food and medical supplies; supplying agricultural goods, seeds, implements, fertilisers et cetera to encourage food production; helping with education or health. Most of our aid effort was concentrated on providing experts in tropical agriculture. We recruited advisers in cattle-rearing, sugar, citrus fruits and coffee, several of whom had been involved in our colonies in Africa until they achieved independence. Their remit was to improve productivity and to help with training.

The Embassy also supervised the allocation of about a dozen volunteers from VSO (Voluntary Service Organisation) and GSO (Graduate Service Organisation), school leavers on a gap year and university graduates respectively. Several VSO volunteers were attached to the agricultural advisers, others were teaching in schools, while some girls were doing social work among Indians. The system had much to commend it. The volunteers were guaranteed reasonable working and living conditions and received a small salary. Their work was extremely valuable and in the process they gained much experience and knowledge. There were few problems for the Embassy to sort out and for me it was helpful when one of the VSO volunteers took an interest in my study of the Andean lakes.

During my time in Moscow, the Prime Minister had been the most distinguished among many visitors and this had caused a great deal of preparatory work for the embassy staff, including myself as Ambassador's Private Secretary. There had never been any question of a visit to the Soviet Union by a member of the Royal Family - for good historical reasons. In Bolivia it was different. Towards the end of 1961, the Ambassador was warned of a visit by HRH the Duke of Edinburgh as part of a tour in South America; the aim was to promote British interests among countries where Britain had played an important role in securing independence. He was to spend four days in Bolivia. This inevitably involved a great deal of preparation, with every visit being planned down to the smallest detail.

It was a colourful programme. Prince Philip arrived, appropriately for a naval officer, on a steamship across Lake Titicaca, landing at the Bolivian port of Guaqui early in the morning. I was not among the welcoming party as my responsibility throughout was to go ahead to check on arrangements shortly before his arrival at the various places he was to visit. The first was to Tihuanacu, an archaeological site dating back to pre-Inca times. He arrived in the royal train, a steam locomotive with high chimney stack, much well-polished brass, whistles and bells, drawing two equally ancient carriages; one of these was already old when it was specially fitted out for a visit to Bolivia by the Prince of Wales in 1930. This was also appropriate for British companies had been responsible for the construction of Bolivia's railway network, as elsewhere in Latin America, and there were still a few British rail engineers living in Bolivia.

For the visit to Tihuanaco we had been offered two Land Rovers by the Bolivian Mining Corporation, but neither had arrived. Since my Land Rover was the only one there, it was decided that Prince Philip should ride in it. I was annoyed when the Director General of Antiquities jumped into the driving seat without so much as a 'by your leave', but he got his comeuppance when he did not know how to start the engine; Prince Philip had to do it for him.

The train continued to the station in La Paz, where a vast crowd was waiting to greet him which was estimated, perhaps with more than a little exaggeration, at 150,000. In the evening a short reception for the heads of diplomatic missions was followed by a formal banquet at the president's palace, for which full evening dress was required. The next day, visits were made to a hospital and museum. The latter was in an Indian part of the town and His Royal Highness was greeted with characteristic Bolivian enthusiasm, from arches of peasant cloth hung antique silver coins, cups and portraits, and showers of confetti. That afternoon, he visited the University and the stadium for a performance of folk dancing. My task here was to raise the royal standard as he arrived. Unfortunately there was a knot in the rope and it was with some difficulty that I got the flag up. Gilbert and Jane Holliday laid on an elaborate dinner that evening, followed by a reception.

There was no shortage of Land Rovers for the excursion into the countryside outside La Paz. We had arranged for a chauffeur to take Prince Philip's vehicle but he insisted on driving himself, which he did at considerable speed. We began at the Chacaltaya observatory, at an altitude of 17,500 feet (5,334m). He was not affected by the altitude, although he told me he felt a bit poorly when we first arrived. One or two in his suite were less fortunate and his Private Secretary needed oxygen. The next stop was the British-owned Milluni mine, with a colourful march-past of Chola women, babies on their backs and miners with their weapons, led by three of them performing an amazing goose-step which would have put Hitler's guards to shame. (The military goose step had first come into use in Prussia in the 18th century and been adopted throughout the world, with Chile the first Latin American country to introduce it to its army in the 20th century.)

The next stage in the journey was to descend to Cuticucho in the tropical Zongo valley. This was put in doubt by reports of bad weather, but we decided to take a chance and set off. Fog and rain shrouded the Zongo pass but lower down it cleared quickly. This is a difficult and scary road down a steep mountain involving ten or twelve tight hairpin bends, with drops of 2,000 feet over the edge. Prince Philip at the wheel in the long wheel-base Land Rover drove quite fast, but always judging the corners perfectly. Back in La Paz, he had a motorcycle escort but continued to drive fast; he even appeared to be pushing the motorcyclists to the extent that in the end, two of them dropped out.

In my Land Rover I had the Director General of Ceremonial at the President's palace, a young man holding an important position, and two members of Prince Philip's aircrew. The Bolivian official started off in the front seat with the two aircrew behind. On the way down, the Bolivian slept while the aircrew members strained their necks to get a view out of the back to see the superb scenery. For the return journey I suggested that they should change seats so that the aircrew could see more. The Bolivian official went off in some one else's Land Rover and I heard afterwards that he was very angry with me because I had ignored his ministerial rank and status in suggesting he should ride behind. Marcus Cheke, author of *Guidance for Members of the Diplomatic Corps Abroad* would no doubt have nodded his head in agreement, had he known of the incident.

On the last day of the visit there was a small informal dinner at the Ambassador's residence and a reception at the Railway Club for members of the British community. The next morning Prince Philip flew off to Santiago. It had been a very successful visit. The careful planning in the months beforehand had contributed to this success, but most of all it was Prince Philip's friendly and sympathetic manner with the Bolivians, which went down extremely well. At the informal dinner he spoke to everyone. As I noted in my letter home at the time, 'He is a most impressive and easy person to get on with, very witty, at the same time remarkably knowledgeable about every subject under the sun, for example discussing aircraft dynamics and the various species of birdlife in South America'.

Beyond high level visits such as that of H.R.H. Prince Philip, protocol dictates that an invitation to an Ambassador, either from the government to which he is accredited or from another source, may not be that straightforward. He is the representative of the King or Queen and it is in a way his duty to accept it and attend the event. However, there may be various reasons why he may be reluctant to do so. He may already have a conflicting commitment elsewhere which he cannot cancel without causing offence. There may also be political reasons in that his presence would not accord with H.M. Government's relations with the country in question. Or he may be unwilling to give up the time required to accept the proposal. One way out of this dilemma is to ask another member of the embassy staff to represent him. It was thus that shortly after my arrival in La Paz, our Ambassador Gilbert Holliday asked me to represent him at the National Eucharistic Congress in Santa Cruz, attended by the President and the head of the Catholic church in Bolivia, a cardinal. I reported on it in a letter to my parents.

> 'I flew in to Santa Cruz on a Wednesday and found the intense heat very trying at first. At the time, Santa Cruz was a backward town; none of the roads were paved so that in the dry season they were dusty and in the wet, muddy. There were hitching posts along the side-walks for those who came on horseback to tie up their steeds. There was no water supply nor drainage, with just wells and cess-pits for each house. I found the hotel unsatisfactory; the room I had for the first night was damp and resembled a monk's cell, while the next one I moved into was infested with cockroaches. I moved room again to a much better one although it overlooked the main square and here the trouble was disturbance from the ringing of bells and the singing of pilgrims on their way to the Congress.

> 'The National Eucharist Congress was held in an avenue a short way out of town. There was a platform at one end with an altar, a stand for the hierarchy and benches for priests, diplomats and members of the government including the President of the Republic and several members of his cabinet. On the first day, I walked up there for the inauguration ceremony, which got under way two hours late owing to the length of time it took for the cardinal's procession to reach the venue from the cathedral. The next day was taken up with commercial and consular

affairs; I was involved in getting a British subject out of the local prison. Later I heard that a secretary from the American Embassy had had a busy time obtaining the release of an American citizen who had had an argument with the Minister of Defence over the use of the hotel's only bathroom and been arrested for his insolence.

'*After dealing with such matters I decided to take a break to visit a colony of Mennonites, a very remote and aloof sect of Protestants, who went to Russia in the seventeenth century and later to Canada, then Paraguay and finally landed up in Bolivia. They only speak German and are so strict in their views that they will not allow any other book to be used in their schools except the Bible. They live an extremely hard life farming in the pampas near Santa Cruz, and their houses are very small and quite inadequate to keep out the dust storms.*

'*That evening I attended a reception at the town hall in honour of the President. I met up with a local businessman and after supper at his home, we went on to midnight mass at the Eucharistic Field.*

'*The congress had begun on July 9 with the arrival in the city of the venerated image of the Most Holy Virgin of Cotoca, this being a small village nearby which is the sanctuary of the Virgin, patron saint of that region of Bolivia and very highly esteemed by all Catholics. During the congress her image occupied a chapel in the Cathedral. Although it was not specified on the programme, she was brought out at 11.30p.m. and taken in procession to the Eucharistic Field amid the playing of a brass band, the singing of the hymn to the Virgin of Cotoca, and the ringing of bells from the Cathedral, with several hundred people taking part. My friend Ronnie Caballero and I were already in position on the platform when the procession reached the Field, where the Image of the Virgin was greeted with hysterical fervour, the waving of handkerchiefs and a huge press of people who gathered round to touch the Image. The service then got under way and lasted until 2 a.m. with many thousands of Catholics receiving the Sacrament. It was the one function where there seemed to be genuine participation by the congregation of several thousands and was most impressive.*

'*Afterwards I returned to the hotel but could not think of getting to bed until the procession had returned half an hour later, still amid much noise and bell ringing. It was thus 3 a.m. before I got to sleep. At 6 a.m. I was awoken by the pilgrims singing hymns as they made their way out to the Field for a mass. I had to get up soon afterwards to be present at Pontifical High Mass, attended by the President and conducted by the Cardinal himself. It lasted two hours, and I felt very tired and hungry by the time I returned to the hotel for breakfast. My rest did not last long for at 4.30 I had to be at the Cathedral to take part in a solemn procession of the Cardinal, all the Hierarchy (and there were no fewer than 30 bishops and archbishops in attendance and some hundred priests) and lay authorities. The Cardinal, who was late for nearly everything, arrived at 5.30. The procession left the Cathedral with the priests singing Gregorian chants in true tradition. The Cardinal rode in a fantastic kind of carriage, complete with altar, candles and lights, bearing the Holy Sacrament in a gold Monstrance some two feet high, and was followed by guards in uniform. Then came the civilian part of the procession, in which I should have taken a dignified position, as an official representative. But the townsfolk of Santa Cruz pushed and shoved in so unseemly a way that the event lost much of its solemnity, and I and my American colleague hopped out and walked round another way to the Eucharistic Field. That evening I attended a dinner given by the Organising Committee. It was nearly all members of the Hierarchy. I am now used to dining in the company of twenty or so bishops and we broke up, after lengthy speeches, at about 1 a.m. It had been a long day.'*

Santa Cruz had been hot but La Paz itself enjoys a very agreeable climate, in some respects more akin to that in temperate regions. There are two seasons; winter (April to August or September) is dry, with little rain, plenty of sun and cold at night. I kept a record of temperatures at my flat. In June 1962 the thermometer fell below freezing in La Paz for three weeks and maxima readings were between 50° and 60°F. Summer (November to March) is wet, with most rain falling between December and February. Heavy cloud suppresses the sun's heat and average maxima were just 10°F higher than in winter and it reached 70°F (21°C) on only five days in 1962. In La Paz at least, strong winds are unusual, the prevailing quarter being east in summer and west in winter. The strongest winds are encountered in sudden squally storms, may come from any quarter and can be very dangerous for small boats anywhere, but especially on the expanses of Lake Titicaca. Higher up, they may bring rain, hail or snow.

Understandably, the climate changed as one went higher. At the official meteorological station at El Alto at 13,175 feet (4,015m) much lower temperatures were recorded. There were also wide variations from year to year as information provided by the Bolivian Directorate of Meteorology showed. Higher still in the valleys of the Cordillera, differences were even more marked. Accounts of visits to the glacial lakes often referred to the contrast between strong warm sunlight at one moment and a snowstorm at the next. One day at Hichucota it hailed for an hour, with thunder reverberating round the cliffs on each side, and then the snow started to fall. Another time, after skiing at Chacaltaya at 17,500 feet (5,334m) we went on to fish a lake high in a glacial valley. It was so cold that the line froze in the rings of the rod. Despite that I landed a fish of nearly four pounds. At this time, snow was common above 14,000 feet but never stayed long once the storm had moved on. The snow line in the 1960s was around 17,000 feet (5,181m). As almost all the peaks of the Cordillera rise to over 19,000 feet (5,791m), they are permanently covered in snow. Since then, climate change has caused glaciers to recede and the snow line will no doubt have risen too.

While pure statistics may have their value, they convey little of the actual conditions experienced by anyone walking in the mountains or fishing on the lakes. They differ from those familiar to hikers and fishermen in Britain. In the tropics, the sun rises straight up, at right angles to the horizon, passes overhead or very nearly so, and drops straight down. Darkness comes soon after the sun has dipped below the horizon, and this effect is accentuated by altitude, where the air is thin and does not reflect so much light after the sun has set. Also, on account of the thinness of the air, places in shade are cold, even if the sun feels intensely hot out of it. Temperatures fall rapidly at sunset, or even if the sun is temporarily obscured by a cloud. There is therefore no warm evening twilight, an important time in the life cycle of many insects. I have often begun the day's fishing with bright sunshine but had to give up an hour or so later when clouds have come down from the mountains with squally winds and driving snow, rain or hail, and possibly thunder and lightning as well. Driving in these conditions on rough tracks can be scary. Elsewhere in Bolivia, the climate varies from Mediterranean-style in towns like Cochabamba or Sucre to the torrid heat of Santa Cruz.

The altitude also has some curious physiological effects. It seems more difficult for the human body to withstand cold, particularly when it is windy and wet, than at sea level; I often had to seek refuge in my Land Rover from wind-driven snow or rain, when I would not have done so under similar conditions in England. One's hands suffer from cold if they get wet when the sun is not shining. Also, altitude lessens one's capacity for physical exertion; quite apart from the breathlessness which afflicts one even after living for several months in La Paz, the body seems less able to take long periods of quite gentle exercise such as walking or rowing a boat. When making depth surveys of lakes, we found that three hours, added to the total of four hours driving, were about as much as we could comfortably manage in one day.

I had brought a range of fishing tackle with me as I knew that there was good trout fishing to be had. Within a fortnight of my arrival I had met a keen fisherman at a reception. He was Father José Farroiola, secretary to the Papal Nuncio in La Paz, and we arranged to go to Hichucota, a lake high up in a valley of the Cordillera, along with a friend of his, Father Jordan Bishop of the Dominican Brotherhood. On the appointed day, the Nuncio's battered Jeep rolled up shortly after 9.30 in the morning. It was my first of many fishing expeditions and I wrote home enthusiastically about it:

'It was a beautiful day, hot sun, white clouds and good visibility and with Father Jordan driving the Jeep, we reached the Altiplano at about 10.30, and set off along the Pan American Highway, northwards towards lake Titicaca. The road is appalling, rutted with loose gravel on it, and owing to the Jeep's wheels being out of alignment, we could not go above 30 mph. We made one stop for the fathers to remove their vestments, and continued for over an hour along the dead flat Altiplano, with ranges of snow-covered mountains on our right and ahead of us. We then turned up a side road and proceeded along a track which I would never have recognised as a road, going through streams and ponds and winding up into the mountains. When we finally came in sight of the lake, I was amazed by the beauty of its setting. It lies, about three miles long by half a mile wide, between two steep mountains, with other mountains blocking the end of the valley, some 4,000 feet higher than the lake, with snow and glaciers on them. I have never seen such a beautiful lake in any country that I have fished in. It was 12.45 when we arrived and so we began with lunch, provided by Father José, a good meal with wine, coffee and so on; he had even brought small coffee cups with him, and enough food for us all. The bottle of beer I had in my rucksack had been broken going over a bump.

'It was delightful sitting by the lake. The sun was very intense, but it grew cold as soon as it went behind a cloud. I tried with flies and the fish took well and we enjoyed a good day's sport. The sun was already going down when we decided to leave at 5.30. But then the car would not start and when we lifted the bonnet to look at the engine, I was appalled by the pieces of wire and string and bits of wood keeping it together. After ten minutes it started but would only run on two or three cylinders. I saw bubbles coming out from one of the sparking plugs. And so we set off for home in second gear, changing into low range to negotiate rivers and bogs. It was a nightmarish journey and after a while, it was obvious that we were going to run out of petrol. Luckily a Bolivian army bus came along and gave us a tin. We then reached a mission on the Altiplano where we turned in at 9 p.m. The Franciscan monks gave us whisky, and we telephoned for the Papal Nuncio's car and chauffeur. At 9.45, we set

129

off again. The chauffeur must have been drinking for we came down into La Paz at a fantastic pace for that road, and I would really have been quite nervous, had it not been for the two stiff whiskies which I had enjoyed with the Holy Fathers on the Altiplano.'

Trout fishing was to become my main leisure occupation and almost every week-end and holiday I set off into the mountains. It might be thought that I neglected my work in the office. This was not so; in my letters home I frequently mentioned having to work on Saturdays in order to keep up with correspondence and report writing. My Ambassador never complained that I spent too much time by the water's edge, although once or twice eyebrows were raised; he was himself a fisherman and we went on many fishing trips together; he and his wife Jane were good friends and we got on well in the office and out of it. In addition there were other activities on offer. In Moscow I had enjoyed singing in an Embassy choir and wished to continue in La Paz. I began by joining the choir of the American evangelical church and attended services most Sundays. During my second tour, however, I found that my limnological research left me little time for Sunday church services and I had to step down. As Gilbert put it nicely in a poem he read out at my farewell party:

'Selby Martin went to church,
Sang loudly in the choir,
But limnological research
To Selby's heart lay nigher.'

This was not the end of my singing as I had already joined a German choir of some thirty members conducted by a remarkable musician, Martin Moesgen. There was a substantial German community in Bolivia, roughly divided into three generations. First there were Germans who had migrated to South America to avoid Nazi persecution. Then there was a group of former Nazis who had fled Germany immediately after the war to avoid being brought to justice for their crimes. I do not recall meeting any who unsurprisingly would have identified themselves in that group, but a visiting businessman complained of being kept awake in his hotel by rowdy singing of the Horst Wessel in a nearby flat. Finally there were Germans of the current generation who were in business, on aid projects or office work. There was a German pastor and we would sing on various occasions including funerals and on one occasion at a party in the pastor's house to celebrate his birthday. Jane Holliday also organised play-reading evenings. These were taken seriously. Copies of a play, usually a Victorian melodrama, were sent out in the Diplomatic Bag and carefully rehearsed before being presented.

The outing with Father José Farrioila to Hichucota had taken me for the first time across the Altiplano and into the foothills of the Cordillera Real. The Altiplano is part of an inland drainage basin stretching from southern Peru into north Chile; much of it is arid and featureless, like a landscape on the moon. Lake Titicaca, an immense sheet of water occupies the northern end, 100 miles long and 30 miles wide. It is the highest lake in the world with a steamship service and is one of the most important inland waters, comparable with the Great Lakes of North America or Lake Baikal in Siberia. It is fed by streams from the surrounding mountains and drains through the river Desaguadero into lake Poopó, a shallow brackish lake, where it spreads out into the salt flats of Uyuni and disappears through seepage and evaporation. The land around Titicaca, once covered by the lake, is fertile and supports the cultivation of barley, potatoes, other root crops and the native cereal quinoa. It is densely populated by Indians of the Aymara tribe, notable for their women's colourful dress and bowler-style hats.

The nature of the glacial valleys is very different. They owe their origin to the two most recent periods of glaciation. The first glaciation of this region left moraines between the mountains of the Cordillera and the Altiplano several hundred feet high. These were cut through during the second glacial period; at this time the glaciers retreated irregularly with moraines being deposited at intervals up the valleys, resulting in the formation of a series of lakes or areas of marshland.

In comparison with the lands around Lake Titicaca, the most striking feature of this region is its desolation. The absence of trees and bushes, the scarcity of plant life, especially around the higher lakes, the towering snow-covered peaks and the lack of man-made features give them an air of remoteness and grandeur. There is almost no arable land and the population is extremely sparse, with widely scattered villages of a few adobe huts and occasional isolated farms depending on livestock for their existence. Llamas, alpacas, sheep, guinea-pigs and horses provide wool for clothes, food, and dung for fuel; the melancholy pipes of the shepherd are often heard. Such arable cultivation as there is depends largely on a system of irrigation channels inherited from the Indians' Inca ancestors. The water for these is taken from the lakes and controlled by simple barrages; the barrages do not affect water levels from a fishing point of view. At this time, the Indian population was so sparse and their way of life so simple that to all intents and purposes the land and the lakes remained untouched by any form of human activity. We found the Indians friendly and helpful, only to be avoided if they were celebrating a feast and fuelled by excessive alcohol.

Earlier, miners seeking minerals high up in the mountains laid down primitive tracks up the valleys and it was these which enabled us to access the lakes. All the same, one had to take care. Heavy rain would often bring down screes of shale blocking the tracks; crossing these required judgement. Just how far could one lean the Land Rover to one side without tipping it over the edge? I usually carried a shovel in the car to smooth out the track if this should be necessary to get by.

The differences between the lakes and the fish found in them had inspired me to carry out some research into the limnology of these waters. I assigned a spare room in my flat to serve as a laboratory and got in touch with the Natural History Museum, the Freshwater Biological Association and Liverpool University. They were interested in the idea and offered advice and equipment in their respective fields. However, it was clear that to pursue research I would need a boat. It would have to be small enough to fit into my short-wheel-base Land Rover, but sufficiently sturdy to withstand rough waters. While in England on leave I came across and ordered what seemed to me the most suitable boat; it came in two parts, the prow with oars and rowlocks would fit into the back of the Land Rover, while the hull could be strapped onto the roof. On arrival at a lake, the two parts would bolt together, to be taken apart again for the return journey.

I had booked to return at the end of my mid-tour holiday on the Pacific Steam Navigation Company's *Reina del Mar*. By the standards of the day, this was a large liner, built some ten years earlier; my cabin was luxurious, the food on board excellent with a high standard of service from officers and crew. We sailed out of Liverpool and I was booked to leave ship at the Chilean port of Arica. We were due to call at various ports on the way. This was at the height of the Cuban Missile Crisis, when the Soviet Union declared its intention to station nuclear armed missiles on Cuba and the United States was threatening preventive action. We followed events with much anxiety as we sailed through the Caribbean.

Fairly soon after setting sail I noticed that the boat I had ordered was badly packed; for protection it had no more than loose sheets of plywood tied round with string. Unless I could do something about it, serious damage was inevitable. The ship's carpenter was unable to help for lack of materials and I would have to set about mending the crate myself. The first opportunity for finding suitable timbers was at Cristobal at the north end of the Panama Canal. I asked the PSNC agent on the quayside to put me in touch with a timber merchant but all he could do was summon a taxi to take me round the town. Apart from finding some pieces of wood on a tip and an old packing case, I had no success until, on returning to the quayside, I came across a pile of planks lying on the ground. The person responsible for these was a tough American who listened to my problem and allowed me to take away five twelve-foot planks without charge. These, with the other oddments I had picked up, enabled the ship's carpenter to put together a sturdy packing case round my boat, strong enough to cope with any amount of rough handling.

On boarding the ship, I had feared that three weeks at sea would be boring. This was not the case. There was the usual range of entertainment; parties, dances, deck games, swimming pool and a cinema. My fellow passengers were a pleasant lot and I enjoyed the company of those at the same table as myself in the dining saloon. These comprised the ship's Chief Officer, a railway engineer, an amusing petrol station proprietor on a jaunt before moving to Tasmania, a young lady, Kathleen, on her way out to join her husband in Lima and another, Jill, who was also on her way to rejoin her husband; she told me they had earlier divorced but decided to try living together again for the sake of their young son. She was notable for an unusual preference for bright purple clothes and long finger nails which she used as sugar tongs or to stir the ice in her vodka.

For these reasons I did not find the journey boring. In addition, on most days I spent two hours studying Spanish and an hour practising the piano in the lounge if there was no-one else around. I also set about marking up a long nylon rope, sewing on coloured bands at ten foot intervals to use for measuring the depth of the glacial lakes I was to study. I had brought my fly-tying kit with me and spent time making fishing flies.

It so happened that Jill, one of the fellow passengers at the dining table, occupied the cabin next to mine. She showed great interest in fly-tying and invited me into her cabin to show her how it was done. I duly moved in, set up the vice and other materials on her bedside table and demonstrated the creation of one of my favourite flies, a Peter Ross. I worked away at this while she lay on her bunk watching. Eventually the fly was complete so I packed up my materials, wished her 'Good night' and returned to my cabin. Only later, after she had gone ashore at Cristobal, did rumours about her conduct on board begin to emerge. She had allegedly forced her attentions upon certain of the ship's officers, in particular the Chief Engineer. Also one of the stewards had been caught in a particularly compromising situation with her and had been dismissed. She had suggested to Kathleen a similar assignation with a deck steward but she would have nothing to do with it. I later wondered whether Jill really had been so interested in fly-tying.

Eventually we docked in Arica, a small port where a lighter had to be used to transfer cargo ashore. I watched as my boat, along with cases of wine, whisky and groceries, were loaded into a large net and lowered by crane into the bottom of the lighter. One side of the net was then unhitched and the baggage tumbled out. Wine leaked out and it was clear that one or more bottles had been broken, while others might well disappear before delivery to my flat. My boat was unharmed. As I wrote home: 'I do not mind if I lose wines and whisky provided the boat is alright.' And so it was.

Not all our expeditions from La Paz were up into the mountains. Gilbert and Jane Holliday invited me to join a group organised by a Swiss anthropologist, Ernest Buechler, on a ten-day trip down the Rio Beni on balsa rafts. This river flows in a north-easterly direction through the tropical lowlands of Bolivia before joining the river Marmoré and eventually the Amazon.

Our party of eight met up at El Alto airport with a large quantity of equipment and after a long delay took off in a Dakota DC-3. The flight over the Cordillera took us through a spectacular landscape of snow-covered mountains and glaciers, partly shrouded in mist, and three-quarters of an hour later we landed at Covendo, a distance of 75 miles NE and a drop from 13,175 feet to 1,640 feet. We were immediately struck by the oxygen-rich air we breathed and the intense heat of the tropical jungle.

We stayed the night at the Covendo mission, founded 150 years previously. Its purpose was to improve the life of the Mossetene Indians who live in the area, as well as introducing them to Christianity in which respect it had been successful. The atmosphere in the mission was one of happiness. Everything was run for the common good, with little distinction between religious and everyday life. The Mossetenes were cheerful, friendly and easy-going and more likeable than the Indians of the Altiplano. The next morning we started by attending mass in the church. It was a large church with only two pews probably put out for our benefit, the rest of the floor being covered with mats of dried palm leaves. There was a large congregation of men, women and children, who separated off with children at the front, then women and finally men at the back. Music was provided from three or four home-made violins, accompanying a most extraordinary-sounding choir quite unlike European singing.

After the service, we loaded up the two rafts and set off down the Alto Beni river. Until then I had always associated balsa wood with neat square pieces glued together in the nursery to make models. Our rafts were made from the dried trunks of balsa trees; their structure was admirably described by Gilbert Holliday in an article he wrote for *Country Life* magazine (September 10, 1964):

'The craft we were to use are locally known as callapos. A callapo consists of two or more balsas or narrow rafts. A balsa is built of seven logs (neither more nor less) of the light, buoyant balsa wood, riveted together with pins of iron-wood. The stern is square and the bow pointed and bent upwards into a prow. Two or more of these Balsas are united by cross beams lashed on with fibre. On top of these are bamboo poles running parallel to the balsa logs. These are covered with mats of woven fronds of a species of bamboo, making a comfortable platform some six to nine inches above the water level. The platform is protected by a triangular structure of bamboo poles, also covered with mats lashed to them and giving about six feet of headroom at the peak. We had two rafts, one of three and the other of two callapos, with a beam of nine and six feet respectively.'

The balsas were manned by members of the local Mossetene tribe recruited by the missionaries with whom we had spent the night. There were eight, one at each corner of the balsas armed with a paddle some eight feet long. They were expert at guiding the rafts down river, communicating with each other in the Mossetene language of which we understood nothing. Yet there arose a sense of understanding between them and ourselves; they were responsive and looked after our welfare with dedication. Most of the time we floated down on a smooth surface. Occasionally we had to negotiate rapids which put their skills to the test; on one morning alone there were twenty. Some presented little more than the occasional bump against stones, others were frightening. As Jane Holliday described it in her book *Cocktails and Cockroaches*:

'The most formidable challenge occurred in a gorge where the river was compressed between the rock faces of a vertical fault. Excitement mounted amongst our balseros whose cries grew more and more wild and triumphant as the river started to roar. We hung on to whatever was handy and said a prayer or two. We plunged at speed over the first weir-like fall and into the whirlpool below. Something went wrong however. We failed to shoot across the vortex of the whirlpool and were rapidly heading for destruction on the huge boulders bounding the pool, smooth and black and menacing. With remarkable presence of mind, and as one man, they started paddling in reverse and got us out of the whirlpool stern-first and just in time. Our respect for our saviours grew by the minute.'

Each evening as the sun began to drop down behind the trees and before the mosquitoes had turned out in force, we would come ashore to set up camp on a sandy beach. The balseros quickly erected a framework of bamboo poles cut down at the riverside to hold our mosquito nets and set about preparing our supper, partly from ingredients we had brought with us, partly from local produce such as the meat of monkeys or fish from the river. We generally slept well and arose at 6.30a.m. The Mossetenes began the day with a short service kneeling on the sand. A good breakfast followed and at around 9 a.m. the captain would bless the rafts for the day's journey. This was the best hour as the sun broke through the mist and it was still fairly cool. The balseros knew the route well for on the third day of our trip, they grabbed spears, bows and arrows and rushed over to an arm of the river where they shot or speared fish lying in a pool. We would go ashore in the early afternoon, set up camp and prepare supper. Each evening Gilbert read an extract from Jerome K. Jerome's *Three Men in a Boat*.

Gilbert and I had brought our fishing tackle with us. We baited our hooks with evil-smelling bits of fish and we each caught a fifteen pound bacú, an ugly bottom-feeding brute with long whiskers. Another fish was lost when it got off and undoubtedly it would have been even bigger. Members of the party had their own special interests: plants, butterflies, shooting or fishing. It was also pleasant during the day to sit in the shade on board the raft, playing bridge and sipping whisky. Swimming was a delight, but only up to a point. One day we were attacked by swarms of flies. That evening, a fish was landed on a set line which caused dismay among the balseros; it was an ugly, leathery flat-fish, an Amazonian sting-ray, with a sting of such powerful venom that it can paralyse a man in a few minutes. The balseros cut off the sting to use as a poisoned tip on an arrow. That put an end to our swimming; we could not risk stepping on a sting-ray. By this time also, the sun was extremely hot and we were plagued by vicious insects, marihuis, by day, and in the evening mosquitoes descended on us.

Eventually we arrived in Rurrenabaque 180 miles away from Covendo and 880 feet lower in altitude. Our rafts, now soggy, were chopped up and the balseros went on their way. In the afternoon we took off on the return flight to La Paz, passing over some of our campsites and other recognizable features. We covered in an hour the same distance by air as it had taken us ten days by water. It had been a remarkable experience and we flew back to La Paz, sad that our expedition was over but glad to be home again.

On one or two occasions I had reason to visit Sucre, formerly Chiquisaca until renamed in honour of the Venezuelan general Antonio José Sucre who, with Simón Bolívar, had played an important part in the liberation of Upper Peru in the early years of the 19th century. The first trip was with the Canadian Ambassador, John Pick, and his Commercial Secretary, Bill Jenkins, with their respective wives, from the Canadian Embassy in Lima. We planned to spend a night in Cochabamba before continuing to Sucre for a couple of days, then on to Potosí. We set out from La Paz early in the morning to drive to Cochabamba, a distance of 430 kilometres, with the car packed to the roof with several suitcases, three tins of petrol and food. The road was in quite good condition although twisty as it traversed several ranges of mountains. Continuing the next day, we had only 340 kilometres to Sucre. The first 120 kilometres were on the Santa Cruz highway, at that time the only paved road in Bolivia. Thereafter, the road deteriorated with steep winding roads over a succession of mountains and along a seemingly endless river valley. Finally we climbed up onto a plateau by moonlight and arrived in Sucre late in the evening.

The Central Bank of Bolivia kindly invited us to stay in their flat. It was comfortable and we were well looked after, sometimes too generously with extensive meals being produced when we really only wanted a snack. However, there was one drawback. Immediately opposite our rooms was a similarly prestigious building with a pediment at roof level containing a clock. It struck each quarter, followed by the hour.

Although disruptive of sleep, it reminded me of my interest in clocks. I did not expect to find English clocks in Bolivia so far from the UK. I was mistaken. My friends and I noticed a clock shop in Sucre and on entering were amazed to find a huge pile of old clocks of all ages and origins and all in poor condition. Clock repairers are notorious for taking a long time over mending clocks; it appeared that all these clocks had been brought in by their owners and the shop had never got round to carrying out the necessary work; their owners had either given up or forgotten about them. They were now for sale and among them were two or three 18th-century bracket clocks. Their history would have gone back to the prosperous days when the silver mines of Potosí resulted in owners setting off to Europe to fit out their houses with good-quality furniture, paintings, carpets and decoration. We bought some fine examples of antique clocks to take back to La Paz, eventually to be restored. On a subsequent visit to Sucre, I went back to the shop to find that all the remaining clocks had been cleared out. At least I had rescued the more important English ones.

My fishery researches turned out to be even more interesting than I had anticipated and were undertaken during the close season when it would not have been right to fish, although a lot of people did. In all, I sent 150 insect samples to the Natural History Museum, as well as forty-two consignments of stomach contents and whole fish. These were sent in a copper box provided by the museum, preserved in diluted alcohol. The waters surveyed were visited on many occasions and at different times, but the results for the main ones can be summarised.

Rainbow trout were introduced to Lake Titicaca by the Americans in about 1941 and they quickly established themselves, increasing in size and numbers until they reached a peak in 1953. At that time, it was possible to catch trout weighing up to twenty-five or thirty pounds and a day's fishing was considered poor if some ten to fifteen fish between ten and twenty pounds had not been caught. Good sport was also to be had fly-fishing in the Suches river which the trout ascended to spawn. After 1953, fishing deteriorated to reach a point when one could troll for two or three days without catching a single fish.

The purpose of introducing trout had been to provide food for the Indian population but there were problems. At first the Indians, accustomed to fish for native species, found their fine nets being broken by huge trout, which they thought were evil monsters and threw back. Only later was their commercial value appreciated and fishing for them by any means, including dynamite, became common. Their nets on the river Suches were so closely set that no fish could possibly get up to spawn. When a Ministry of Agriculture launch approached the Suches river to attempt to control fishing, it was shot at. A further problem was that as the trout continued to grow in size and number they threatened the survival of native species. That the latter were a major source of food for larger trout was shown by the difference in the quality of the flesh. Larger trout from Titicaca were plump, with a layer of thick fat around the stomach and back. The flesh was orange in colour and rather too rich for good eating. Smaller trout from Lake Titicaca and other lakes were leaner, there was no fat and the flesh was bright red from feeding on shrimps.

Fishing on Lake Titicaca was difficult. Although the trout were large, there did not seem to be many of them. Our friends Ronnie and Betty Clark had a motor boat and kindly took me out to troll along the shore but we caught little. Once or twice I borrowed his light folding boat and launching it at the Yacht Club I fished round the reeds nearby. It turned out better than trolling; I soon had a fish of 3¾ pounds and after a break for tea, I hooked another on a yellow plug bait. It tore off about fifty yards of line and eventually came to the net, weighing in at 9½ pounds. Three weeks before I had lost an even bigger one, which I estimated at between ten and fifteen pounds when the line broke. An Indian told me that he had caught this fish with my bait in its mouth and it had weighed eleven pounds.

Introductions of trout to other waters followed at different stages, with varying results. The Hichucota lake to which Father José had taken me was in fact one of two. A second lake some five hundred feet higher up the valley and separated from the lower one by a series of waterfalls also had trout in it. Both lakes had similar geological characteristics. The lower lake was very deep, going down to 130 feet throughout its length except for shallower areas at the top and bottom ends and at a shallower band in the middle. The upper lake was slightly less deep but with similar bands of weed along the shores. It was more difficult to reach as the track gave out soon after leaving the lower lake; in order to get my boat to it I employed an Indian to repair the track as far as he could but this still left a few hundred yards to cover on foot. Despite the similarities, the two lakes were quite distinct from a fishing point of view; the lower one yielded large numbers of small fish, the upper one had very few fish in it; we only caught two there and they were large, at five pounds and seven pounds. A study of scales from fish of both lakes by Dr J. W. Jones of Liverpool University showed that fish from both lakes were of a similar age. In the lower lake, the food supply was insufficient for the large number of fish while in the upper one, numbers were held back; either fewer fish had been put in in the first place or the lake lacked suitable areas for the fish to spawn. In both lakes food supply was similar as shown by the stomach contents of the fish we caught; it consisted mainly of freshwater shrimp which lived in a band of weed growing at a depth of between fifteen and thirty-five feet.

The best and most interesting fishing we enjoyed was on Hampaturi, one of two reservoirs supplying water to La Paz. It had been built in 1945. Although only an hour's journey from the city, it was not easily found and it was unfortunately some time after my arrival before I discovered how to get there. A track off the main road to the tropical Yungas valleys climbs up round a shoulder of a mountain at about 14,500 feet (4,420m) and then drops down into the Hampaturi valley, ending up at a disused tin mine just above the reservoir. I had heard that Americans had been catching trout with spinners from a boat, and on my first visit, the Indian caretaker who lived in a hut near the dam assured us that there were fish there. He had a small rowing boat from which he used to troll a spinner on simple tackle. My friends and I confirmed that there were good trout there to be caught on both spinner and fly, particularly at the top where the stream flowed in.

When we went again, it was late in the season and a brilliant sun shone all day. We began to fish after the sun had dipped behind the mountains and it soon became apparent that there were plenty of trout about. Several large fish assembled at the mouth of the stream and were taking flies as they hatched out. We caught several up to four pounds in weight.

Shortly after this the Indian caretaker evidently decided that visitors from La Paz were depleting his stock and built an immense wall across the track not far from the top of the hill. This meant leaving one's car at the wall and walking three miles down to the lake, a trip which took three quarters of an hour going down, with a drop of five hundred feet. Climbing back up took over an hour and at that altitude it was an extremely arduous walk.

I had previously obtained permission from the municipal authorities to fish there and the wall did not prevent me, although it effectively put a stop to those, mainly Americans, who had relied on taking a boat with them and trolling a spinner for their sport, a method that I found unsportsmanlike and disliked.

At the beginning of the next season, we found that the wall had been dismantled, presumably to allow normal access for maintenance, and the caretaker's boat had been taken away for repair. For a few weeks we were able to drive down to the lakeside, but then the rains came and a landslide blocked the road at a point near where the wall had stood, and we were walking again. This turned out to be a blessing. Only a few friends and myself keen enough to go to such trouble ever went there. On one occasion I borrowed a child's bicycle small enough to fit into the back of my Land Rover, to ride down on and then to push back with tackle and fish loaded onto it. It was a wonderful season with good hatches of fly and whenever we went, there was a strong chance that we would find the inlet end of the lake full of feeding fish, undisturbed by the spoons and spinners favoured by American anglers. Apart from the Indian caretaker, we never met any Bolivians, who as a rule did not fish. And then one day even the caretaker ceased to appear; we learned later that the unfortunate man built himself a raft while his boat was being repaired, he went out on it one stormy January night and had drowned. We felt very sad that our friend had been lost in that way.

There were several factors which favoured trout in this reservoir. In the first place, the number of fish benefited from very favourable spawning grounds on the gravel beds where the stream flowed in at the head of the lake. Secondly, it was relatively shallow. The dam had been built across a flat valley floor and as it was thirty-five feet high, the lake behind it would be no deeper than that, unlike the natural glacier lakes which were deep and steep-sided. At that depth, a type of weed flourished which was an ideal habitat for shrimps, molluscs and other invertebrates on which trout feed. Another type of weed, found in every other lake I visited and thought to be less productive, was not seen. The rich feeding for fish accounted for their unusual size.

From an angler's point of view, the great advantage of Hampaturi over other lakes was the presence of plentiful fly life. There were three species. The most numerous was a large mayfly, the nymphs of which lived in the stream and would float down into the lake to hatch; here the trout gathered to feed on both the nymphs and the flies as they emerged. We never found out where the flies mated or when they laid their eggs. It was nevertheless clear that the stream was an essential part of the ecosystem.

We introduced trout to Taipichaca, a smaller lake in the Palcoco valley to the south of Hichucota, transferring some three hundred recently hatched fry caught by the Indians in the stream below. A year later we caught two fish of a good size. Scale readings again showed two years of slow growth followed by rapid increase. Other lakes which we tried only occasionally yielded similar results. There were also trout in the river on the way down to the Yungas. They were comparatively small, but their diet was more varied; one fish had in its stomach a snake longer than itself.

To summarise, for the best fishing conditions there needs to be a balance between the number of trout stocked or produced from spawning and the amount of food available for them. If there is only limited food available, the fish may be numerous but they will be small. Conversely, good feeding but limited spawning capacity will result in a few larger fish. In the case of Hampaturi, both spawning and food supply were excellent. Scales were sent to Dr. J. W. Jones, Reader in Zoology at Liverpool University, who kindly helped with the survey. In the case of a 4½ pound fish he commented: 'This, as far as I can see, was only just beginning its third year of life, the scale read 2+, with two very definite winter bands. It seems to me that the fish in Hampaturi are faring very well.'

However, results from scale readings from fish in the tropics may be open to question. In temperate latitudes, bands on scales are determined by the seasonal rate of growth dependent on food availability; also by spawning. In the tropics differences in food availability are less marked, while the trout, originating in latitudes with more clearly defined seasons, seemed more random in their spawning. Both Dr Jones and another biologist, Dr Margaret Brown, cast doubt on the reliability of scale readings in the tropics. All the same, the results of scale readings seemed consistent and provided the information I was seeking.

The size and population of fish in any given water may change over time if conditions change. Correspondence with fellow anglers after I had returned to England certainly suggested this. The trout in Titicaca had unexpectedly become more numerous, although much smaller. In Hichucota, the trout had increased in size from an average of a few ounces to over a pound; this was attributed to a reduction in numbers caused by heavy fishing by Americans trolling with spinners; in one case thirty-five fish had been taken out in one day. On Hampaturi, the fishing had been poor, with fewer fish and no hatches of fly; no explanation was offered.

The information arising from the survey was well received. However, there were difficulties over collating and publishing it. As Dr Greenwood from the Natural History Museum explained: 'The biological data are not weighty enough for a scientific journal, and particularly because your samples were either too small or not repeated over a sufficiently long period. Nevertheless your data are important and in many cases unique and it would be a tragedy if they could not be permanently preserved in print.' The answer would be articles in non-scientific publications and I ended up with a long article in the Royal Geographical Society's *Geographical Journal* in December 1965.

No angler can resist the lure of far away lakes, high in the mountains, teeming with vast fish; he will go to any lengths to travel there to try them out. So it was with Alasdair MacKenzie and myself, and a brief expedition to the lakes in the Apolobamba mountains became my last expedition before leaving Bolivia. It lay in the north-west corner of Bolivia bordering the Peruvian frontier. The Cordillera Real which contains the lakes so far described ends at its northern end with the peak of Illampu, at 21,036 feet (6,412m) one of the highest in Bolivia. Thereafter comes the Sorata Gap, about fifty miles wide, and beyond it the Apolobamba range. It is geologically similar, but with a more gradual slope up from the Altiplano. There are several glacier lakes leading up into the mountains and they are longer than those found in the Cordillera Real. Lake Suches, the largest glacier lake in Bolivia, is fifteen miles long and Lake Cololo five miles. These two form the headwaters of the Suches river which flows into Lake Titicaca and is the only one large enough to provide spawning grounds for trout.

It is a remote area and difficult of access. We travelled in a long wheel-base Land Rover, taking with us a drum of petrol, spare parts, four cases of food and drink, and camping equipment. At Puerto Acosta the Bolivian Wool Board (COMBOLFLA) provided a room for us to sleep in. The next day we visited the wool sorting plant, where alpaca and llama wool from local herds was graded and sorted for export to Liverpool. From there we had intended to cross to the next valley, Charazani, but lost our way; after one and a half hours we stopped to ask an Indian for directions and were told that we were on the road to La Paz. We turned back and after driving across an immense and featureless plain we arrived after dark at the village of Ulla-Ulla. The Indians were surprised to see us arriving so late and turned out to welcome us with obvious friendliness; they soon arranged for us to have the use of a hut with a table and chair and there we spent a comfortable but cold night.

Next day we set out in warm sunshine for the village of Pelechuco, halting on our way to boil eggs in a hot spring and later to fish in Lake Cololo which yielded a 9½ pound rainbow trout; it was in poor condition but we kept it for research purposes. We continued up to the pass at 15,866 feet to cross into the Suches valley. Here it was cold and windy and the descent down the other side was one of the most frightening I experienced; it was extremely rough, with hairpin bends of such sharpness that one had to back up on each turn to get round them. At Pelechuco, the question of our lodging was resolved by the kindness of a visiting Franciscan friar who let us sleep on the floor of the parish hall. He joined us for dinner and told us of his work with the Indians. His job was a difficult one, having to minister to Indians who were wholly superstitious in their approach to religion. He was constantly being visited by Indians in varying states of intoxication with requests for special masses.

Our final destination was Suches, with its large lake reputed to hold monster trout. We again lost our way and were fortunate on returning to Ulla-Ulla to pick up an intelligent young Indian with relations in Suches who would not only show us the way but help us with finding accommodation. Even so, it was not an easy journey; we lost the track more than once and our guide had us stop frequently to talk to local people, probably to seek further directions. After an hour driving over open countryside in what we assumed to be the right direction, we finally arrived at a small group of huts on the crest of a moraine; it was Suches, previously an extensive gold-mining town going back to Spanish days, but now consisting of only six adobe huts; one was a schoolroom for local children and into another one we were invited to spend the night. At an altitude of 15,390 feet we had expected it to be very cold, but warmer weather had set in.

We cooked up our usual modest meal on a primus stove but our repast was disturbed by the entry of the village cacique with his rod of office which he laid down on the table as if to stay for some time. He was very drunk and we were only able to edge him out with the gift of a few eggs and a tin of preserves. We thought it possible that either he or other members of the community might return later to cause us difficulties.

Our fears were confirmed when, half-an-hour later, there was a pushing and banging at the door, which we had fastened. This went on for some time until eventually we gingerly opened up to see who was there. We found only a couple of horses who had entered the village and were perhaps trying to get into their usual stable.

Our fishing in the lake was disappointing. We had a few small trout on spinners, all around a pound and a half in weight, and only one on a fly. No doubt there were big fish there but they had not appeared to justify the stories of monsters about which we had heard. After a second night in Pelechuco, this time without disturbance, and another in Puerto Acosta with the Wool Board, we returned to La Paz. This was a very different trip from the Alto Beni. We had experienced the remoteness, desolation and cold of the high Andes and much enjoyed our fishing even if it had not come up to the expectations which had lured us there in the first place.

It is said that there is no life without change. Fifty years on from my time in Bolivia, I was in touch with a Bolivian fisherman in La Paz, who updated me on the situation. An increase in the population has brought more pressure on the lakes, and fishing has become commercialised. Rainbow trout are raised in cages in lake Titicaca, much as salmon are in Scotland, and there are hatcheries to provide alevins for stocking the main lakes. In these, laying nets has harmed the quality of rod-and-line fishing. In Hampaturi, a suburb of La Paz has moved nearer to the reservoir where we fished. Caddis and mayflies still hatch but you are lucky to find a fish that has escaped the nets. Four more reservoirs have been built higher up the valley where the fishing is better, but here again, net fishing is still a problem for the angler.

At Hichucota, there is now a proper road most of the way. The trout are much the same size as before. Two Indian communities, one on each side of the lake, are in dispute over fishing rights. The lake is stocked by a company who then rent out nets for the fish to be caught and sold. In the higher Hichucota lake, conditions are much as before. It is not stocked and there are only a few, large fish to be found there.

Tourists who come to Bolivia hoping to fish for trout do not find it easy. They suffer from the extreme altitude and feel unwell. And when they are taken to a particular lake or river, they may find that the fish have been scooped out by nets just before they got there.

The much larger population now living around La Paz and elsewhere need to be fed. The farming of trout in Titicaca and the extensive use of nets provide an important food source; it is hard to argue against that. For the sporting angler, the Andean lakes have lost much of their attraction and fishing for dorado in the subtropical rivers to the east has more appeal. Trout fishing for sport can only be viable if there are waters where fishing is strictly controlled by common consent, with a system of permits and the resources to enforce conditions. In Bolivia this is plainly not possible.

One day in March 1963, the Ambassador Gilbert Holliday summoned me to his office to say that I was to be recalled to London towards the end of that year, some six months before I was due to leave. While I looked forward to getting back to England for a home posting, I was very disappointed to lose those six months with all the fishing and research on which I had embarked, as well as the company of many friends. I was fortunate to have been in Bolivia at a time when there was so little pressure on the fishing; it had indeed been a wonderful place in which to spend two and three-quarter years of my life and I noted in a letter home that I would probably never have another posting like it. Certainly a few years in London did not appeal, although it turned out to be far more rewarding than I might have expected.

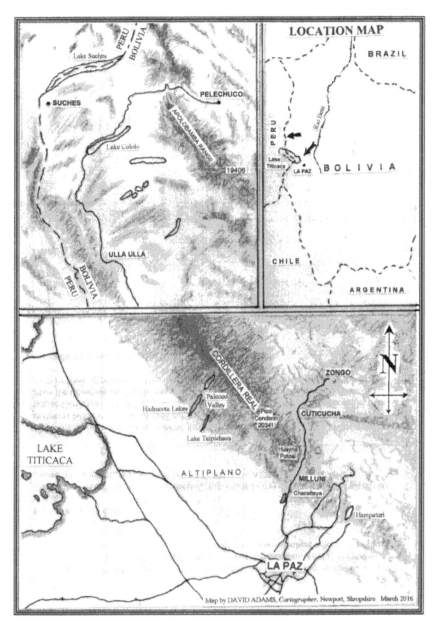

The area around La Paz, Bolivia

Illimani dominates the city of La Paz as night falls

Railhead at Guaqui on Lake Titicaca.

The locomotive that brought HRH Prince Philip from the port of Guaqui to La Paz

Prince Philip at Milluni tin mine, speaking to the director Ronnie Clark, with Ambassador Gilbert Holliday behind him

Marchpast by local children in welcome to Prince Philip at Milluni

The road to the Yungas

Steam locomotive on the Antofagasta railway

Rail car in which the author travelled from Potosi to Sucre

Hampaturi Reservoir supplying water to La Paz

A Mayfly which provided good sport on Hampaturi

Aerial view of Hichucota lakes (Bolivian Military Geographical Institute)

Lower Hichucota lake

The author measuring the depth as part of a research programme

An outing with Dick and Mary Sturgess and friends' children on Hichucota

On the way to upper Hichucota

Fishing in upper Hichucota

Rainbow trout from Lake Titicaca. The larger one weighed five pounds

A moraine under the surface of the top Palcoco Lake

Condoriri in 2010 (Alan W Shave)

Shearing llamas at Puerto Acosta. The wool was exported to Liverpool

A street scene in Santa Cruz

Loading balsa rafts at Covendo on the Alto Beni river

Setting up camp on the Alto Beni

Mossetene Indians catching fish with bow and arrows, and spears

Gilbert Holliday putting together his collection of pressed wild flowers

Chapter 9

Three Defining Years: then Pakistan and the Himalayas

Anyone returning to London after a few years away needs to find accommodation at short notice. It is fine if you already own a property and have let it out to rent on a contract with a specific termination clause. That was not my situation on returning from Bolivia and I was extraordinarily fortunate to be able to return to the same lodgings where I had lived in the 1950s in Kensington Park Road, Notting Hill.

My landlady was still Sybil Drew, with whom I had stayed as a student in Cambridge and in Notting Hill when she moved there in about 1955. She slept on the first floor and her mother on the ground floor. There were four of us; Peter Hamlyn, a solicitor, my brother David who was then practising as an architect in East London, Mark Lucas, a somewhat aloof young man who kept to himself and whose main hobby was the guitar, and myself. It was a good arrangement. We would arrive back from work around 6 p.m., enjoy a glass of South African sherry in one of our rooms and then go out somewhere for a meal. On Friday night we would disappear home, in my case to Broadstairs returning to London first thing on Monday morning.

To travel to the Foreign Office in Whitehall was straightforward. The simplest and quickest way was by Underground on the Circle Line. Foreign Office hours were from 10 o'clock to 6 o'clock which avoided the main rush-hour. On a fine day I would walk to work and it was a pleasant route across Hyde Park to Green Park and then through St. James's Park, which took an hour. Alternatively, I would cycle in following a quieter route through the back streets north of Hyde Park. Within a few months I had bought myself a car which was an ancient Morris Minor Convertible, but I preferred not to drive in London if I could avoid it. There was no parking difficulty; I would drive into Downing Street and enter the courtyard through the arch opposite No. 10. Nor do I recall any security arrangements; we just walked in through the main entrance, greeted the uniformed wardens who stood at reception and only offered proof of identity if required.

I had been assigned to the Latin American section of the American Department, with responsibility for several South and Central American countries, including Brazil, Venezuela, Peru and Bolivia. With Dick Slater as head of department and George Hall as his deputy, we had two main interests to promote. The first was to try to encourage British firms to invest in Brazil and Venezuela. These two countries were comparatively wealthy, with reasonably efficient administrations and likely to expand their economies, offering opportunities for British exporters. The second interest was in dealing with the few remaining British colonies which were approaching independence and had problems with neighbouring countries. The most urgent of these was British Guiana.

The territory of British Guiana had seen several changes in ownership over the years, predominantly with Holland and France, reflecting the course of events in Europe. In 1831 it became a British colony but retained the Dutch constitution. The western boundary had been determined by Robert Schomburgk in 1840 but Venezuela had not accepted this; the matter was put to arbitration in 1898 and the tribunal awarded ninety four per cent of the disputed territory to Britain. This arrangement was formerly accepted by both parties in 1905. So matters rested until 1962, when Venezuela renewed its claim to the Essequibo district, arguing that the 1898 tribunal had been improperly influenced by external pressures.

Our role was to support British Guiana as it approached independence, while still remaining on good terms with Venezuela, an important supplier of petroleum. It was suggested by Venezuela and accepted by Britain that experts from each side should undertake an in-depth review of all the historical evidence and come up with recommendations. For us, a distinguished retired Ambassador, Sir Geoffrey Meade, was invited to carry out the necessary research. Sir Geoffrey was a kind, quiet-spoken gentleman, who nevertheless was thorough in his work. On the Venezuelan side, three Jesuit priests tackled their role with enthusiasm. To me it seemed that this was a three-against-one contest and I had misgivings as to where the research would lead us, not because there were weaknesses in our case, rather that the zealous ferreting by the three priests would produce an overwhelming and confused mass of documents.

In the event, independence approached and from our point of view offered a way out of the dilemma. It might have come sooner, but for political considerations. In an election in 1953, the People's Progressive

Party had won a majority of seats in the Legislature under Cheddi Jagan, a dentist with left-wing views, who was not welcomed by either us or the Americans. The constitution was suspended, troops moved in and the Governor assumed direct rule. Further elections again resulted in a left-wing majority, until 1964 when the main opposition party, the People's National Congress under Forbes Burnham formed a coalition with another party and took over.

A conference was held in London in November 1965 to work out the terms for full independence. This was agreed and Guyana became independent on May 26, 1966. A Service of Thanksgiving and Dedication was held on June 7, 1966, at Westminster Abbey attended by Their Royal Highnesses the Duke and Duchess of Kent with the Dean and Chapter of the Collegiate Church of Saint Peter in Westminster. The National Flag of Guyana was taken in procession and laid on the altar. Venezuela's claim to the Essequibo region was not resolved but fell into abeyance. Guyana was no longer a British Imperialist colony, but an independent country and a member of the United Nations. For Venezuela, circumstances had changed and a pursuit of its claim would have been vindictive.

Another British territory with a problem was British Honduras, the whole of which was claimed by Guatemala. The problem caused so much trouble that at one time we broke off diplomatic relations. We maintained a military presence in British Honduras but in the end the territory gained independence as Belize. So far as I am aware, Guatemala's claim has been quietly shelved.

Even at this time, Argentina was laying claim to the Falklands but not to the extent of threatening invasion, nor were they campaigning to the extent that has followed since the war of 1982. There was no question of surrendering sovereignty over the islands but it was thought that there would be scope for negotiating closer links between the two countries over such matters as air services and trade. Nothing came of this proposal for the good reason that the Falkland Islanders had no wish to become more closely associated with a country which was unstable and unlikely to drop its claim.

Only a limited diary was kept at this time but one or two entries reflect frustration at the constant pressure of work in the office. May 27, 1965: 'The office continues to be a dreadful grind; last Thursday worked until 9 p.m. and last night until 9.30p.m., having started in the morning at 9. Today I complained to Dick Slater, the head of department, that so much paper as a routine, was excessive. He thinks of asking for another person in the department, which we badly need......I find this so depressing and often think of chucking it up and looking for something else. I have no time for anything else such as music, reading, writing and little social life. Thank goodness I can get home for week-ends still, to fish.'

I must have been in a really bad mood when I wrote this, for in fact I had plenty of opportunity for a social life; I had piano lessons and found time to practise at Sybil's where she had a lovely Blüthner baby grand and Peter, David and I would enjoy our evenings out. I also joined a Scottish dancing club in Chelsea and attended an evening geology course at an adult centre near the Elephant & Castle.

It was about this time that I was invited to become a Resident Clerk at the Foreign Office in Downing Street. I would have shared a flat with other Resident Clerks on the top floor, with responsibility for dealing with urgent matters out of office hours. Once a month I would be on duty over the week-end and required to stay around. I declined the invitation. After five years abroad I did not want restrictions on my activities, particularly fishing in the Kentish Stour, and I preferred to remain in my bedsit at Sybil's along with my brother David and friends. I was also nervous of the prospect of having to deal with emergencies at week-ends or in the middle of the night on issues and about countries of which I had no knowledge. Had I been more dedicated to my work and more ambitious, I might have accepted.

The family was still living in Broadstairs. My father was by then in his late seventies but still running his business along with my brother John and would usually get up early to visit a building site before breakfast at 8 o'clock. He and my two brothers were members of the Stour Fishery Association which had fishing on the river for several miles above Canterbury and were closely involved in its organisation. I was not a member but fished the river, either as a guest on the Association's water, or on the public stretch above Canterbury. In summer the best time was in the evening and the family would set off with a picnic after a quiet gin and lime in the garden. If I was fishing the public stretch, my parents dropped me off on their way further upstream and picked me up late in the evening. This was a beautiful reach of the Stour, bordered by water meadows close to the city of Canterbury and with fine views to the city walls and the towers of Canterbury Cathedral. We had fished it after the war and caught some fine trout, often on a minnow. By now, we fished only with fly; there were hatches of Mayfly and Blue Winged Olive which brought the fish up to feed and offered the angler excellent sport. These fish had been stocked by the Tonford Fishing Club on their stretch of river immediately above and moved downstream. I was very pleased when one evening I landed a trout of just under four pounds which was an exceptional fish on that river and I had done better than the rest of the family on the Association's water.

149

In July 1965 I saw a notice in the local paper about a planning application to develop the land between the river and Wincheap for industry and warehousing. Much of it was in private ownership and the application was for the compulsory purchase by the council of just over thirty acres. The area was to be divided between light industry, warehousing and public playing fields. The latter space was liable to flood and to negate this they declared 'it is the council's intention to raise the level of the land by tipping and to lay it out in due course for playing fields and amenity open space.'

I was horrified and sent in a strong objection, arguing for the protection of the water meadows and open space, with fine views to the city and the cathedral. Basically I wanted the site to be left as it was and sought support from local environmental organisations. The inspector approved the council's proposals, which were concerned more with public ownership of the land than with its development. My arguments were presumably included among those that he considered to be 'of small weight or irrelevant to the main issues'. It is evident that my objections should have come at the earlier stage of the draft Local Plan. I knew nothing about this and was inexperienced. But I had learnt quite a lot in this my first planning campaign.

A much more serious threat to the River Stour at this time was a proposal by the East Kent Water Company to increase abstraction from boreholes from three million gallons a day to nine million gallons. Any river may be polluted and its condition is determined by the extent to which polluted water is diluted with clear water from springs or other clean sources. There may be efficient sewage works but the effluent emptying into the river contains nitrates and phosphates which cannot be eliminated. If dilution is insufficient, fundamental changes in the river quality occur. The main one is the excessive growth of the alga *Cladophora glomerata,* or flannel weed. This in turn brings about radical changes in the river's natural life. Rooted weeds such as Crowfoot and Dropwort are stifled; mayflies and crayfish disappear. The river can become unsightly and evil-smelling due to the decomposition of flannel weed so that fishing, bathing and boating can be unpleasant and even dangerous for health reasons. Increased abstraction at the level proposed would have tipped the balance against the river's future.

David carried out his own surveys and engaged Dr. Margaret Brown, an eminent Oxford biologist, to prepare a detailed biological report on the river, not just on the Association's water but on the whole river from Ashford (a main source of pollution) down to Sturry a couple of miles below Canterbury. I helped where I could but was posted abroad

150

before all this was put to a public inquiry. The Association's case was presented by a distinguished barrister with experience in such matters. The decision was for permission to allow only three million gallons a day of additional abstraction. It was something of a victory and the river was saved, at least for the time being. This was one of the first cases to be brought against water abstraction on chalk streams and increased nationally an awareness of the need to protect our rivers.

In La Paz I had sung initially with the choir of the American church and later with a German choir. I had enjoyed it and was keen to carry on in London. I heard of a choir based in Whitehall, the Treasury Singers, who were happy to take in people from other government departments. I joined and took part in practices once a week during the lunch break. I do not recall any more formal performances, except one day before Christmas we sang to the Chancellor of the Exchequer, James Callaghan. The carol with reference to gold seemed fitting and we sang it with gusto.

Now that I was back in London, there were opportunities to go skiing with friends. It was some years since my first skiing trip while a student at Cambridge, when a group of us went to St. Anton-am-Arlberg in Austria. Arrangements had been made by Innsbruck University; a professor looked after us for the fortnight and taught us. This was obviously very different from cross-country skiing which I had enjoyed so much in Finland, while in Bolivia I tried no more than a single run down at Chacaltaya because the ski-lift was out of order.

In 1966 a group of us went to Zermatt for a fortnight. At that time, Zermatt was a relatively small village, dominated by the Matterhorn. There was no traffic - cars and lorries were not allowed and there were only occasional trains. The skiing was excellent; one could take the narrow-gauge railway up into the mountains and come down through forest and pasture, ending the run within a few yards of the village centre. It is said that you should never return to a place you have enjoyed previously; it will invariably be a disappointment. Certainly this was so in the case of Zermatt when we returned forty-five years later. The town had expanded extensively up the valley; while some of the new houses retained an Alpine style, others had not and were of an ugly 'modern' design which clashed with the Alpine vernacular. No longer could we walk the streets in peace; although there was still a ban on motorised transport, many hotels had minibuses to ferry their guests up and down the valley.

It was through the Scottish Dancing group in Chelsea that the next skiing trip took place. One of the members, Lois Streatfield, arranged a trip to Sölden in Austria in February, 1967. There were about fifteen of us; we stayed in a pension which gave us breakfast and each evening we dined in a restaurant where we sat together at a long table. Even at that time of year, there was little snow in Sölden so we took a cable car up the mountain to Hochsölden. We were allocated classes according to our ability and experience. The instructor in our group took us on some quite demanding runs and looking back as we crossed a steep traverse, I noticed that a girl was struggling. I moved back to give her a hand; it was Rachel, the red-haired girl who sat opposite me at the other end of the dining table.

On returning to London we went out together for meals or the theatre and two months later went to Islay in the Inner Hebrides for the May week-end holiday, staying at a hotel in Bowmore. We were lucky to have hot sunny weather, so hot indeed that the deer were wading into the small lochs to keep cool. I suggested that we should cross over by ferry and climb one of the Paps of Jura. I had not realised that Rachel was not good at heights but she tackled the steep ascent without complaint. Once at the top I proposed to her and despite any misgivings she might have had over the climb, to my great joy she accepted.

Rachel's parents had been in Malaysia for many years, where her father had been an administration officer in the Colonial Service. He had retired before the war and Rachel was born at Petworth, the third of three daughters. On leaving school in Salisbury, she had gone to the École de Commerce in Neuchâtel, Switzerland to improve her French and then attended a Cordon Bleu Cookery School for three months. In 1957 a job came up for a post with Humphreys and Glasgow, engineers, in London and a year later she moved to Montreal where she found a job on arrival with an investment company. The following year she took six weeks unpaid leave to travel with two friends across North America in an ancient Dodge. After a further six months she accepted a job in Paris as a bilingual secretary with Schröders bank in their representative's office. While Paris has much to offer, it can be a lonely place, as I had discovered when staying with a Russian émigré family before going to Moscow. Rachel found the same and accordingly transferred to Schröders London office, sharing a flat with a number of friends in Redcliff Mews near Earls Court.

By this time I had been posted to the High Commission in Pakistan under the exchange arrangements with the Colonial Office when the two government departments combined to form the Foreign & Commonwealth Office. I had bought everything I would need such as tropical clothing, crockery and cutlery, wines and spirits, and my luggage was about ready to be sent off. The Head of Personnel was still John Henniker-Major and I made an appointment to request that I take leave after one year to return to England to get married. He insisted that my departure should be delayed by a month so that I could get married first and take Rachel with me. I am for ever grateful for this example of the Foreign Office's care for the interests of its staff and we set about making the necessary preparations with all haste; we had five weeks before the wedding and ten days after it for our honeymoon. For Rachel it was particularly difficult having to buy suitable clothing for the tropics in a very short space of time.

With many friends living in London and our families a long way from each other, in Kent and Hampshire respectively, a wedding in London was the best solution. The problem was finding a church prepared to accept one of us as a regular worshipper on the electoral role which was not easy as we both tended to go home at week-ends. As it happened I had been to Sunday services at All Saints, Margaret Street, on a number of occasions and loved it. It is an outstanding example of the Gothic revival, designed by William Butterfield and dating from the middle of the 19th century. The architecture and the pattern of worship, still more the music and singing of the choir, appealed to me; the church at that time ran its own choir school. For these reasons I had become a Friend of All Saints and on that basis the vicar was pleased to hold our wedding service there. The reception afterwards took place at a near-by hotel. At that time, it was the custom for guests to wait for the departure of the bride and groom before leaving themselves.

For our honeymoon we had booked to stay at a castle on the Isle of Skye belonging to a man who had been at Wellesley House with me during the war. As can so easily happen in Scotland, it rained for nearly all the week. It was nevertheless a happy time and at the end of it, we came back south and boarded the plane for Karachi. We arrived at the height of the monsoon to stay a night with the Deputy High Commissioner. The streets were under water and any exploration on foot was inadvisable, if only to avoid the risk of falling into a manhole, the cover of which had been stolen. Our first experience of the way of life in Pakistan was early the next morning, when we were woken by the entry into our bedroom of the bearer; he was magnificently attired in a white uniform, his head surmounted by a white turban. He was bringing in our bed-tea, or 'Chota Hazri'. We flew on to Rawalpindi and were taken to our house in Islamabad, the new capital of Pakistan replacing Karachi in that role.

Not much of Islamabad had been built at that time; it was mostly wild country and the baying of jackals at night was normal. Government

153

offices were there, so also residences for foreign diplomats and officials. Our house had on one side a government minister, with his security officials, while on the other side was waste ground. It was previously the residence of a colleague who had been posted to Mongolia and we were happy to stay on there. It was an upside-down split-level house: three bedrooms in the basement, each with a small bathroom, sitting room, dining room and kitchen on the ground floor, with another bedroom above that which was much too hot in summer, but pleasant in winter. The servants' quarters were in a yard to one side. It was in fact a sensible design, since the bedrooms in the basement were cooler and we had air conditioning in one as well as in the living room above. In an attempt to alleviate the intensity of the heat, we bought enough earthenware flower pots to cover the whole roof; this made some difference but it was December before the climate cooled.

Fortunately we had numerous servants to run the household, all in a distinct hierarchy. The bearer, Ali, was in charge; then came the cook, a hamal (assistant bearer), sweeper, and a night-watchman/gardener. The latter in fact slept on a bed just outside the front door and we presumed that he had paid off local thieves to leave us alone, for we never had any break-ins. Sadly, we had to replace Ali who had been working for British families for fifty years. After Jessica's birth in May, we also engaged an ayah (nanny).

The unusually heavy monsoon and floods had caused both delay and damage to our luggage as it sat on a quay in Karachi. Our piano, some pictures and other things were either destroyed or damaged, while thunderstorms continued in Islamabad. As I told my mother in a letter home:

'At 3 a.m. we were woken by a thunderstorm. It was one of the most violent storms I have ever experienced. There was a colossal wind blowing and the rain was solid, driving horizontally. Looking out of the window, one felt more that one was at sea; features round about could only be dimly discerned in the constant flashes of lightning. The noise of wind, rain and thunder was deafening. We went upstairs to find Ali, our bearer, clad only in pyjama trousers cut off at the knees moving furniture, assisted by the watchman. It was pandemonium. The water driving against the veranda door on the top floor was streaming in, cascading over the stairs and falling onto the stairway below before running out into the garden through the basement. All the ground floor rooms were more or less flooded and we had to lift the carpets and move the furniture. One window was blown out and smashed, and another plate window was broken by a bamboo blind which broke away and was

blown into the next garden. It took an hour to sort things out and so it
was 4 o'clock before we returned to bed.'

The High Commission offices in Islamabad had not yet been completed. To get to work, we had to drive in to Rawalpindi where we occupied a rather seedy-looking office block with its own car park beside it. I have vivid memories of wondering at the queue of Pakistanis waiting to sign in for migration to the U.K. It troubled me; I could not imagine how these people, mostly illiterate, middle-aged men from distant villages would cope with life in England. It was a controversial political issue and I felt at the time that Enoch Powell had reason to warn of rivers of blood on our streets.

As a member of the economic and trade relations department in the High Commission I was involved in aid projects, but also in promoting exports. The two were linked; government funding for specific projects was usually conditional upon equipment being supplied by British manufacturers. From an organisational point of view, the promotion of British exports was cumbersome. Pakistan's capital until 1958 was Karachi, which was the country's main commercial centre. The move to a new capital in Islamabad, in the north, was in part prompted by the perceived need to separate government officials from industrial and commercial interests and the opportunities for corruption. Our mission there was led by a Deputy High Commissioner nominally responsible to the High Commissioner in Islamabad but largely independent. In addition, East Pakistan came under the High Commissioner's umbrella and remained so until independence as Bangladesh in 1971. It was important to the UK for its production of jute, which was exported to Dundee for processing which was a curious relationship dating back to Victorian times.

My opposite number in Dacca was Robbie Robinson. He and his wife Pauline had stayed with us in Islamabad and invited us to return the visit in January when I went there on official business. We met a wide range of business interests and visited Narayanganj port where peasants were coming in their boats with loads of jute for shipping to Dundee. By this time, however, several jute mills were opening up and Dundee's jute industry was already in decline. In Khulna we went round yet another jute mill and then on to a cold storage and packing plant where river and sea prawns were prepared for export around the world. A sideline was the supply of frogs' legs to France but this was seasonal and in January there were no frogs on offer. Despite the great deal of business activity around Khulna, we were not impressed. I described it as a poor town, with large numbers of underfed children living in crowded hovels made of straw mats. We returned to Dacca by a river steamer, the *Kiwi,* which had been built in Calcutta in 1930. The engine was situated mid-ships with three pistons driving a crankshaft, the axle of which went right across the ship ending with the paddles. It was fascinating to watch the three pistons lunging backwards and forwards, but one felt sorry for the man who had to keep shovelling coal into the boilers day and night. On board there were eight first-class cabins accommodating fourteen passengers, with deck accommodation for some six hundred people who slept wherever they could find room. We had thoroughly enjoyed our visit and flew back to Rawalpindi much refreshed.

I visited various towns in an official capacity but the most memorable trips were the private ones into the Himalayas, with trout fishing in mind. The rainbow trout in Bolivia had been introduced by Americans, whereas brown trout in Asia and Africa were brought there by the British. There are allegedly trout in a river in the north of Afghanistan but I was told by a Pakistani fisherman that these were indigenous; the river that now flows into the Aral Sea had once flowed into Europe and shared European species.

The nearest trout fishing to Rawalpindi was in the Kaghan valley about 150 miles to the north. This was the destination for our first fishing expedition and we spent a week-end there. I was fortunate to get Friday off and Monday was a public holiday. Leaving Rawalpindi at 3.30p.m. on Thursday, we drove to Balakot, where we arrived at 7.30p.m. having had a flask of tea on the way. After a night in a rest-house, we set out at 6.30a.m. the next day. The Kaghan valley at that time had not been spoilt by excessive tourism. The landscape is magnificent, with steep mountains on either side. There is little rainfall, with most falling as snow in winter, and avalanches are common. The valley was open only between June 1 and October 15. The inhabitants were farmers who took their herds of cattle, sheep and goats up to the mountain pastures in summer; we met many of them on our travels.

The road was rough, dirty and extremely precipitous and we had to hire a Jeep from the government transport service, with a driver. As recounted in my letter home 'He was very nice man and like all the drivers up there, he was very good and careful, and neither Rachel nor I felt at all nervous'. This took us to Naran where we had booked to stay in a tourist rest-house. We had been advised to take food with us, but this upset the manager who prided himself on his cooking and indeed depended on it for his living. A local ghillie took me fishing but scorned my flies; the fish didn't and I was lucky to catch one. Naran is at 8,000 feet and delightfully cool after the heat in Islamabad and the following

156

day we hired a Jeep to take us some six miles up a rough road to Lake Saiful Maluk at 10,500 feet. It was a popular site for walkers but as we wanted to spend some time there we took the Jeep both ways. We walked round the lake and on up the valley. I fished a spot where the stream enters the lake and caught a fish over two pounds in weight. On our way down, we stopped at a glacier to collect some ice and packed the fish into an insulated ice box to take back to Rawalpindi. I regretted that the valley was not nearer to Rawalpindi as it took us nine and a half hours to return.

Rather more ambitious was a trip we undertook in August of the following year to the Himalayas north of Rawalpindi. It is an area of disputed boundaries and political tension following the Indo-Pakistan war the year before. The bone of contention was, and still is, the province of Kashmir, with both countries claiming sovereignty. India took possession at the time of partition but this was not accepted by Pakistan, which launched an attack into the northern area from Baltistan and made some territorial gains. A ceasefire was agreed and it is this line that now forms the *de facto* boundary between the two countries. Because of this sensitivity we were followed and watched by a member of the security service on a bicycle; he was a pleasant individual very different from the goons I had experienced in Moscow.

Previous to partition, communication with Gilgit had been through Kashmir down a tributary of the Indus. It was a long and arduous journey and a number of rest houses were built along the route so that travellers could spend the night in them on their way. The rest houses were neglected until taken over by the Pakistan Tourist Board for use by visitors such as ourselves.

Our original idea had been to go to Skardu but we had to postpone it because of the uncertainty of flights at that time of year. So we went to Gilgit instead and on arrival we booked a Jeep to take us up to Astore, a small village sixty-eight miles away, where we had heard there was trout fishing. I called on the Resident and Political Agent and secured a fishing licence from the Commander of the local army regiment called the Gilgit Scouts. The Jeep was rather too small for our party, consisting of Rachel and myself, Jessica our daughter who had been born three months before, our bearer Roshan, the driver and the driver's mate, a general handyman and mechanic. Jessica was in a carry-cot on our laps, a bit perilous as there was no door and she risked being swept out if a bend was taken too sharply. Our luggage was kept to a bare minimum. My letter home recounted our experiences:

'We loaded the Jeep and left at 10 o'clock. The 68 miles to Astore should not have taken long, but the road is very windy, narrow and in places steep as it skirts round cliffs and ascends mountainsides in a series of hairpin bends. We did 18 miles in the first hour and by 12 o'clock reached a little village called Bunji. Here there is a Northern Scouts barracks, and we borrowed the guardroom at the entrance to have a picnic lunch and feed Jessica, who slept all the way. Thus far our route had been down the valleys of the Gilgit and Indus rivers but shortly after leaving Bunji, we entered a narrow defile crossing the torrent by a suspension bridge, which seemed narrow and precarious although perfectly safe. Then the Jeep developed gearbox trouble and we had to wait in the gorge while the driver and mechanic worked on it, not at all pleasant because of the strong wind and dust. But after an hour, we continued on our way. The remaining 25 miles took three hours as we climbed up and down and bumped along the very uneven road. In places, there was just room enough for the vehicle to get round and under outcrops of rock overhanging the road.

'On arrival at a rest-house after a long day's journey, one can often feel a bit depressed by the absence of amenities. This was the case at Astore. The rest house was shut and we had to wait an hour for the warden to arrive. Then the water was very muddy, and it took long to obtain drinking water and water for washing Jessica. We lit a fire in our room and made do on a tin of London grill and a stiff whisky followed by a Guinness with Camembert cheese. We had hoped the next day to go to a rest house at 10,000 feet on the slopes of Nanga Parbat, but it was cloudy and cold the next morning with slight rain and snow on the hills about. Astore is at 8,200 feet (against 4,600 feet in Gilgit and 1,800 feet in Rawalpindi). We also discovered that there is no trout fishing in Astore or near it, and were advised to go to Gudai, seventeen miles away in a side valley. So we set off for Gudai, having recovered from the previous day's journey. Roshan was travel sick, but we were OK and as usual Jessica slept what must have been an uneasy sleep in a carry-cot across our knees.

'The journey to Gudai was straightforward and took one and a half hours. After three quarters of an hour, we turned off into a valley and followed up a beautiful little river, with gin-clear water of a bright blue-green colour. The rest house at Gudai was better than that at Astor. We occupied the main room, with a wash-room and toilet, the sort that has to be emptied twice a day. Water, hot and cold, was brought *from the kitchen and river respectively. The kitchen was a shack with a stone hearth burning wood. Amidst the squalor, the smoke and the flies, Roshan coped magnificently, producing excellent meals at all times.*

'There is a noticeable change in scenery and climate between Gilgit and Gudai. Gilgit has virtually no rainfall, perhaps five inches a year in winter. The mountains are stark and dry, and vegetation depends on water from the river. Gudai at 9,000 feet seems to catch quite a lot of rain from the monsoon. While it is not verdant, there is still quite a lot of greenery, with pine trees on all north-facing slopes, and other trees, including magnificent walnuts, in the valley. We had a little rain, but most of the time it was fine and sunny, with temperatures in the 60s Fahrenheit by day and colder at night.

'On our first day, we badly needed some trout for dinner and I set off with spinners and fly to try to get some. I fished for about three hours without success and was on the point of giving up when some trout began to rise in the pool I was fishing, and I had two around one pound in weight. I was surprised to find that there were prolific hatches of ephemeridae (mayflies) with lots of flies coming off the less turbulent pools all afternoon. There were two main species, a kind of March Brown and a small light olive. It was very pleasant to return to the rest house with the trout for dinner to find a blazing fire, all warm and cosy, and Jessica just about to be put to bed.'

We stayed for three full days going for walks once domestic matters arising from Jessica had been sorted out. There was a limit of six fish in a day and this was soon reached; the fishing was good especially in the late afternoon and evening when the light is beginning to fade. As in Bolivia, twilight does not last long in these tropical latitudes. The one trouble we had was the mass of flies which tormented us. As Gudai is a staging post, horses are tethered outside the rest house each evening and attract flies which find their way into the rest house. It was also difficult to obtain any sort of food there. There was no meat and we had trout for one meal every day. For the other main meal we had a tin of tongue or something similar, and Surprise peas. Roshan found some fresh peas and broad beans, which are grown as a crop. He also procured apples and delicious apricots.

The journey back was less strenuous and we were entertained on arriving in Astore to find a polo match in progress. The local people attending the match were also entertained by the sight of Jessica; a white-skinned, red-haired baby was an usual spectacle for them. The next day we came to a place where a landslip was about to occur; a stretch of road some twenty yards long had sunk three feet and had cracks in it. It was clear that the whole section would fall away into the river a thousand feet below in a matter of a day or so. We crossed gingerly on foot while the Jeep came through with some difficulty.

We had travelled to Astore because of uncertainties over flights to Skardu and it was a most inviting prospect when we heard in September that Skardu was again approachable by air. It is the capital of the Agency of Baltistan, to all intents and purposes a part of Pakistan. It lies east of Gilgit at an altitude of 7,600 feet. The Indus river valley at this point is seven miles wide, flat and sandy, and drops little over fifteen miles. The whole country is mountainous and includes the Karakorum range with some of the highest peaks in the Himalayas. The climate is dry with only about 5 inches of rain a year, all in winter, with snow on the mountains.

On our trip to Astore we had taken Roshan, our bearer, but this time we decided to take the ayah, Mary. The flight was exciting. It took us due north from Rawalpindi but after passing Nanga Parbat, it turned east up the Indus valley through a steep gorge, giving us magnificent views of the mountains all round. About ten minutes before reaching Skardu, the plane passed a spur of mountain and then dropped quickly into the Skardu valley. The plane was a turbo-prop Fokker Friendship, ideally suited for this kind of approach.

We had gone to some pains to prepare our holiday, booking a rest house through the Airport Development Agency who looked after visitors, asking them to reserve accommodation and meet us with a Jeep. We had also sent off luggage a week beforehand consisting of all our bedding and provisions. On arrival, there was no one to meet us, no transport, no accommodation and no advance luggage. After an hour or so a man from ADA turned up brandishing the telegram which, he claimed, had only just arrived. After another hour a Jeep arrived to take us to our rest house at Katchura. It was on the edge of a small lake, with trees all round and behind it almost vertical mountains. We liked it so much that we managed to stay on longer than intended. It was large and well appointed. Our meals were prepared by the chowkhidar who turned out to be a good cook. Fortunately we had brought with us enough baby food to last for two days and some beer packed into my waders and we bought food for ourselves at the local shop. Later I set up tackle and caught a nice trout for our dinner, which we enjoyed eating by the light of a hurricane lamp, and spent as comfortable a night, fully dressed, as was to be hoped for. Our luggage turned up the next day.

The lake was an unusual place for fishing. There was an old boat which I managed to bale out and for which I found a piece of wood to serve as a paddle. As was nearly always the case during our stay, the water was dead calm and the sun beat down from a cloudless sky until the afternoon when it was obscured by the mountains. Soon after starting, large numbers of red and blue damselflies appeared and began laying their eggs, hovering over the water about a foot above it, either singly or in pairs. The trout cruised around just under the surface in gin-clear water, occasionally leaping high to seize one. The nearest imitation of a damselfly I had was a large, dry Mayfly. It was difficult; the trout were very shy, but I managed to catch two. In the evening it was rather cold and very dark; there was an eclipse of the sun, about three-quarters of the disc being covered at 4.30p.m. This cast an eerie gloom over the scene and the trout did not seem to like it. It was odd; the sun was still shining on the mountains opposite but without producing any light.

We were very hospitably looked after by one or two people at Katchura. I again quote from a letter home:

'First among these was a man called Wali Mohammed Khan, a contractor supervising the installation of a new water system at the rest house. He kept on giving us fruit and other foodstuffs to a quite embarrassing extent, and really did his utmost to look after us and see that we had all that we needed. On Monday afternoon he took us off, accompanied by about fifteen other locals, for a walk to Katchura village and to show us a second lake. This involved a climb of about 800 feet and several miles distance, and at that altitude we found it quite hard going. The village is situated on a moraine at the mouth of a valley with a stream coming down to provide irrigation. As a result, it is very fertile, with numerous little fields and orchards of apricot, apple, walnut and other trees scattered about among enormous boulders left behind by the glacier when it melted. The houses are bigger than elsewhere in Pakistan, consisting of two storeys, the lower one of mud brick being mainly for the cattle and the upper one, of wattle and daub, for living accommodation. Some attention had been given to doors and windows, and there was a certain amount of carving'.

The lake that we saw was an eerie place. It was about a mile and a half long by a quarter of a mile wide. The water was bright blue-green, clear and very deep. The banks are extremely steep and except for one small section consist of huge boulders jumbled together. There are said to be trout in it, but we were discouraged from fishing; according to local legend, the lake is inhabited by a monster, half-human, half-beast, which lures people into the depths; no one goes near it.

Two days later we decided to explore the valley which goes up from Katchura village to the mountains behind. In the village itself the river rushed down in a torrent over rocks, but we had heard that higher up it is slower with pools for fishing. Again, it was hard work climbing up to the village and for a mile or two beyond as we rose around 1,000 feet. But then we came to a place where a moraine and a landslide had long ago blocked the valley, and thereafter it was flat and broad with the river winding down in a series of long flat pools. We continued for a further three miles beyond the village of Tsok until we came to the end of the flat area with its fertile fields and the valley again rose sharply towards the mountains and glaciers. On the way back I caught trout which we gave to the local women, who allowed themselves to be photographed, a favour not normally offered in Pakistan.

Our return to Rawalpindi was delayed for a day, possibly because of a backlog of passengers who had booked onto earlier flights; we were told that the pilots had gone on strike because they did not consider that the aircraft were being adequately serviced. It was annoying in a way but we took advantage of it to visit the Shigar valley, a journey of eighteen miles, first over a desert then through steep hills. The valley itself is green and beautiful, renowned for its apricots and grapes. On our return, we found that a medical captain from Skardu hospital had taken charge of Jessica because she had been crying; he maintained that our ayah Mary had mistreated her. It was untrue but we could hardly complain; he had invited us home for dinner and we spent a very pleasant evening with him.

Travel in Pakistan had been for us a great pleasure and privilege. It is often the way that people are more relaxed and hospitable once you get away from the pressures of a big city. It was certainly the case in Pakistan. Our arrangements did not always work out as planned but we were always warmly welcomed and treated with courtesy and generous hospitality.

The posting to Rawalpindi is normally for a spell of four years with home leave of two months after the first two. Towards the end of our first two years, we began to lay plans for our holiday. We were keen to go skiing and booked up for a fortnight in April at a resort in Norway, reckoning that the snow would be better there in April than in the Alps. Jessica would stay with Rachel's mother Geraldine, aided by a nanny. We were also planning short stays in Broadstairs and Williton in Somerset with our respective mothers. Then in February, when all was arranged, the High Commissioner told us that we were unexpectedly to be posted to East Europe forthwith, probably to Bulgaria. This left us very little time to sell our two cars and the piano, all of which were taken up by a diplomat from Ghana. We also had to abandon some of our planned holiday, including the skiing trip to Norway.

The political situation was becoming increasingly tense. Although the officials and professionals whom we knew were very friendly, there were layers of society less favourably inclined towards Great Britain, at one stage Pakistan had even left the Commonwealth. Riots seemed to break out without any real justification, at least in our eyes. When the American magazine published on its cover a picture purporting to be an image of the prophet Mohammad, rioters quickly appeared on the streets of Lahore and the offices of the British Council were attacked; no distinction was made between the USA and Britain.

In November 1968, students rioted in Rawalpindi, burning vehicles and stoning government buildings. In the scuffle, a student was killed by the police, stoking up unrest still further and a curfew was imposed over most of the town. The issue was ostensibly trouble with students who wanted to legalise the importation of contraband. The *Pakistan Times* deplored the violence and in its editorial attacked the Muslim League, the main opposition party. Even as we left Islamabad for the airport, severe rioting had again broken out on the streets of Rawalpindi. A few weeks afterwards President Ayub Khan, who had ruled Pakistan for eleven years, was forced to resign. We were glad to be moving back to Europe.

Chapter 10

Under Communism again in Bulgaria

While it had been disappointing to cut short our holiday arrangements, we were pleased with the prospect of living in Bulgaria, a country about which we knew practically nothing.

The Balkan countries lie between the territories of historic empires and over the centuries their history has been determined largely by competing interests including Greek, Roman, Byzantine, Mongol, Austro-Hungarian, Turkish, Russian and Soviet; one only needs to recall the consequences of the assassination of the Austro-Hungarian Archduke Franz Ferdinand by a Serbian in 1914. Bulgaria is at the eastern end of the Balkan complex and its history relates mostly to neighbouring Byzantium, the Ottoman Empire and to Russia, with territorial disputes over Macedonia to the west. The Bulgars arrived in the area in the sixth century to combine with Slavs and the country enjoyed a measure of autonomy within the Byzantine Empire until overrun by Turkey in the fifteenth century to become part of the Ottoman Empire. Turkish rule was brutal. Christianity was suppressed, monasteries looted and many Bulgarians were forced to adopt Islam and change their names accordingly. Oppression continued down the years, largely unnoticed in Western Europe. An uprising in 1875 led to the brutal massacre of thousands of Bulgarians, whether or not they had been involved in it. Britain's foreign policy at the time was dictated by the desire to support Turkey against Russia. Gladstone, however, campaigned for public support for the Bulgarian cause, publishing a critical pamphlet *Bulgarian Horrors and the Question of the East*. Russia declared war on Turkey in 1877 and after a bitter struggle, Bulgaria gained independence in 1878.

In the Second World War, Bulgaria had sided with the Axis under pressure from Germany. At the end of the war, the Communist Party emerged and Bulgaria became a member of the Soviet bloc as a People's Republic. After Stalin's death, a change in Soviet policy led to Todor Zhivkov's appearance as First Secretary of the Communist Party and

164

Prime Minister, with Bulgaria remaining a determinedly communist state until 1990, reflecting Soviet Russian styles of security and economic and political administration.

Links between Bulgaria and Russia went back long before the advent of communism. The language was similar, both countries using the Cyrillic script introduced by two monks from Macedonia, Cyril and Methodius, who took Christianity to the Slavs. The Alexander Nevksy cathedral in Sofia had been built as a memorial to Russian soldiers who had died in the 1877-78 war; it was named after the Russian prince who had won a battle against the Teutonic knights on frozen Lake Peipus in 1242, the so-called 'Battle on the Ice.' Another Russian Orthodox Church was built near the Shipka Pass, again a memorial to those who perished in the war of liberation.

We had driven to Bulgaria in a new Triumph 2000 estate car, specially adapted with a metal shield below the engine to protect it from rough roads, and an electric heater in the cooling circuit to prevent it being frozen up. The journey had taken ten days, with overnight stops in Germany with friends, at an Alpine hotel in Austria and at bed-and-breakfast accommodation in Yugoslavia. Throughout the journey we admired the scenery and as we crossed into Bulgaria we realised we were entering a country of exceptionally beautiful landscapes. There are several ranges of mountains and Sofia itself lies at around 2,000 feet. It all looked very promising.

Compared with our missions in Moscow and Rawalpindi, the embassy in Sofia was quite small, though possibly slightly larger than I had encountered in Bolivia. The Ambassador's residence is a magnificent building designed by Lutyens and completed in 1913. The offices were in a three-storey brick building next door, anything but magnificent, but they served their purpose. Accommodation for staff was scattered around the area. We were assigned to a spacious flat on the fifth floor of a block on Lenin Prospect. It was occupied entirely by members of the diplomatic corps. We had a Polish couple on the same floor as ourselves and immediately below us an East German family with a daughter about the same age as Jessica. Since we did not recognise the German Democratic Republic and so had no diplomatic relations with it, we were not supposed to talk to this family. In practice our respective children played together and we got on well with them, albeit at a tactful distance.

My letters home make it clear that here too there was a lot of work in the office. As in Moscow, we were also involved in a great deal of entertaining, attending colleagues' receptions and dinner parties and laying on corresponding events of our own. It was a busy life and we were extraordinarily fortunate to have two outstanding Bulgarian staff to help us, the cook, Slavka, and a maid, Milka. Slavka produced meals of the highest quality for a large number of guests, while Milka helped her as well as carrying out other domestic duties. They were both utterly reliable and Milka in particular made our life easier by baby-sitting and looking after our children if we were away for a day or two. Slavka had an allotment some miles outside Sofia at Pobit Kamuk where she entertained us to lunch several times during our stay in Bulgaria.

Near the door to the block of flats on Lenin Prospect was a sentry box always occupied by a policeman on shift duty. His job was to keep an eye out for Bulgarians who might be visiting but more importantly to alert the Bulgarian security service DS whenever certain residents went out. We were invariably followed; if I took out the car, a Russian Volga would emerge from a side street and engage with mine. We were constantly watched, while in the office the same security considerations prevailed as I had known in Moscow; we would never discuss confidential matters indoors and files had to be locked away every time we closed the office. This could be a problem. One day we had a visit from a UK minister and we felt that his two brief cases with his papers should be securely locked away for the night. He was not amused when he found out about this as one of them contained his pyjamas and washing kit.

All this prompted a comparison with my earlier experiences in the Soviet Union. There were of course significant differences in geography and climate. While the landscape round Moscow was generally flat, Sofia was dominated by Vitosha at 7,200 feet, snow-covered in winter and offering skiing, simple but none the less enjoyable. Both cities experienced extremes of temperature, Sofia perhaps less so and for shorter periods. Being 13° of latitude further south than Moscow, Bulgaria as a whole had an almost Mediterranean feel to it; winter days were longer and spring came early. Whether these differences affected the national temperament is uncertain. Nevertheless we found Bulgarians bright and cheerful, more so than Muscovites who, in the 1950s, were a drab lot and reluctant to talk to foreigners unless and until they had reason to get to know them personally; they were then friendly and hospitable. Allowance must be made for the appalling suffering of the Russians during the war and an oppressive security regime which had been bearing down on society since the 1920s.

To us it seemed that the Bulgarian security apparatus was more lenient over relations with western diplomats; there was no feeling of being in a glass cage as I have earlier described diplomatic life in Moscow. While western diplomats had to take sensible precautions in their relations with

Bulgarians, I felt less threatened in Sofia by the secret police than I had in Moscow. The United Kingdom was at cold war with the Soviet Union, but not with Bulgaria; it made a difference. In Sofia there was no forty-kilometre limit beyond which western diplomats needed to seek permission to travel. We were indeed followed wherever we went but the goons were less expert and more obtrusive than their Russian counterparts had been in Moscow. On one occasion, we had been invited by our maid Milka to visit her in her home. The goon, this time a woman, had followed us closely and when we went in, she had the nerve to follow us up to the house and stand outside peering in at us. I noted in my letter home that one gets used to it and the people we saw did not seem to get into trouble.

We were sometimes followed onto the slopes of Vitosha by a man and a woman, inappropriately dressed, the woman in particular staggering over the rough ground in high-heeled shoes. Once we were taking photographs of spring flowers for the author Oleg Polunin for his book on the flowers of the Balkans. A few minutes later we met an Austrian friend who was the United Nations' medical representative in Bulgaria. He told us later that our goons had stopped him, thinking he was a Bulgarian, and somewhat aggressively had cross-examined him on what we had been up to.

Nevertheless, it seemed as though the Bulgarian government were keen to show the world that the communist way of life was supreme and that any deviation from it would be punished. Almost every street had its communist party office exercising authority over residents in the area, with the inevitable red banners and images of Lenin displayed in the window. Once on our way back to Sofia we gave a lift to a Bulgarian who told us that he had just been released from five years in prison for having tried to leave the country without proper authorisation. On another occasion we gave a lift to an army officer on our way down from skiing on Vitosha; when he heard that we were western diplomats he was very worried, hid from sight as we passed a police checkpoint and got out at the earliest opportunity.

To their own people, the Bulgarian secret police, the DS, were even more oppressive than their Soviet equivalent the KGB and earned a reputation at home and abroad for their brutality. We heard that a doctor in Sofia, known to the embassy, had been prosecuted for listening to the BBC's World Service, put on trial and executed. A few years after we had left Sofia came the case of Georgi Markov, a defector from Bulgaria who in 1978 was working for the BBC World Service in London. While on his way to work he was hit by a poisonous pellet shot into his thigh from an umbrella and died four days later. It was never established exactly who was responsible, but it seemed likely that the DS, in conjunction with the Soviet KGB, had carried out the assassination. Another Bulgarian defector in Paris was attacked in a similar way but survived. Pope John Paul II was the object of an assassination attempt in 1991 and there was speculation that the Bulgarians were involved at the behest of the KGB who feared that his influence in his native country Poland would undermine communism in that country and beyond (as indeed was the case). So far as is known, this has not been proved.

The most extreme example of Bulgarian intransigence was perhaps the ridiculous regulation that no man entering the country should have long hair. Young men returning to Western Europe from Istanbul by train were inspected and if their hair was too long, they were obliged to get out of the train at the frontier station and have their hair cut on the platform, even though they were in transit. On one occasion, twelve students were removed from the train and told to have haircuts. One of them set about cutting the hair of another and a third tried to take a photograph. His camera was taken away from him and when a militiaman appeared, there was a scuffle. He was charged with injuring the man, who had had a tooth knocked out in the fracas.

The trial took place at Svilengrad on the Bulgarian-Turkish frontier and the student and his two lawyers came down from Sofia. The courtroom was pokey with gaunt wooden furniture. Despite his nervousness, the student performed well, as did his two lawyers. The judgement was a fine of 200 leva (about £42 at that time) and no prison sentence. The militiaman was reprimanded for not behaving more considerately to a foreign traveller who understood no Bulgarian. The outcome seemed reasonable; the judgement could have been much more severe.

The authorities discouraged religion but were less oppressive than one might have expected in a communist state, due to a relaxation by Todor Zhivkov of the persecution carried out under his predecessor Chervenkov. We visited many monasteries, usually open and with a priest in charge. At Chiprovitsi, a remote village near the Danube town of Vidin, we found that the monks' rooms had been converted into rooms for children who used it as a holiday camp. It looked bright and cheerful and we were soon surrounded by children wanting to know who we were. The church was still in use and children attended services in it. There was a bell tower and beside the bells there were the skulls and bones of Bulgarians killed by the Turks, no doubt a reminder of the years 'Under the Yoke'.

On a later visit to Bulgaria in 1980 we went to the Sokolov monastery at Etera near Gabrovo. It was a working monastery for nuns and the whole place was being rebuilt. Near the church were two, large, painted notices, one of them quoting from a speech by Georgi Dimitrov in 1947, in which he paid tribute to the role of monasteries in the struggle for freedom from the Turks; he had been proud of the Bulgarian Orthodox church. Monasteries in communist times have tended to become the site for hotels, pioneer camps and general attractions for tourists.

We had also been surprised by an exhibition and concert in the crypt of Alexander Nevsky cathedral in Sofia. We had heard about this privately and it appeared to us unusual that the authorities had allowed an event with such strong religious connotations. The programme began with a lecture in Bulgarian about a monastery at Mt. Athos in Greece. Then a group of eight young men performed Bulgarian music from the 13th to 16th centuries. Finally a chamber orchestra played a modern suite, each movement of which had a religious title inspired by the icons on display.

There were a number of villages of Turkish origin in the south-east corner of Bulgaria. It was supposedly out of bounds to western diplomats but shortly before we left we were keen to visit the area. We took the road to Plovdiv and evaded our goons by driving slowly on the winding road until we arrived a few kilometres from the turning we needed to take. We then accelerated hard and turned off before the goons had caught up with us. After climbing up a long way through the forest, we came across an attractive little village in open countryside, notable for the fact that it had a mosque. It was simple in design yet beautiful inside. When we arrived, it was prayer time; there were seven old men there, one of whom climbed up into the minaret to intone a prayer. After having our picnic lunch outside the village, we returned and were invited into the cowshed of a co-operative farm and given sour milk and some rubbery cheese to taste. The elderly couple told us that all the villages round there were entirely Mohammedan. Certainly that village had no church, only the mosque, despite its name being Sveta Petka (Saint Peter). We also heard that there were very few communists in it, although those that were in effect ran the place.

Little publicity was given to the way that the Turkish community were treated by the authorities. Turks with Islamic names were made to change to Bulgarian ones and were pressured to integrate more closely with Bulgarian education and culture. It was claimed that many were in any case Bulgarians who had been Islamized under the Ottomans. In later years, this became a big human rights issue, when the Bulgarian government used force to get them to change their names, made them speak only Bulgarian and abolished Turkish-language local newspapers. After the fall of the communist regime, the area became more accessible;

there were still separate Turkish and Bulgarian villages with little love lost between them.

My post at the Embassy was Head of Chancery and Consul, a position later renamed as Deputy Head of Mission (DHM). In the former role my responsibility was to oversee the reporting of political matters to the Foreign Office in London, in the latter to look after the interests of British and some Commonwealth nationals and to support them if they got into trouble. If the Ambassador was away out of the country, the Head of Chancery became Chargé d'Affaires *ad interim*. When we arrived the Ambassador was Desmond Crawley. He was a delight to work for, relaxed yet diligent in his duties, and with a great sense of humour. He was inclined to be sceptical over the street sense of members of the clergy and it was ironic that his last posting before retirement was to the Vatican as Minister to the Holy See.

After the Crawleys had left, I was in charge during the interregnum until their successors arrived. Desmond had pointed out that until his successor had presented his credentials, he would continue to be paid an Ambassador's salary while I would benefit from an enhanced entertainment and other allowances. Shortly before his successor Donald Logan was due to arrive, we were informed of an intended visit from a junior British minister involved in agriculture. Donald sent me a telegram suggesting that he should come out earlier than planned in order to be in Sofia to receive him. I had to point out in my reply that until he had presented his credentials, he would have no standing and would not be able to take part in meetings and other arrangements. He arrived as planned and turned out to be generally a pleasant and friendly person, although inclined to be rather abrupt. He was more enthusiastically engaged in his approach to Anglo-Bulgarian relations than his predecessor but could also be difficult.

Donald may have been demanding in some ways but he and his wife Irene were outstandingly generous to the staff in laying on entertainment for us. When we were due to leave Sofia at the end of our tour, he kindly allowed us to go earlier than we should have done so that we could take part in a family holiday in Scotland. He went on to pursue a distinguished career in the diplomatic service, ending up as UK representative to a conference on the Law of the Sea.

Life in a communist country with constraints imposed both by the local authorities and ourselves could be stressful and it was important that the well-being of the embassy staff was looked after. Because of this we enjoyed certain privileges. We were allowed to adapt office hours so that the Embassy could close at lunch time on Friday, with extra time added onto the other days of the week to make up for it. There was a diplomatic club with tennis courts, while in winter the ski resort of Aleko on Mount Vitosha was only half an hour's drive away. The Embassy also had a delightful chalet in the mountain resort of Borovetz, where one could spend a week-end or longer with opportunities for skiing and walking. At the time, posts abroad were occasionally visited by an inspector from London to check up on the Embassy's work and, even then, to consider possible economies. We had one such visit from an inspector during our time and were successful in convincing him that such facilities were essential for the welfare of the staff.

The interregnum between the Crawleys' departure and Donald Logan taking over lasted almost three months. In some respects it was a burden, especially when we had to lay on receptions and dinners for visitors from the UK. On the other hand, it came with certain privileges and we enjoyed ourselves. One memorable occasion was the visit to Sofia by a group of eight MPs. We invited them to dinner at our flat and Slavka laid on an excellent meal. All went well until our Defence Attaché took exception to one of the party praising the communist system and a lively and somewhat embarrassing argument ensued.

The week after was marked by an international competition for opera singers. A British singer, Margaret Curphy, was taking part and coincidentally a group of Bulgarian singers were about to go to Glyndebourne to appear in a production of Eugene Onegin. This provided an opportunity for entertaining a wide range of Bulgarians, more or less involved in opera. We used the embassy residence and were surprised by the unusually large number of guests who accepted our invitation and turned up. In a communist country one needed two requisites to get round the security service's constraints on locals attending events by western embassies. First there needed to be a sound reason to justify the event, in this case the opera competition. Secondly, the party had to be given by some one for whom refusals or failure to turn up would be seen as an insult in diplomatic relations; an Ambassador or a senior staff member had more success than a junior officer. This applies equally the other way round, as I discovered when I failed to attend a reception by the Soviet Ambassador to mark the centenary of Lenin's birth on April 22, 1970 and was roundly criticised for it by the Soviet cultural attaché. Western Ambassadors had agreed beforehand to ignore it but later the French Ambassador had changed his mind; he had told other Ambassadors but not me, merely a chargé.

Shortly before Donald Logan presented his credentials, the Embassy received an invitation from the Bulgarian government to attend the

Festival of Roses. He could not go himself but asked us to go in his place and kindly lent us his car and chauffeur. In my subsequent letter home, I wrote:

> 'The roses are grown in a valley in Central Bulgaria to supply Attar of Roses for the perfume industry. There are many extensive fields of them and the petals are gathered in the early morning before the essence evaporates. They are a small double rose, of a light purple hue and very strong smelling.
>
> 'We were met outside the town of Karlovo and the principal guests, but not us, were garlanded with roses by five beauty queens; we were given bouquets by children. After the ceremonial opening of the festival, we climbed into Jeeps and were driven slowly into town, while bystanders threw flowers at us and clapped sporadically. In Karlovo, we were shown onto platforms in the centre of the town to watch a procession. A crop-spraying helicopter flew along over us spraying out strong-smelling essence of roses. The procession was good, having more the character of a folk festival than the propaganda efforts which we see in Sofia. There were political slogans but none of them objectionable. Groups of dancers and musicians playing peculiar instruments came past, and there were three orchestras lined up on the opposite side of the street from us; a school orchestra with trumpets, horns and brass, a civilian band and a military band.
>
> 'The procession lasted an hour and a half and we were then taken off to hear some dull speeches, but at least were sitting outside in the sun in an orchard of walnut trees. That over, we went to the hotel to have a really good lunch.'

Soon after this, Donald Logan presented his credentials. It was a very formal ceremony, with a military guard of honour, and the Ambassador wore his full diplomatic uniform. Unlike the fine weather we had enjoyed at the Festival of Roses, it was raining most of the morning and very cold. After he had reviewed the guard, we all went inside the National Assembly building where the Ambassador made a speech and handed over his letters to the President of Bulgaria.

The Logans were away for a fortnight towards the end of our stay in Sofia and I was again left in charge. It so happened that during his absence Heads of Mission were invited to accompany Todor Zhivkov on a trip to the Black Sea arranged by the Bulgarian government. It was to celebrate the adoption of a new constitution under which Todor Zhivkov, following a referendum, was elected President of the State Council.

> 'The party consisted of heads of diplomatic Missions and their wives.

172

We had a special flight from Sofia at 8 am to Tolbukhin, where we were taken in coaches, about 80 of us, to the hotel and had a big breakfast. There was then a meeting at which the Party First Secretary for the province spoke about farming. The Head of State, Todor Zhivkov, then also spoke and I asked a question which was the only one to be asked.

'We then went on to the tourist resort of Albena, where we wandered round in a flock and had lunch. This was a big affair with eight courses; caviare (vodka), fish (wine), steak & mushrooms (wine), sweetbread, pudding, yoghurt, fruit, coffee & cake (brandy). There were some rather nice Bulgarians at our table from the local Party organisation.

'After lunch, which was a long affair, we went by coach to another Black Sea resort called Golden Sands, where we were provided with hotel rooms. We had two hours to rest and Rachel and I went for a walk along the sand and had a delightful swim in the sea which was beautifully warm. Then we changed and went by bus to the Euxinograd Palace, a beautiful French-style château built by the king before the war. Dinner was served at about twenty tables outside, again a long meal of soup, fish, steak, ice cream, fruit and coffee, with wines. There were fountains and a stage where; at the end of the meal, an orchestra put on a musical programme with classical, folk and 'pop'. There were fireworks, toasts, and when we left, we were given a present each. In our case, it was a basket each, with four bottles of very good Bulgarian wine.'

The next day a special plane brought us all back to Sofia. It had been a delightful outing, very well organised and nothing had gone wrong. The children meanwhile had been with Slavka and Milka at Pobit Kamuk, where Slavka's garden was located.

A few months after our arrival in Sofia, Rachel was pregnant again and we made arrangements for her to go into the maternity wing of the hospital when the time came. It was late one evening in December, with snow on the ground, when she was admitted. I was a bit anxious since the wife of a member of staff had given birth in the hospital and had suffered a wretched time there. A long report about it was on her file in the office. Although I normally had access to personal files, I was banned from reading hers because it would only increase our anxiety.

Regulations regarding access by visitors were severe. We had to decide on the child's names before Rachel went in. We had referred to it as 'sausage' up to that point, but now had to decide on two sets of names; it had been made clear that she would not be allowed to leave hospital until the child had been named and given a Bulgarian birth certificate. Nor were husbands permitted to visit the hospital. So I waited at home until around 1 a.m. when the telephone rang to tell me that she had given birth to a boy. The doctor invited me to come round, gave me a doctor's overall to wear and I was unobtrusively taken into her ward. This was a small room for six patients, all the others Bulgarian, wearing identical pyjamas. Rachel had been having lessons in Bulgarian and very soon she found herself able to talk to her fellow patients. Moreover, her Bulgarian was more colloquial than mine; I had been using official Bulgarian as it appeared in the newspapers and formal correspondence. Rachel had gone shopping with Slavka to the local markets, where Bulgarian in general use had a strong Turkish influence dating back to the years of Ottoman occupation. She had in a way enjoyed her experience in the ward but was very glad to come home again. Timothy was later baptised in our flat by the visiting priest from Bucharest, there being no Anglican church in Sofia.

I suppose that consular duties are never routine. There were not many British visitors to Bulgaria at this time and there were few cases requiring embassy assistance. The young man who photographed hair cutting on a railway station was certainly unusual. So too was the case of an Indian Swami, who came to Sofia and spoke in public about his philosophy. Two rather unkempt young men came to the embassy to complain that their car had been confiscated. They were leaving Bulgaria with their Master, the Swami Dev Murti, who had been working in Bulgaria for four months in a circus, demonstrating his exceptional strength by tearing up steel plates and allowing lorries to drive over him. When the two Englishmen reached the frontier, the customs officers found concealed in their car a large amount of Bulgarian banknotes. They knew nothing about them. The Swami, who arrived half an hour later in his Mercedes, said he had hidden them there for safe custody. He was promptly arrested and the money confiscated.

He called at the office one day with an English lawyer and explained his philosophy. It consisted of meditation, a vegetarian diet, no smoking or drinking, no meat or kissing, daily exercises and a strict regimen in all things. He had studied medicine with Gurus in India and claimed to have cured a large number of people with his medicines and exercises. Normally he gave the proceeds from his demonstrations towards founding a yoga centre. He had not been able to do this in Bulgaria, nor could he bank the money without special permission. So he had put the money in his friends' car since his own had been damaged in an accident and could not be locked.

The trial took place in a small village about twenty-five miles from Sofia. The judge was an extremely intelligent and able young woman of about thirty assisted by two jurors. There was a prosecutor and a court secretary who typed everything down as statements were made. The court had a difficult time of it, for the Swami, a large, bearded and unkempt looking man in Indian robes, had difficulty in presenting his arguments coherently. His initial deposition of evidence took about two hours, for he went into the greatest detail of what he was doing and all the notable people in Bulgaria whom he had cured of their ailments. He had numerous files, none of which he was able to produce at the right moment.

The court adjourned for lunch. We went to a rather crummy restaurant to eat a normal lunch while the Swami stayed in the court room and munched an apple or two. Cross-examination of witnesses was a lengthy procedure and the trial did not end until 7 p.m. He was found guilty, sentenced to three years imprisonment suspended for five years, fined Leva 2,500 (about £500 at that time), had his Leva 21,000 (£4,000) confiscated, also his car. This sentence seemed unduly harsh but at least he had had a trial. It emerged during the proceedings what a numerous following he had attracted during his time in Bulgaria, no doubt an embarrassment to the regime who allowed no ideologies besides Marxism-Leninism. Perhaps for that reason his visa was suddenly terminated and he was given only fifteen hours in which to leave the country.

Our main pastime was travelling round Bulgaria enjoying its magnificent scenery, the churches, monasteries and historic towns. I had taken fishing tackle with me and hoped to fish for trout in the many rivers and lakes. This had not worked out as I had wished. On one of our first outings we had seen the Isker river below Samokov; it looked ideal water, flowing slowly through a broad valley. I attended a meeting of the Union of Fishermen. I was told that foreigners were not allowed to join; I was not accorded a warm reception, indeed, it was distinctly frigid. Not long afterwards we went up a valley at the end of which there was a reservoir reputed to hold fish. We could not go all the way to it as there was a police barrier for which one needed a pass. We heard from a fisherman we met there that the reservoir was kept for members of the government. I tried to get a pass without success. There was another high lake about an hour's drive from Borovetz on a rough road. At the end I was told by a warden that fishing was prohibited as the lake had just been stocked. I left my tackle behind and after a steep climb I eventually reached the lake. It was very small, only two hundred to three hundred yards long and one hundred yards wide, shallow and free of weeds. Sure enough, it was full of minute trout.

One of the most interesting sites in Bulgaria is the Rila monastery. We booked a week-end there, partly to look at the monastery but also to try fishing in a lake about three hours walk away. As it was wet and misty, this was out of the question. I tried a small stream, the Rila river, without success, and only got very wet. Later the same day we walked up a side valley for a picnic and I again had a go with fly although I still had no success. Finally, on our way home I tried in a promising-looking place on the Rila river where a sluice formed a large pool and many flies were hatching on it. An hour's fishing there produced nothing. It was exceptionally cold for July with an air temperature of 54°F while in London it was 82°F.

We took a week's local leave to travel to Lake Ohrid, which lies between Macedonia and Albania. It was not easy to fit our luggage and ourselves into the car and in addition we had Slavka with us, who as ever was a great help. Neither the hotel we stayed in overnight on the way nor the one in Ohrid were up to the standard one would have wished; the food was poor and the service even worse. The impression we gained in the Ohrid hotel was that they could not care less and did not know how to run a hotel; indeed, there was no manager. Despite all this, we enjoyed our stay, all the more when we were joined by the Sturgess family, two of whose daughters had been bridesmaids at our wedding. The town had several churches of great interest, with frescoes dating back to Byzantine times in the 10th to 13th centuries. Another unusual church is at Sveti Naum at the top end of the lake. The monastery had been converted into a hotel and Rachel and I decided to move into it, glad to get away from the modern horror we had booked into.

Lake Ohrid is about fourteen miles long and three to four miles wide, surrounded by steep wooded mountains. The water is bright blue and very clear. One morning we got up at 3.30am to go fishing in a hired rowing boat:

'The Ohrid trout live at a great depth and never come in to shallow water to feed. They can only be caught by trolling at a great depth with spoons and therefore are of little interest to the sporting angler. But we were anxious to catch one and had arranged to be picked up by boat at the hotel at 4 o'clock in the morning and to fish for five hours. We did so and a splendid morning it was. The boatman caught one trout on his tackle and told us that our own was of little use. He had the usual Ohrid equipment which was usually a weight of 3½ pound similar to the weight from a grandfather clock, on about 50 yards of forty pounds breaking strain nylon line. At two yard intervals from the bottom were droppers of about nine pounds breaking strain with a mepps spinner on each. There were twelve such droppers altogether thus ensuring that trout were covered at all depths. The system is illegal for sports fishermen, but

176

it is cheaper to chuck the whole lot overboard than to pay the fine if
they are caught. The professionals use four such lines at a time, i.e. 48
spinners all at once. Not surprisingly the fishing has gone off a lot in the
last few years, with pollution as a contributory factor. The fish caught
by the boatman weighed 1¼ pounds and was indistinguishable from
a brown trout except for being rather silvery, with distinctive red spots
down the lateral line.

'Part of the fun of this excursion was in talking to the boatman, an
extremely intelligent and knowledgeable instructor in swimming and
water-polo at a local school, and a very pleasant and friendly person;
we learnt more about Macedonia from him than during the whole of
our stay.'

The behaviour of trout in Lake Ohrid may be due to its geology. It
was formed by land dropping between two parallel faults, and is known
technically as a graben lake. It is extremely deep and the sides are so steep
that the water is 230 metres deep only 300 metres from the shore. There
is therefore little shallow water with weeds encouraging invertebrates
on which trout feed. Presumably they rely on other deep-water species.
I spent an hour next day talking to the director of the research institute
on the lake but unfortunately did not note down what he had told me.
Since those times, much research has been carried out into the different
species of fish in Lake Ohrid, spurred on by pressures from overfishing
and pollution.

The stay at Sveti Naum was not as peaceful as we had anticipated:

'On arrival for our peaceful two days we found that a big folk festival
on the occasion of the saint's anniversary was in full swing. The inside
of the monastery was full of people from the surrounding districts, many
of whom had brought with them sheep, calves or chickens as presents
for the church. The family would carry the sheep three times round the
church with a peasant band playing behind them; about fifty sheep were
presented in this way. Many peasants were settling down for the night
outside the monastery with bonfires, and there was music and dancing
until very late, starting up again at 3.30a.m; in fact I don't think they
stopped all night. It was very interesting to witness a celebration of this
kind with the peasants participating, and not something laid on for
the tourists. In the church itself, a service was being conducted by the
Metropolitan of Macedonia, and peasants were kissing the relics of the
saint. St. Naum was one of the disciples of Cyril and Methodius; the
latter invented the Slav alphabet while working in Moravia, and their
two disciples, Naum and Kliment, returned to Macedonia and began to

copy and translate scriptures and teach around 960 A.D.'

On an earlier journey, we had stopped at the monastery of Bachkovo about twenty miles from Plovidv where we had been attending the annual Trade Fair to meet British exhibitors. While we were there, a farmer and his wife came in with a live sheep. It was held in front of an icon with a candle burning over its head, while the priest said various prayers and repeated seven or eight names. He told us afterwards that the peasant had taken a vow to present a sheep to the church if various difficulties, such as the illness of his children, were resolved. This had apparently happened, as the farmer had brought in his offering which we saw being blessed: the prayers were for the family and the names were those of his children. It was an interesting and refreshing occurrence to witness in a communist country.

After leaving Sofia on return posting to London, we later returned as ordinary visitors on two or three occasions. The first was in 1980 on a camping trip through Hungary, Romania and Bulgaria. We found everything much as we had left it, except that the country seemed tidier, brighter and more prosperous. Richard Dales, then Head of Chancery, generously invited us to stay. The same staff were still working at the Ambassador's residence. In some ways, life at the embassy seemed easier and more relaxed, with fewer restrictions. In other ways, things were harder with food, especially vegetables, becoming more difficult to obtain. Slavka and Milka were delighted to see us again and entertained us to extravagant meals. On a walk in Lenin Park, we were nostalgic about the different features where the children had played nine years before.

In 1994, a group of us from Shrewsbury spent a night in Sofia before changing trains on our way from Athens to Bucharest. A bag containing money and tickets was stolen as we waited on the platform. It was reported to the Embassy, who replied:

> *'Unfortunately the extremely unattractive side of the new Bulgaria is the massive increase in crime rates. This is a phenomenon general to virtually all the post-communist countries in this region. The police here are quite unable to cope and at many levels probably corrupt anyway, since they earn such low salaries and living costs have risen so sharply.'*

In 1998 we returned once again to Bulgaria on a week-long tour of the country organised by a travel agency. We had time in Sofia to revisit the area where we had lived when we were members of the Embassy. The block of flats looked down at heel; the park was woefully neglected; benches had been broken and not properly repaired, if at all; street lamps had been smashed; the ponds were empty, fountains not working. Graffiti had been scribbled on the Russian war memorial, a piece of vandalism I found highly offensive given Russia's part in liberating Bulgaria from the Turks and then in defeating the Nazis, with whom Bulgaria was allied in the Second World War. Since that time, the monument has become a centre for anti-Russian protest, for example over the arrest of the Pussy Riot girls in Moscow, and Russian intrusion into the Ukraine; there are many campaigning for it to be removed.

Such disruption as that caused by a radical change of regime is common all over the world. We believe that the situation has improved since that time and Bulgaria is now an important tourist destination, popular among those wishing to buy a property abroad. Despite the peculiarities and constraints of living in a communist state, we were there at the right time.

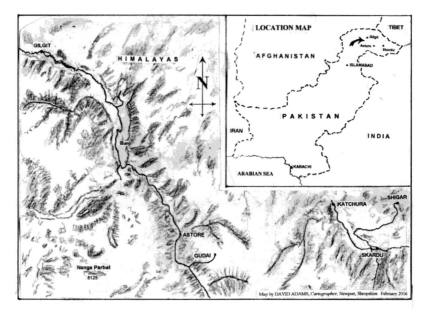

Pakistan and the area of Baltistan visited by the author

The Kaghan valley at Naran in north Pakistan

A nomad crossing on a ridge above the Kaghan valley

Loading Jessica into the Jeep on the trip to Astore

The rest house at Gudai

The lake at Skardu with the welcoming rest house beside it

Rachel with the ayah Mary holding baby Jessica

High up in a valley above Skardu. The local women had no objection to being photographed

Donald Logan taking the salute before handing over his Letter of Credence as HM Ambassador to Bulgaria (author's archive)

Donald Logan addressing the Bulgarian Head of State (author's archive)

At the allotment of our cook Slavka who entertained us generously

A military parade was held to mark the twenty-fifth anniversary of the Bulgarian Communist Party's accession in 1946

The state shop Univermag, the equivalent of Moscow's GUM

A Turkish village in south-eastern Bulgaria

Lake Ohrid in Yugoslavia was visited for a short break

Timothy had been born in Sofia and was with us for a family
photograph with Slavka just before we returned to England

PART 3

Chapter 11

A Year at Leeds;
Learning about Languages

On arrival back from Bulgaria I had been posted to the East European Department of the Foreign Office and we needed to find somewhere to live at short notice. As for any one with a job in London, there is a wide range of possibilities from a flat or small house in or near the centre to somewhere in the suburbs, or beyond in the countryside provided the travel time is reasonable. We spent much time looking at various options and decided to take a house in the Sussex village of Ticehurst. It was a pleasant place to live with a number of shops, a church and a school; the nearest railway station was at Wadhurst on the Hastings line and the journey door to door to the Foreign Office took just over an hour.

Fairly soon after moving in we considered buying a property in the village. A wing of Ticehurst Manor came on the market and we were interested in it. If we stayed on in the Foreign Service, it would suit us well. We were also attracted by an advertisement in the Sunday Times for a farmhouse in the north of Scotland near Loch Watten, notable for its trout fishing. It attracted us as a holiday retreat, especially if we were serving abroad and needed a base for home leave. At £3,000 it seemed a very attractive proposition and I arranged with the owner to travel up to look at it. The idea was to take an overnight train on the Friday, view it on Saturday and return south on Sunday. However, a few days before I was due to leave, I fell ill with 'flu and had to cancel the expedition. Perhaps it was as well; as time went by we gave more serious thought to our future and whether or not I should resign from the Foreign Service.

I am often asked why I decided to give up the Diplomatic Service with the prospect of a rewarding and prestigious career. After a hesitant start, I had indeed established myself at a reasonably senior level and so far as I knew, reports from my heads of mission would have been favourable. I had ahead of me the prospect of some good postings abroad accompanied by a wife eminently suitable for a diplomatic life, being bilingual in French. We both loved travelling and even if I would not attain the highest posts, as I had been warned on completion of my probation, we could look forward to world-wide opportunities to visit other countries. Why give it up?

It was not an easy decision and a number of different factors combined to tip the balance in favour of leaving. I had a feeling that I was not achieving much. By then, I was a relatively senior First Secretary, due for promotion on my next posting to the rank of counsellor. Too junior to be put in charge of an embassy, I could expect to be sent to larger missions in big cities. We did not believe we would enjoy life in places like Washington, New York, Rio de Janeiro or the capital cities of Europe. When I had applied to MI6 fifteen years earlier, my interviewer commented on my interest in the countryside and had told me I would be unsuitable for postings in large embassies where MI6 officers would most likely be operating. I think he was right. Then there was the interminable round of cocktail parties and official entertaining, which were an inescapable part of diplomatic work. It was a way of life that did not appeal; we now had two young children and wanted to settle more permanently at home.

The main reason, however, was that I just wanted to teach. As the Germans say: 'Nicht ein Beruf, sondern eine Berufung.' (Not a career but a vocation). I had come across children in several families in Moscow and La Paz and felt that teaching would be both rewarding and enjoyable. To test the ground I went to visit a school where the head master had moved into education from a senior post in the Foreign Office. I also applied for a year's sabbatical to take up a job in a school to see how I got on; this was turned down by the Foreign Office on the grounds that if I took a year off, it should be spent on some activity directly related to foreign affairs.

There were good reasons to take a Postgraduate Certificate of Education before applying for a teaching post. Methods evolve over time, I had been away from language studies for seventeen years and to attempt to go into a classroom using methods from my time at school would have been foolish. There was also a political consideration. A PGCE was not obligatory for teaching in an independent school, but the situation could change. It would have been frustrating if all new teachers were required to hold that qualification and I had missed the opportunity to acquire it.

It would have been a particular pleasure to go back to Cambridge for my course but by the time I applied, there were no places left. Instead, I registered at Leeds University for the academic year beginning in

October, 1972. We bought a small semi-detached house in Cookridge, some seven miles from the city centre. It was in a quiet cul-de-sac and within twenty minutes of our arrival, neighbouring children had come over to welcome us. We found Yorkshire people open and friendly and we enjoyed their company during our stay in Leeds.

From the outset I had wanted to teach in an independent boys' boarding school such as I had experienced myself. At the time there was an undercurrent of prejudice against the independent sector and my fellow students, mostly half my age, found it difficult to understand my preferences. Our studies, a combination of specialist language teaching and general advice, were well worthwhile and in the second term, we were placed in local schools to practise. So that I could experience how the state system worked I asked to be assigned to a comprehensive. Instead I was put into Leeds Grammar School to practise teaching in the junior half with boys from eleven to fourteen. This was certainly the right decision for me and besides the classroom, I enjoyed going to morning chapel and supporting at rugby matches in which any of my pupils were taking part.

We had lectures on general educational topics but it was the language theory and teaching methodology that I found most helpful. This involved a study of language learning and the theories put forward by various authors who wrote at length about two key elements of language acquisition which are conditioned learning (what you learn from your parents at home) and conceptual learning (from study at school or elsewhere).

Conditioned learning is the universal way in which children learn to speak and what they learn will reflect their parents' style of speaking at least in the first few years of their life. Absorption of language is strongest in a child's earliest years but declines as it grows up. It may not disappear altogether; some adults have a remarkable gift of becoming fluent in a foreign language without having to study it - simply from what they hear. Languages have existed since the Tower of Babel was knocked down and many have learnt them by this process.

The role of conditioned learning was well illustrated by an incident when we were travelling on a ferry from Helsinki to Stockholm. Finnish is difficult as a foreign language since neither grammar nor vocabulary relate to other European languages. We happened to be sitting at a table with a Finnish couple and their seven or eight year-old son. There are fifteen cases which are used, amongst other things, to express movements towards something, e.g. a house, into it, out of it and away from it, as well as location within, but also in idioms. The young boy talked a lot

182

and clearly gave no thought to the cases that he was using, nor indeed to other grammatical constructions. But on going to school he would have had to grapple with them if he was to learn to speak and write accurately; the same applies to any language, including one's own.

Another element of conditioned learning is accent. Accents vary both in the UK and abroad and reflect regional differences. It is curious that local accents survive despite the use of standard English in television and radio. In European countries, the differences are marked, often for historical reasons, but even where the accent is strong, people will use standard speech when speaking to a foreigner or a fellow national from a different area, or in formal situations. Local accents are respected and carry none of the class connotations which used to exist in Britain in the past.

I had studied German at preparatory school for two years before moving on to Marlborough. When speaking German in the classroom I apparently used a Viennese accent for this led to some teasing from both teacher and pupils. The reason for this must have lain with my prep school teacher who had probably picked up his German in Austria at some time between the wars and had then passed it on to his pupils. It no doubt embarrassed me at the time but it illustrates an important aspect of language learning – the student's ability to pick up speech through hearing it. I had made no conscious effort to imitate my teacher; I merely spoke and acquired the accent I had heard. This, after all, was how I learnt to speak English with an accent acquired from the way my parents spoke. All children do this.

One occasionally comes across adults who have unconsciously picked up an accent from people they come into contact with. The daughter of a friend in Wales, who went to work for a few months at Laura Ashley's factory in Carno, came away with a distinct Welsh accent. It soon disappeared when she left that environment to study medicine. For myself, acquiring a local accent has always proved difficult; when I was staying with friends in Germany, they admired my command of grammar and a rather old-fashioned 19th-century way of talking, but suggested that I should go to see a theatre speech therapist, which unfortunately I had no chance to do.

On retirement I volunteered to help with reading in a local primary school and the use of the local accent was an issue. Should I require a child to use what one might call 'Queen's English' in its reading accent? One boy in particular failed to pronounce the letter 't' in phrases like 'little beetle' resulting in what is termed a glottal stop. Should I correct this? I finally decided that I should; he would no doubt continue to use the glottal stop in his conversations with family and fellow pupils. But reading aloud implies formality and I did not feel it wrong to ask for a more formal pronunciation. I am sure that many would disagree.

Conceptual learning is quite different and is determined by a person's innate ability to acquire certain skills and knowledge through study. At first, these will be relatively simple but as learning ability develops, more complicated structures can be absorbed. The ability to learn conceptually varies from person to person; some are better at it than others. It is this variation in ability and the different elements in a foreign language with which the teacher has to contend.

Of the various elements in language study, possibly the most important and difficult is grammar, that is understanding sentence structure. I attribute such ability as I may have for learning foreign languages to the cult of Latin that prevailed at my preparatory school during the war in Scotland. Beside learning gender rhymes and singing them to Gilbert and Sullivan tunes, we studied Latin grammar in depth, so essential if trying to translate English texts into Latin or *vice versa*. Latin involves six cases for nouns, German has four, Icelandic and Russian six, Finnish fifteen. English has hardly any and training in the use of cases in a foreign language is important if a thorough knowledge of grammar is to be achieved. Latin at a young age is a good start.

Confirmation of the value of a knowledge of Latin came to me later from an unexpected quarter. During a short break at Rydal Hall in Cumbria, a fellow guest recounted how during the war he had come to work at Bletchley Park. When interviewed about his academic background, he mentioned that his main experience lay in Latin and Music. He was immediately taken on and required to learn Japanese so that he could work on intercepted messages. Japanese is one of the most difficult languages for Europeans to learn, but for him an expert knowledge of Latin provided evidence of conceptual learning skills.

When I went to Marlborough College in 1947 to sit the scholarship exam, the German paper involved advanced grammatical constructions, requiring an extensive knowledge of vocabulary, tenses and the use of the subjunctive, a demand on linguistic knowledge far beyond that needed for present-day GCSE, even A-level German. I still have the paper; for example 'Translate the following into German:

'*If I had only known that I should have come.*'

Many years later when I had to learn Russian, I came across grammatical concepts which were totally unknown to me. There is nothing like them in Latin. I struggled with them and still do.

Vocabulary is another hurdle which has to be overcome. A child picks it up easily enough. For an older pupil or an adult it is difficult and success will depend upon academic ability. There are various ways of learning vocabulary. When studying Russian, I wrote out cards with the English on one side and the Russian on the other and would spend time, sitting under a tree in Hyde Park if the weather was fine, going through my stack of cards.

That is not the end of the matter. Unless the words are repeated and put into use, they may not stick. To a certain extent, this can be done passively by reading literature in the foreign language at the right level, edited if necessary. Approaching the end of my Russian course I embarked on a translation into Russian of Conan Doyle's *Hound of the Baskervilles*. To start with, it was difficult and I had frequent recourse to the dictionary. After a while, I knew the words I had been looking up and became so involved in the story that I almost forgot that it was not in English. That was encouraging but I would have needed to repeat these words actively if they were not to be lost with the passage of time.

Someone attempting to speak in a foreign language which they are in the process of learning translates in their mind between their own language and the one being studied. It takes much practice to cut out this mental translation process and think in the foreign language. More difficult still is trying to interpret one foreign language into another direct. I certainly found this to be the case when attending a diplomatic reception in Sofia and found myself trying to interpret between a Spanish-speaking Cuban and a Bulgarian official.

I faced a similar challenge in 1994. We were travelling with a small group of boys from Shrewsbury School in eastern Europe. On reaching the Lithuanian-Polish frontier there was a long queue of vehicles waiting to cross. We explained to the Lithuanian border official that we could not afford the time to wait and were invited to bring our cars to the front. We had expected to be asked to donate a few dollars for the privilege and had prepared for this by putting varying amounts of dollars in different pockets. But no. The border officer produced a plastic container with instructions in German and invited me to translate them into Russian, the language much used in the former Soviet republics at that time. It was all about the application of undercoat when painting a plastered surface, an area of language about which I knew nothing in either language, nor indeed in my own. I got the main point across about not diluting the fluid, made up the rest as best I could and we were sent on our way with no dollars having changed hands.

Our time in Leeds was not solely determined by my studies at the university's teacher training department. The city had much to offer, among other things the annual music competition, and we frequently went to concerts. We joined an arrangement with our neighbours to baby-sit for them and they would do the same for us. And you do not have to travel far to reach the wonderful landscapes of the Yorkshire moors. At the end of our stay we sold our house in Cookridge and prepared for our move to Shrewsbury where I looked forward to putting into practice the training I had received on the PGCE course.

Chapter 12

To the Community at Shrewsbury School

Seeking a post to move on to had been a preoccupation in my third term at Leeds. The Cambridge University Careers Department willingly helped alumni in their later years as well as students still at university. They circulated notices of vacancies and through them I was put in touch with Sherborne, Marlborough and Shrewsbury. Sherborne appealed as it was not far from Williton, where Rachel's mother was living. However, the interview with the headmaster did not go well and in any case he wanted younger graduates straight from university.

In 1973 Marlborough was looking for a Head of Russian and if I was taken on, I would also be expected to run the Air Section of the CCF. At the same time I had applied to be Head of German at Shrewsbury, for German was my main subject. After interviews the headmaster, Donald Wright, told me that he would telephone me the following morning to let me know if he was able to accept my application. In the meantime I had to decide whether to take the job if offered, or accept the one from Marlborough. I sought advice from Michael Coates, a fellow pupil at Marlborough and Clare College, Cambridge. He warmly recommended Shrewsbury as he thought it would suit me because it had a pleasant and friendly atmosphere. He was in a good position to know, having married the daughter of a housemaster there. The next morning at 8 o'clock the telephone duly rang; I was offered the post and accepted.

Donald Wright had been appointed Headmaster at Shrewsbury in 1963 and set about introducing radical changes to the way the school was run, so as to bring it up to date and in accordance with the prevailing trend towards liberalisation in the 1960s. Part of his programme was to recruit staff from outside professions to complement many who had gone straight into teaching from university, in many cases to the same school they had themselves attended. The post I had applied for, Head of German, had already been filled, but I was accepted to take over the language-teaching periods of the assistant chaplain who was due to leave

187

at the end of the Michaelmas term. This suited me well, as it meant I had half the normal timetable and it gave me time to settle in to a new and unfamiliar career.

Every school is different in its location, site layout, activities and the manner in which it is run. Shrewsbury was one of many schools throughout the country founded during the reign of Edward VI, many bearing his name. It is doubtful whether Edward VI had much to do with this since he was only fourteen at the time. The country was run by an autocratic ruler, Edward Seymour, Duke of Somerset, motivated by a determination to establish Protestantism in the church and in public life. The dissolution of the monasteries by Edward's father, Henry VIII, had closed down seats of learning associated with them and there was an urgent need to open new schools. Shrewsbury was founded in 1552 (the same year that Cranmer published his Prayer Book) and Edward VI is recalled as its founder in the annual Carol Service.

The school was established in the town centre opposite the castle and from the early 17th century it was housed in a magnificent stone building, now converted into the town's library after extensive restoration by the County Council. With the town's increasing prosperity in the 19th century after the arrival of the railway, the school flourished, particularly when the Public Schools Act of 1868 named it as one of seven prominent boarding schools which had been examined by the Clarendon Commission set up in 1861. It had outgrown its buildings and the playing fields in the meadows along the river Severn were no longer adequate; it had to move.

Across the river stood the former workhouse, built in 1765 as the Foundlings' Hospital, but then vacant. The Army had considered taking it on as a barracks but decided it was not really suitable for several reasons, one being a fear of infection from people who had been buried there. The headmaster of the time, Edward Henry Moss, saw this as an opportunity to move and negotiated the purchase of the building and a large area of land around it, to be turned into playing fields. The workhouse was adapted by Sir Arthur Blomfield and turned into classrooms, while his son Reginald Blomfield designed the chapel and the main boarding house. A library, science block and fives courts appeared along the ridge overlooking the Severn. Boarding houses were built in a semi-circle at the eastern end of the site and behind that, the Kingsland area was developed for up-market housing, converting what had once been a rather disreputable area into residences for the wealthy.

The school continued to expand in the 1920s with the purchase of three large private houses to the west. These became housemasters' residences with wings added to accommodate boys. Other buildings were built along Port Hill Road to provide a sanatorium and further staff accommodation. An old rubbish dump was earthed over for playing fields. In this way, the school was completely self-contained on a single site with some of the finest playing fields in the country.

On appointment I had been told by Donald Wright that all members of staff were expected to live in school accommodation or within five minutes walk of the school site so that boys could visit their tutors on foot. After six years living in government or rented property, we wanted a home of our own and were fortunate to find a house within that distance. Because of this there were very few cars on site and there was hardly any traffic; bicycles were the norm.

Michael Coates' recommendation of Shrewsbury for its friendly atmosphere was justified. It was indeed a happy school, both within the Common Room and between staff and boys. The maintenance of the school as a community was encouraged. Once a term, a dinner was arranged, mainly for recently appointed staff and wives who were included so that they could get to know each other and become involved in the school community. Rachel helped to run the school's second-hand clothes shop. Boys grow out of their clothes quickly and it was only sensible that, if in good condition, these should be available to others at a time when clothing, usually made in the UK, was a big expense for parents. Rachel also took on cooking instruction for boys in the Sixth Form; she had done a Cordon Bleu cookery course after leaving school and was well qualified to teach. More formal guest nights were held for local personalities who helped out at the school as a way to thank them for their contribution, for example, officers from nearby Copthorne Barracks who were involved in the CCF.

Obviously there were occasional differences between members of staff which had to be resolved but in general this was achieved in an amicable way. The only more serious difference arose from the existence of a private dining club which some members of staff were invited to join. It was named the Trimmers after George Savile (a former pupil at the school), the 1st Marquis of Halifax. He was a prominent political figure in a somewhat tumultuous time in the 1680s and skilfully adjusted his policies to take advantage of the prevailing scene. He sought to justify inconsistencies in outlook in his book *The Character of a Trimmer*. The club had been founded in 1937 and was intended as a relaxation for married staff, particularly housemasters, to give them an opportunity to get away from their houses and to enjoy a good meal. Membership was not open to all but not long after our arrival, I was invited to join. Meals were formal. The first one I attended was at an Oxford college. Another was held in a railway coach belonging to the Bulmer cider family in Hereford, another high up in the South Shropshire hills. Both the food and drink laid on were of the highest order in both quantity and quality. The arrangements for the meetings were supposedly confidential but details inevitably leaked out. No problems had arisen since the club's foundation, but this was a time when existing institutions were open to challenge and it was beginning to prove unpopular with some staff, especially a number of bachelors who saw it as a secret cabal influencing school policy. It was not, but the fact that it was seen as such was divisive and out of character with the informal and friendly ethos of the school. A couple of years later the Trimmers was quietly closed down.

I must admit that I was very nervous when I entered the classroom at Shrewsbury for the first time. My very first lesson was for French to a set of thirteen-year old boys. One is naturally expected to speak in French and when a boy came in five minutes late, I asked him why he was late: 'Pourquoi es-tu en retard?' His reply was lengthy, detailed and in perfect French which turned out to be much better than mine. I was taken aback. How could I teach such able pupils? It turned out that he had just come from a school in Paris. While his spoken French was faultless, there were points of sentence structure that he had not then mastered.

My teaching was confined to classes up to O-level and GCSE, for the good reason that I lacked qualifications after so many years away from academe and there were others better qualified than myself to take on more advanced levels. For German, I was fortunate in that the school was using a BBC course *Frisch Begonnen* which I knew from Leeds. This combined spoken language with pictures on a screen. It comprised three parts; a film strip which had to be loaded into a projector, a tape of conversations related to the picture and a book with texts, grammar explanations and word lists. This combination provided plenty of opportunity for practising spoken German in the classroom, while the book had material in it suitable for homework. It was not easy for the teacher, who had to set up and operate both projector and tape recorder and then dismantle it all at the end of the lesson. Doing all this was a nuisance but results were encouraging.

I noticed that some boys were inclined towards the Romance languages such as French, Spanish and Italian, while others clearly preferred German and were better at it. Were the former descended from the Normans who occupied the country after 1066, I wondered, while the latter came from Anglo-Saxon or Viking roots? It would be an interesting research topic to analyse the DNA of professors and lecturers in these languages to find out their origins.

For Spanish I was initially asked to take on a set of good linguists who were taking O-level in one year. Presumably uncertain of my competence at the end of my first year the school authorities had asked the Oxford & Cambridge Examinations Board to comment on the performance of my pupils. The results were satisfactory but the Board noted that the pupils had been taught by some one who had learnt Spanish in Latin America. It was true; my Spanish had been learnt in Bolivia and it seemed to me remarkable that this should have been reflected in my pupils' written papers for at that time there was no oral test. South American Spanish is distinct from that in mainland Spain and evidence of this may have come through in the dictation and comprehension tests. When visiting Spain in later years I had great difficulty in understanding what people were saying. On one occasion I met a young man in a museum in Madrid and understood him perfectly as he came from Mexico.

Occasionally I was asked to teach A-level Russian literature to a student while my colleague Peter Holgate looked after the language side. At that time, Russian was not officially offered as a subject and both Peter and I took this on in our free time. Results were good and when our students achieved A grades, the school was quick to recognise them as the school's achievements. After retiring, I was invited to teach A-level Russian literature to two Russian girls at Adcote School, not that their Russian was in any way not up to it, rather that they needed to know how to handle questions in the A-level exam. I had no qualifications for teaching Russian literature having never studied it at school but, as at Shrewsbury, it worked out well.

When teaching a foreign language the two aspects of acquisition, which are auditory and visual (by ear and by eye), need to be balanced so far as is possible. My language studies at Cambridge had left me poorly qualified in listening and speaking; it was soon after the war and taking a year off to study in Germany, now an essential part of university study, was out of the question.

The consequences of imbalance were brought home to me when I undertook the teaching of Swedish to Arthur, a boy who was desperately keen to learn the language. There were family connections with Sweden and at the age of eleven he had travelled there, fallen in love with the country and was determined to learn the language and go on to a Swedish university.

I was delighted to do this but soon discovered that I knew virtually nothing myself. I had read the works of around fifteen 19th-century authors at university, but that was many years before; nothing I had leant then enabled me to carry out simple day-to-day tasks such as booking a hotel room, ordering a beer or finding out train times. I had to make good the deficiency and at the end of the first year I booked into a Swedish-language summer course in the beautiful university town of Uppsala. On arrival I found that I had been placed in the top set on the basis of my knowledge of grammar and vocabulary. I understood not a word of what was going on and immediately asked to be moved down. The reason for this error was the severe imbalance between my knowledge of grammar and vocabulary and my complete lack of spoken Swedish.

Even in the lower class, it was four days before I could understand what our teacher or the other pupils were saying. Then quite suddenly it all came; this helped my ability to speak and my knowledge of words came into its own. One has to persist. I had taken with me a small pocket radio, on which I listened to a news broadcast daily at 7 a.m. and again at 8 a.m. before going into the school; this helped a great deal when our teacher played a recording of the same broadcast as part of her lesson. The imbalance had been corrected, at least to some extent.

It was teaching Arthur Swedish that brought me to consider more carefully the nature of language courses. I had begun by buying copies of *Colloquial Swedish - the Complete Course for Beginners*, with accompanying tapes. It worked well for a few weeks but I then realised that this was totally unsuitable for proper language learning. It contained eighteen chapters, each one introducing a new aspect of grammar and another area of vocabulary. The material in the first chapter was inadequately repeated in the second and, as we moved on, the backlog of unrehearsed material grew bigger. At half-term, I dashed off to a specialist language bookshop in London and bought *Nya Mål*, a course in three volumes, each with its own book of exercises and CD recordings. This proved very effective.

The series *Colloquial Courses for Beginners* cannot be expected to provide a sound foundation of language. However, they are excellent for revising a language already well known, for example, if one is going back to the relevant country on holiday after an absence of several years. I have used them for Slovak, Czech and Polish thinking that a knowledge of Russian would make things easier. This was true, but only to a limited extent. The language learnt in this way and tried out in practice was quickly forgotten.

An entry in a catalogue for travellers *Travel Paraphernalia and Outdoor Leisure* featured perhaps the simplest solution to learning a language:

'*LEARN A FOREIGN LANGUAGE-NATURALLY. Being able to*

communicate with the locals when travelling abroad really enhances a trip. Now you can learn enough to get by using the same method you used as a child. You learn through listening and speaking without the pressure of memorising or writing. Play the CD's in the car, at home or download them to your MP3 player and join the millions of people who learn a new language.'

I have not had occasion to try it out but doubt whether I would have got very far, although others might.

Setting of pupils according to ability is essential and I suspect that many of the complaints about being poorly taught at school stem from a failure in setting. On one occasion I was given a German beginners' set of late entrants in the Lent term, where there were wide differences of ability; some boys were very gifted, particularly one pupil whose father was a German-speaking Czech, others much less so. The exam results measured against those who earlier in the year had been put into sets reflected this as they covered a far wider range than was the case for the boys in other sets; some scored as highly as scholars, others were way down in the list.

Advances in technology have made a huge difference. At Marlborough just after the war, there were no tape recorders or other audio-visual aids. The nearest we got was a weekly twenty minute French programme on the BBC Home Service. Our teacher in the Sixth Form, Dr William Rutland, would once a week bring a wireless set into the classroom. It was mains-operated and required him to make the connection by standing on a chair to remove a light bulb and plug it in.

The invention of tape recorders was a great help in teaching as it enabled a teacher to balance better the audio and visual aspects of language learning. By the time I arrived in Shrewsbury, the language laboratory had come into fashion and a room in the languages department was equipped with one. There were twenty-four booths, each with its own tape recorder, headphones and microphone. The teacher's console had a master tape recorder, from which a recording could be transmitted simultaneously to all twenty-four desks, also a set of switches, one for each booth. The teacher could press the switch in one direction to listen to a particular booth without the boy being aware of it, and the other way to speak to him. At the start of the lesson, an exercise would be sent out from a tape and the students would get to work on it. It might, for example, ask a question with a pause for the student to answer, followed by the correct answer which the student would then repeat.

The material was limited in subject matter, vocabulary and grammar to tally with the ability and level of experience of the students. There is little if any value in putting out material which is either above or below the students' capacity to use it; in either case, boredom and frustration soon set in. As a teaching method, there were many benefits. The recordings were by native speakers and in repeating sentences the students were imitating a genuine accent as well as engaging in oral practice, albeit in an artificial way. The teacher could help if there were problems and the option of listening in was more than just a matter of ensuring that a student was behaving. The language laboratory enabled all pupils to speak at the same time in the foreign language.

The main problem arose through breakdowns, either of the tape recorder, if the tape broke or came adrift, or of the headsets which were not robust. These problems could sometimes be overcome by moving pupils to different booths if there were less than twenty-four in the class. Despite this, I set high value on the laboratory as a teaching aid, especially with younger pupils better able to acquire accent and intonation from a tape. I was upset when I overheard my head of department tell a visitor that he had little use for it except in the Sixth Form: I would say that in some respects the reverse is true.

Television opened up a completely new area of language-learning activity. A programme recorded on a tape or disc can be chosen to suit a particular standard of ability, much as in the language laboratory. Watching a screen will encourage a student and help in understanding the accompanying dialogue, while maintaining concentration. There is, however, a danger that the visual will take over to the exclusion of the audio; the story may be followed from the screen but little language is learnt. This was brought home to me when I went to a local cinema to watch a performance of *Die Meistersinger von Nüremburg* transmitted live in high definition from the Metropolitan Opera in New York. It was a fascinating spectacle with the cameras moving from one part of the stage to another and including close-ups of the individual singers. I left the cinema wishing I had heard more of the music; it was of course there, but the visual image had distracted me.

Many years ago, the BBC produced a series of Spanish programmes on a video tape *España Viva*, which rehearsed specific structures and were within the range of GCSE pupils. This was complemented by a further five programmes, mainly in English, on cultural topics such as the poetry of Antonio Machado. Using these programmes provided a change from normal lessons and widened the students' general knowledge. Things once went wrong for me when using *España Viva*. There was only one room with a television/video tape player in the department (shared also with the English department) and it had to be booked beforehand. One day the TV kept jumping channels, with my Spanish programme suddenly disappearing off screen to be replaced by a Test match commentary. After repeatedly switching back to no effect, I became increasingly grumpy and had to abandon that lesson in the belief that the television had developed a fault. Only later did I learn that one of the boys had a wrist-watch with a built-in zapper; he was more interested in cricket than Spanish.

The value of standard TV programmes in a foreign language is debatable. A student needs to have reached a very high standard to understand fully what is being said, even if the picture gives a clue. English sub-titles are better, if these are accurate and appear just before or at the same time as spoken words. One of my pupils had the misfortune to suffer a broken leg in an accident in the south of France. He enjoyed watching television and speaking French to the nurses and his language skills had improved noticeably on his return. My own experience of Swedish television was less encouraging; with concentration split between watching and hearing, I concluded that radio on its own was more helpful.

While the content of educational television programmes needs to be set at the right level for those studying a language, so too should the course being used in the classroom. On arrival at Shrewsbury, I came across a French course *Langue des Français* by Watson in three volumes. This was an offspring of traditional Latin textbooks and must have been in use many years previously. Each lesson had a text, a vocabulary list, a grammar explanation and basic exercises such as 'Translate into English...' and 'Translate into French...' There was little scope for oral practice until a supplement for use in the language laboratory appeared in the 1980s. The school had abandoned this course and replaced it with a more interesting and up-to-date one which was better suited to the linguistic needs of the time and the syllabus for GCSE exams.

In an attempt to encourage interest in contemporary issues and teach appropriate vocabulary another course appeared in the 1990s which featured the environment, conservation, air travel and other topical matters. I was invited to use this course with a bottom set (out of seven) of thirteen-year olds. They were not good linguists and the course was way beyond them, in both vocabulary and content. Using it effectively was beyond my own ability as well and in desperation I switched to Watson's *Langue des Français*, enough copies of which had been gathering dust in a cupboard. This was successful; words and grammar could be explained (in English of course) and the simple translations were well within the pupils' grasp. Some sense of achievement began to replace frustration and behaviour also improved.

There is a huge variety of courses available for schools and one replaces another almost as frequently as changes in ladies' fashions. The best I have come across is an English course for Norwegians written by our home-exchange partner in Sogndal. It is well structured, uses appropriate language and has subject matter of interest to children. For example the boys had a good piece about an English football club, for the girls matters of dress or theatre might be appropriate.

However hard teachers and students work in the classroom and whatever methods are used, there is no substitute for visiting the country in question and staying there long enough to benefit from classroom learning. Shrewsbury School used to have an exchange arrangement with a school in Hamburg. Boys would spend a fortnight staying with German families in the Easter holidays and receive their exchange partners in the first fortnight of the summer holidays. The right time to undertake this exchange was in the second year of learning German. By that time, enough knowledge had been acquired for maximum benefit to be gained from being in a German-speaking environment; moreover, it was immediately before O-level exams.

Repetition is essential in language acquisition. A child learning to speak from his parents will persistently repeat a word, usually a noun such as 'tractor'. The student on a language exchange is in effect using his auditory ability to extend his knowledge and skill to communicate. I pointed out to my pupils that they would hear more German in a fortnight's exchange in Hamburg than in two years in the classroom. I also encouraged them to get their Hamburg partner to go round the house describing all that they saw in the way of furniture and pictures, not just once but several times and make them repeat it.

The exchanges on the whole went well and produced good results. Occasionally there were hiccoughs. One year, boys discovered that the English 10p coin worked in German slot machines where the much more valuable one mark coin was needed. They had picked this up from boys at a Croydon school. The latter had been caught and their passports confiscated until money owed had been repaid. Fortunately our lot escaped, having heard what was happening to the Croydon boys. I also had the case of a boy who disliked German food to the extent of looking into the saucepans on the kitchen stove and making disparaging noises about the contents; I had to go and sort it out. Despite this little difficulty, he went on to study German at university and ended up as head of German at a large comprehensive school.

More problematic was the return visit in the summer holidays when there was a clash between the German boy's stay and the requirement for his exchange partner to attend summer camp in the Brecon Beacons. Some of the German boys enjoyed the experience. Others did not and one can understand the extent of the problem for a boy brought up in urban Hamburg finding himself camping in the Welsh hills and having to undertake demanding exercises, often in bad weather.

Sadly exchange visits no longer take place unless arranged privately by enterprising parents. A number of reasons have combined to bring this about. Children travel abroad more with their parents than was the case in the 1970s and maybe are less adventurous. Parents for their part are less willing to undertake the task of receiving a foreign child in their homes. Finally, higher awareness of the risks of abuse and the question of DBS checks on families abroad have further reduced the popularity of school exchanges. They have been replaced by organised school trips at the initiative of teachers; these are beneficial in widening knowledge of the country and its culture but cannot provide the acquisition of language skills inherent in exchanges.

On joining the Foreign Office in 1956 I studied Russian for a year before going to the embassy in Moscow, then on to Spanish-speaking Bolivia and later, after a spell in London, to Pakistan and Bulgaria. Many years later I met an intelligent lady who was clearly conversant with a variety of foreign languages. She disclaimed suggestions of linguistic brilliance, asserting that she had 'paddled in the shallow waters of foreign language.' I felt I had done the same and my skills lacked depth. In Moscow I continued with lessons, but conversations with ordinary Russians were excluded for security reasons. I also failed to pass the Foreign Office's higher level Spanish exam as the paper included texts from the golden age of Spanish literature, with which I was not familiar.

French, German and Spanish up to GCSE were thus the mainstay of my normal timetable and I also taught some Russian as well as Norwegian, Finnish and Swedish to individual boys at different times. It may sound impressive, but it was not. With a certain knowledge and experience from days in the Diplomatic Service combined with the use of first-rate materials then available, it was not that difficult and a pleasant change from the hum-drum of basic GCSE language teaching.

Chapter 13

On to other Subjects:
English, Biology and Beekeeping

I have sometimes been asked whether it is boring to teach the same thing over and over again. In a way it is, certainly at GCSE level where the language range is limited. Knowledge of the language is not adequate to allow for discussion outside the narrow range laid down in the syllabus. Occasionally boys would ask questions which had nothing to do with the lesson content, for example: 'Were you a spy when in Moscow?' It was only polite to give some sort of answer and we would go off onto a red herring. While the subject up to that level was of limited interest, each set of boys was different and this provided welcome variety and interest.

Shortly after I began at the school, I was asked to take on a form of boys in their first year. I was to teach them both French and English and have some responsibilities outside the classroom. So far as I recall, there was no laid-down syllabus in English and it was up to the teacher to cover any aspect of English that appeared to him important. Obviously, spelling and grammar were essential basics, as well as answering questions in a comprehension exercise, which was part of the GCSE English paper.

Week-end homework was writing an essay, but here again the teacher could decide on the topic to be written about. For me this was an opportunity to extend the range of instruction to include matters of social convention, for example writing an appropriate letter in a given situation. This might be a letter of thanks to an uncle or aunt for a Christmas present or for hospitality. It had to include certain basic elements: thanks, an expression of appreciation, some news item, comment on a matter of concern to the recipient of the letter and a suitable conclusion. This might seem straightforward but was not so easy when the present was something not wanted or even disliked. Another aspect was the correct use of 'Yours faithfully' and 'Yours sincerely' when writing to people outside the family circle.

Once in the course of the year I would ask the form to write a diary for one week. It seemed to me a good idea for them to reflect on their various activities and describe what they did and how they felt about it. I made it clear that they should not include any matter which they would prefer me not to read. For my part, I also kept a diary for that week which likewise omitted any private matters and this was to be passed round for them to read if they wished. Looking back on that time and bearing in mind the question of ethos and community, I was interested to read the final day's entry in my diary for a particular week:

> 'I read Form IVB diaries with much pleasure and enjoyment. It is interesting to see how similarly the boys react to things; we live in a community and are engaged in the same occupations, but on different sides of a fence. These diaries give me an insight into the other side and, I hope, a better understanding.'

Elocution was also taught. It was important that boys should be trained to read aloud in various circumstances, with attention to pronunciation, modulation and intonation. The school ran an annual competition for the Bentley Elocution Prize, requiring a representative from each form in a year group to recite a poem learnt by heart and to read aloud a set passage. It was very gratifying when a boy in my form won the prize for his year.

As a tutor in the Grove boarding house I was responsible for arranging the lesson reader for the year's chapel service on a Friday morning and would insist on the reader turning up early to practise. The larger the audience area, the slower and clearer the reading needs to be, a requirement which was all too easily overridden with a speedy delivery induced by nervousness.

The same considerations applied to giving a talk which was spoken rather than read from a written text. Each boy was told to prepare a ten-minute talk on any subject he liked. On completion of the talk, he would be expected to answer questions and his performance would then be discussed, with reasons given as to why it was effective or not. One boy, a skilled angler, insisted that we should all go down to the river for his talk on the art of fly-fishing, which he expertly demonstrated as he spoke. Literature, both prose and poetry, was studied. My preference was for a collection of twenty short stories by Graham Greene, easily read and discussed, while an attempt to study Shakespeare's Julius Caesar was a disaster and quickly abandoned.

The teaching of English also provided an opportunity to look at subject matter of one's own choice. One year there was to be an exhibition in London on the Vikings. Given my Icelandic studies at university I embarked on a number of lessons on Viking history, backed up by videos. On Field Day a colleague and I took the form to London and boarded a boat for the trip down to Greenwich; it was a most enjoyable day out, although the return journey was less straightforward. It was the rush hour. We were on the Docklands Light Railway and when we reached Bank to change onto the Underground the platform was so crowded that our party had to split up. We met again safely at Euston.

One year a boy suggested in a French lesson that I should take them to France. There happened to be a relevant travel brochure in the Common Room and a visit to Brittany was soon arranged. Two other members of staff joined the party, which included all our family, and we had a great time. Less successful were an exchange trip to Jaen and a separate tour of Andalusia in Spain for older students. Trips to East Berlin and the Soviet Union went well, although I was alarmed when some of the boys decided to see how close they could get to the Berlin Wall before police arrived. Fortunately they did not push their experiment that far.

Outside the classroom a form teacher was expected to take a more general interest in the boys' welfare and activities, for example if there was any evidence of bullying or bad language. My lot were intelligent and hard-working, keen to make the most of their opportunities. They were generally well-behaved; a touch fearful at finding themselves in a new environment and at the bottom of the pile after being near the top in their preparatory school; maybe a bit cheeky but not yet prone to the restlessness of adolescence; above all welcoming the greater freedom they could now enjoy. Some of course had difficulties and one had to be sympathetic and willing to help them get round them; I felt sorry for one boy who asked to be excused writing a letter home because he felt so homesick. I also felt it essential to read the confidential reports from the headmasters of their previous schools so as to be aware of any special circumstances which had to be taken into account.

It seemed to me that the house system was inward-looking, even antipathetic to other houses; there was therefore good reason to encourage boys to visit houses beyond their own. At the time every house had table tennis and a knock-out competition was laid on with a draw determining who played who. The 'draw' was manipulated to favour members of the form playing an opponent in a different house. The final took place in the gym in the last English lesson of the term, with the best of three games to decide the winner. Once that was over, we played round-the-table knock-out so that every one could have a go. Looking back on this, I can see that it was an unusual thing to do during a lesson. Yet no-one ever complained or even criticised the competition. It was characteristic of the school's tolerance of unusual activities and reflected the easy-going atmosphere that prevailed at the time.

Such an arrangement was popular but it did not mean that things never went wrong nor that there were no behavioural difficulties. On one occasion I had made a mistake and wrote in my diary:

> *'After making so much fuss about accurate reading and carefulness, I felt very small even if the boys took it with a good grace. But worse was to come. At the end of the lesson two boys started fighting, one flicking ink all over the other, who retaliated by punching him. I made them stay back for a serious warning, but the incident remained in my mind all afternoon. It has never happened before in any of my forms that two boys have behaved so badly during a lesson and I resolved that any further misbehaviour on their part should be ruthlessly dealt with.'*

I had started with the second form out of six and continued thus for seven years. Later I was transferred to forms of lower academic ability but this made no difference. They were just as rewarding to teach but needed more careful scrutiny lest they should classify themselves as 'failures'. In my diary I wrote that I had been 'promoted' to the lowest form.

Then in 1990 it was suddenly announced that the form system was to be abolished, with responsibilities being transferred to housemasters and house tutors. I was disappointed to lose what had been for me the most rewarding and arguably the most important part of my teaching with wider responsibility for many aspects of welfare. Sadly, English dropped out of my curriculum. I was also somewhat annoyed that the decision had been taken without any consultation with those involved, nor reason given. It may have been to ensure that decisions on A-level choices in the third year should be taken in the house unbiased by the personal interests of a form-master. I may be wrong, but as I say, no reasons were given.

While teaching a form was rewarding and stimulating, it would be wrong to conclude that all teaching was like that. Far from it; discipline is a vital factor for any teacher and some classes are better than others in this respect. Teaching effectiveness can be undermined by a single disruptive pupil. Nowadays lessons downloaded from the internet and projected onto a white board or screen ensure that a teacher can keep a constant eye on the whole class. Before then, one had to write with chalk on a blackboard, back turned to the class, providing an opportunity for a trouble-maker to make trouble. One year the results of a set taking the one-year GCSE Spanish set were disappointing. The course was a challenge for good linguists who had taken French GCSE a year early and it required very hard and uninterrupted work. It had been a difficult set to teach and the fewer A-grades gained that year may in part have been due to my inability to restrain a certain difficult pupil.

One sometimes had to reproach a boy for behaviour which was not disruptive to the class as a whole but might affect his concentration or be simply unacceptable such as yawning, falling asleep, doodling or eating something. One particular case stands out in my memory. There was a boy who sat near the back with a golf ball in his hand which he would gently roll from side to side while I was explaining some point. When I reproached him, he told me that it helped him to concentrate. It did indeed appear to help him and did not disrupt others, so I allowed him to continue to roll the ball. In a later lesson, he turned up without it and when asked why, he told me that a physics teacher had confiscated it. I happened to have a spare one, which I gave him with the warning to be careful where he rolled it next time.

My teaching was not confined to foreign languages and English. One day during summer camp in the Brecon Beacons, I was walking from our base at Neuadd back to Cantref on my own, where the route follows the old Roman Road which rises gradually along the side of Tor Glas before cutting through a gap below Fan y Big and continuing down to the valley. The sun was shining over the hills and no sounds disturbed the peace. I was not thinking of anything particular, my mind just floating around on this and that. On school matters I thought of the General Studies arrangement, under which members of staff offered a series of lessons on a subject in which they had an interest outside the normal syllabus. And then it struck – the idea that I should offer to do a course on Freshwater Biology. The offer was accepted and I then had to put a course together, covering about twelve weeks.

My research in Bolivia into the limnology of the high Andean glacial lakes was a start since I had become familiar with the main invertebrates, even if the species would be different from those I would encounter in Shropshire. The Field Studies Centre at Preston Montford near Shrewsbury offered a course in the techniques for gathering samples and I joined this; it included a visit to Ashes Hollow stream in the Long Mynd. This was invaluable as I learnt not only the methods for collecting samples but also some of the identities of the creatures we caught.

The timetable for General Studies comprised four periods a week, two single ones and a double lesson on Fridays between break and lunch. This was ideal; the single lessons would cover as many aspects of freshwater and the creatures in them as possible, while the double period would provide for practical experience, driving out to different waters equipped with nets and trays and taking a picnic lunch for the more distant destinations.

The single lessons were a challenge as I am ignorant on many matters and had to rely on textbooks from which to prepare them. I depended on three major works: *Life in Rivers and Lakes* by Macan and Worthington and *The Biology of Polluted Waters* by Professor Noel Hynes. The Biology Department acquired sufficient copies of a third work to be lent out to each student. This was *The Family Water Naturalist* by Heather Angel and Pat Wolseley. This covered every conceivable aspect of freshwater biology and sections of it could be recommended for study as homework. The first two provided ample material for the single lessons and, looking back at my file, I am very surprised that I presumed to lecture on so wide a range of topics: these included the geology behind different types of water, the nature of a river from source to sea, fish and their spawning habits, sources of water for domestic consumption with their respective advantages and disadvantages, the creatures that inhabit waters, even such complicated matters as the chemical composition of water and the different types of pollution.

The expeditions to Shropshire waters were easier to plan and great fun. We visited Ashes Hollow, the Shropshire Canal and various local ponds and streams. Our most rewarding site was the River Severn at Preston Boats. The river there is shallow and the stumps from former eel traps are clearly visible when the river is low. We caught and identified various species of fish as well as invertebrates and on one occasion an eel was caught, taken back to the laboratory and kept in a tank before being returned to the river. We had several collecting nets and each pair of boys was given a list of the species which might be encountered and columns for different places from which samples were taken; those from fast flowing parts of a stream would be different from the ones from a still pool.

The National Rivers Authority provided a link between classroom theory and practice in the field. At the time, the NRA was responsible for water supply, sewerage, water quality management and pollution prevention. They had an office in Shrewsbury and the official dealing with the last two kindly agreed to teach my class and myself about pollution and explained how the range of invertebrates in a given stretch of water reflected water quality and the extent of pollution, if any. It was simple: the more common aquatic creatures had a value number; for example, the burrowing mayfly *Ephemera danica* rated a score of ten (only found in the purest oxygen-rich streams) while midge larvae *simulium* are happy almost anywhere and score 1. By adding up the scores from creatures found in a given water, one had an idea of its quality and variations in the score from samples taken at different times could indicate an incident of pollution.

Water contains many different chemicals, but the most important constituent is oxygen, derived from surface contact with the air, from turbulence or from photosynthesis. It is essential for plants, animals and fish and plays an important part in the decomposition of waste. Because of the effects of oxygen, a polluted stream will eventually clear itself after a certain distance provided the levels of pollutants and their composition are not too toxic; it will be accelerated if clean spring water enters the stream, thus reducing the concentration of pollutants. If a river becomes completely depleted of oxygen, anaerobic decomposition sets in, with emissions of methane and hydrogen sulphide, generating unpleasant smells.

All this became real when we paid a visit to the local sewage works at Monkmoor to learn how sewage is treated. We were taken round by a guide who began by showing us how solid objects which cannot be decomposed in the works are filtered out. Most of the sewage is trickled over circular beds of clinker which develop colonies of bacteria, later fed on by worms and insect larvae.

The second method is to confine sewage in closed tanks. With no oxygen available, anaerobic decomposition sets in, producing methane gas. This is used at Monkmoor sewage works to drive a turbine and produce enough electricity to meet its needs. The final effluent goes back into the river. Although biologically clean it contains phosphates which will affect the river ecology, encouraging the growth of blanket weed which, if it is dense, stifles normal plants and adversely affects the food chain from plankton through invertebrates up to fish.

Methods for dealing with possible pollution in sources used for domestic supply were covered in a visit to the Shelton water works, again thanks to the support of NRA officials. Much of the water for Shrewsbury comes from the River Severn nearby. We were shown how this is filtered through sand beds and treated with chlorine before being pumped into the supply network.

On our visits to different stretches of water, members of the group recorded their findings and compared the results. I am glad to say that we did not come across pollution and the main interest lay in the contents of the nets.

At the end of the course, pupils were given a test in the form of a quiz rather than an exam and it was my hope that they left with a greater understanding of aquatic matters and an enhanced interest in the environment. For me it was a delightful, if challenging, change from teaching languages, and I had indulged in a certain arrogant pride in entering the biology building to teach a subject in which I had no professional qualification. Sadly, the General Studies arrangement came to an end six years later with a revision of the timetable and as with my English lessons, my freshwater biology course was discontinued.

Shortly after arriving in Shrewsbury I turned my attention to the possibility of getting started on beekeeping. My father had kept bees in Broadstairs before the war and although Broadstairs, at the tip of Kent largely surrounded by sea, was not ideal, he took a fair amount of honey from the two hives in the garden and another two in a brick storeroom; this was intended for keeping apples but there were two slots in the wall with a shelf behind for hives to stand on. He continued with beekeeping for a few years after the war which was long enough for me to see what was happening although I did not take part. My interest was stimulated by one of my tutors in Leeds who kept bees and was enthusiastic about it.

Writing to the Deputy Headmaster, Michael Charlesworth, in June 1974, I explained my proposal. I told him that a number of boys were interested; I had received an offer of hives from Clive Tanner, a local wine merchant; I enquired about a suitable location and ended up by formally requesting permission to start an apiary on the school site. The proposal was warmly welcomed. A colleague, David Christie, who had experience of bees on Jersey, joined in and we soon had three hives set up on rough grassland at the edge of the site. We had very little equipment and made do with a few veils, a smoker and a hive tool. My own veil was supported by a bowler hat which I still had from Foreign Office days. While working in the Latin American Department, I had been asked by my Head of Department to go out to Heathrow to welcome the new Panamanian Ambassador, for which purpose I should wear a bowler hat. I bought the cheapest I could find and never used it again until I reached Shrewsbury. More equipment, including bee suits and a second-hand extractor, was acquired with grants from the profits of the school shop. It was not long before we were selling our honey to raise more cash.

The idea of a beekeeping society proved popular. Housemasters encouraged new boys to get involved in non-academic activities and at the beginning of the year we would have around thirty members. Not all stayed on, but from each intake emerged a small group dedicated to beekeeping. During the winter terms, we would arrange lessons in the theory of beekeeping including anatomy, sources of pollen and nectar, hive management and so on. These took place on Thursday afternoons in David Christie's classroom. In the summer term, meetings were held at the hives to give instruction in the practicalities of hive management. We were much helped by the introduction of a 'Societies Hour' immediately after lunch on Monday. The number of hives grew to around twenty, with two or three boys taking charge of each.

We were much encouraged by support from the Shropshire Beekeepers' Association, who invited us to attend apiary meetings in summer. We travelled by minibus to learn from demonstrations at SBKA members' homes, usually followed by a delicious tea. The boys had asked for instruction in more advanced aspects of the craft in which neither David Christie nor I were qualified, such as queen-rearing and diseases and I asked Michael Charlesworth, then acting headmaster, for permission to arrange for speakers to come during 'Top Schools', that is, the couple of hours after supper dedicated to homework. I wanted the Beekeeping Society to be on the same footing as other societies which invited in guest speakers, the Bastille (history) and the Darwin (science). Understandably I received a cautious reply. Sessions were to be limited to two meetings a term and, naturally, Top Schools must be done. I was later to come across the same hesitancy when I took boys fishing to Lake Vyrnwy on a week-day evening. Fishing and beekeeping, although welcomed as activities, did not enjoy quite the same status as visits to Stratford to see a play or away sports fixtures involving a late return.

Various incidents occurred in the course of our activities and it was in the early days that we experienced the worst of many arising from our bees. The creatures can become aggressive if disturbed and one evening after one of our sessions, a boy on his way to tea was stung in the eye. It was all the more serious because he only had partial sight in his other eye and we feared that he could suffer serious long-term damage. Certainly his ability to take his exams at that time was impaired. It was a relief when we later heard that he had fully recovered from the sting; if anything, the sight in the other eye had improved.

We had not foreseen this difficulty and it was clear that we had to move the hives to a safer location. Choice was limited by the nature of the school's layout. In the 1920s, the school site had expanded to the west with the purchase and incorporation of three large properties. One of these, Kingsland Grove, included an extensive garden and patch of woodland in an isolated corner. Part was already in use as a duck pen, where boys could keep poultry and between that and the garden of a neighbouring house was a green, wooded area. It was a promising site, particularly as the garden shed could be used as a store for equipment.

The hives were accordingly moved there.

The neighbouring house happened to be the home of Shrewsbury's Member of Parliament, Derek Conway. In 1984, he had complained to Simon Langdale, the headmaster, about the number of bees in his garden. Later in August he wrote to say that he had been stung once, as had their nanny, and his son twice. He feared that his son while running around in the garden, might have a bee enter his mouth with even more serious consequences than the two stings he had already sustained. He asked for the hives to be moved.

It was in response to his earlier request that I had moved three of the hives in May 1984, but the fourth one was more difficult. I had tried to move it the day before the date of Derek Conway's letter; no doubt it was this disturbance which caused the trouble and prompted him to put his complaint in writing. We eventually moved it some twenty-five yards away from Mr Conway's garden wall. The following April, he wrote to me to say that two hives were in view and bees were still visiting his garden. His wife was due to give birth to their second child in July and would be spending much of May and June in the garden. 'I will not have her suffer bees in quantity in this condition and hope that an immediate relocation will take place. I wish to avoid legal action as much as possible but the School must be assured that this will be delayed for a very short while.'

I was upset by the threat of the school being taken to court but appreciated that Mr Conway had a point. Normally bees are not aggressive unless disturbed and trying to move a colony in summer is not a good idea. Nevertheless, we had to do something and immediately arranged to relocate the apiary. There had in any case been difficulties earlier when some bees from the twenty or so hives we had in the Kingsland Grove garden swarmed into the hedge adjoining the playing fields. Bees dislike noisy machinery and had stung groundsmen using mowers, including the headmaster's son who was helping out. We had reduced the number of hives but in the light of Derek Conway's experience and the threat of legal action we now had to find a better location.

Further west from the main school building lay Ridgemount, another former residence extended to provide a large boarding house. It had an attractive orchard, and beyond the house there is a wood on a steep slope above the river Severn. It was decided to split the apiary between the orchard and the wood. A further advantage was the possibility of keeping our equipment in unused rooms for storage and changing into protective suits, as well as for extracting honey. One of our members dug out steps going down the slope through the wood and for a number of years this proved an ideal location for four or five hives, until one day a passer-by on the drive above was stung. By then we had fewer hives. That part of the apiary was abandoned and the remainder were moved to the orchard.

Despite these setbacks beekeeping continued to provide a sound foundation of knowledge and practical experience. The series of theory lectures in the Michaelmas and Lent terms, combined with hive manipulation in summer led up to boys taking the Junior Exam of the British Beekeeping Association if they so wished. This was a thorough exam, involving a written test of twenty questions followed by an oral, conducted by a BBKA examiner, Geoffrey Hopkinson, who came over from Stafford. Sadly, the syllabus was changed after a few years; candidates were required to keep a diary for every visit to the apiary to record what they had seen and done. This was not popular; boys were already under pressure in their academic studies to produce written work and they did not wish to take on additional tasks of this nature. Regrettably we had to give up offering boys the option of taking the BBKA Junior certificate.

Instruction was not diminished because of this although its character changed. Rather than dedicate the whole of a meeting to theory, which was in itself rather too much like a formal school lesson, basic instruction was combined with a practical activity related to bees. These include refining and melting beeswax, making candles and polish, honey tasting, brewing and tasting mead and most importantly the construction of frames. Boys are probably now less well informed than their predecessors but interest in the subject and the enjoyment of a hobby are just as prominent as before, if not more so. And that is what matters.

Over the years keeping bees has become much more difficult, both generally and at the school. The arrival of the mite *Varroa destructor* and the diseases which afflict bees because of it have made it that much harder to keep colonies going. In some years we lost nearly all our colonies and had difficulty in building up the numbers again. There was also less time. In 2002 I wrote, somewhat apologetically as I was then retired, to the Headmaster, Jeremy Goulding, pointing out difficulties which we faced in running the Beekeeping Society. Societies Hour had been reduced to forty-five minutes; there were fewer meetings available because of extended week-end breaks and longer half terms; boys were under increasing pressure from course work, exams, computers and other distractions. Other activities were beginning to take boys away, either compulsorily or by choice. The head master was sympathetic but in practice nothing could be done as it was the way academic work and other pressures were evolving.

Given these constraints, the extent of our activities is more limited, particularly in the summer term. A couple of Mondays with rain or cold preventing us from meeting in the apiary have reduced even further the time for practical instruction and manipulation. Over the years it had always been my intention to move on from the basics to some of the more advanced procedures in beekeeping. We taught about swarm control but were never able to fit in the necessary procedures of brood inspection and hive manipulation. We knew about raising queens but were not able to raise any ourselves. For those of us running the society, there was additional work to be done in the holidays: extracting honey if it came from oil seed rape, treating hives against Varroa and organising the equipment.

The success of any school hobby activity depends upon the availability of staff members with an enthusiastic approach and a desire to pass this on to their pupils. We have been fortunate to have successive masters with a passion for bees, particularly in the Biology department, first Andrew Powell who took over from David Christie when he left, and then Andrew Allott, an enthusiastic beekeeper who later became Head of Biology. Furthermore, each year group of boys provided one or two enthusiasts who took responsibility for helping out with talks. From time to time former beekeepers tell me how much they learnt from beekeeping at the school. I cannot recall anyone saying the same about my French lessons. A child's experiences will inform his or her interests and memories for the rest of their life and any school (as well as parents) should make every effort to ensure that these cover a wide field and give pleasure in later life.

For me it has been a pleasure and privilege to continue to take part in the society many years after my own retirement. In 2014 the Society's 40th anniversary was celebrated with a dinner attended by a number of past presidents. Beekeeping is to my knowledge the only school activity which contributes to agriculture both by the production of honey and to increasing awareness of the importance of bees to the pollination of food crops. Let's hope that it will continue for many years to come.

*****

All members of staff were expected to help with sport, a major element of the school's programme, as in virtually all independent schools. I had never been much good at sport but wanted to make a contribution. There were two Common Room football teams which played against teams from the houses, one very serious, and the other more easy-going. I joined the latter and much enjoyed the weekly game. I refereed house matches, mainly for older boys with limited skills. A colleague and I ran a junior rugby game in the Lent term for a few years and then I moved over to fives taking responsibility for the under-fourteens. Unfortunately I had never played fives at Marlborough but was glad to take it up. One year shortly after the beginning of term, I wrote in my diary:

> 'At 5.15 I played a game of fives with three boys, Richard Lucas, John Easton and Stewart Evans. It was most enjoyable and perhaps the thing I have enjoyed most of all today. To begin with, we were all pretty bad but as time went by the standard of the game improved until by the end we were having quite long rallies. Mr Williams [master in charge of fives] gave us some advice at the end and we had learnt a great deal. As we left the courts the sun was dipping down over the lime trees by Kingsland Hall and the grass of the playing fields was lit up by a most attractive autumnal shade.'

There were matches against other schools to which we drove in a minibus. The trouble with fives matches was that one of the four games always seemed to drag on long after others had finished and it was uncomfortable standing interminably in the cold. Similarly, I umpired the odd cricket match at a very junior level and one year helped with tennis although I was not invited back for the year after.

I had no experience of rowing as a sport and was not qualified to help with coaching crews on the Severn. Perhaps for that reason I was invited to join the 'Impartial Committee' for the Bumpers race which takes place on four successive days at the end of the summer term. Crews consisting of four oarsmen and a cox from each house would line up along the north bank of the river at carefully measured distances. A gun was fired a minute before the start and a second shot set the crews rowing in an attempt to bump the boat ahead of them. If successful, a crew moved up a place for the next race the following day. A cup was awarded to the crew that ended up head of the river.

Judges were positioned at various places up and down the river to watch for any errors. A common one occurred when a boy holding the rope at the start of the race let go of it before the gun went off. The boat would be disqualified. There were also disagreements over whether a bump had properly taken place, especially if there had been two bumps at the same moment, and our job was to work out which one had occurred first. In such cases judges reported back to the Impartial Committee which took a decision. The crew that lost out was bitterly disappointed, so was their housemaster. On one or two occasions a housemaster would be so infuriated with our decision, or the possibility that we would decide against his house, that he would burst into our room in the boat house to argue his case. We had no alternative but to ask him politely to leave.

Trout fishing was not recognised as a 'sport' in the usual sense of the word, but my interest in it gave me an opportunity to take boys to Lake Vyrnwy, where the proprietor Sir John Baynes, whose sons had been at the school, gave us very generous terms to take out boats and fish in the evening. Boys would have to do their homework before we left at about 3.30p.m. and we had picnic suppers with us. The boats had to be back on shore by 9 o'clock to enable us to return to the school by about 10.30. We caught the odd fish and generally all went well. There were two worrying occasions, however. One was when a severe thunderstorm broke out. It is not sensible to fish in the middle of a lake using a carbon fibre rod when lightning is striking round about and we had to move in to the shelter of trees around the edge and stop fishing. Another time, one of the boats was late returning and as it approached from a distant bay, I noticed that the rowing was irregular. It turned out that the two boys had taken their supply of beer and spirits with them and were not sober; one of them had to be taken to hospital on return to Shrewsbury.

The West-Mid Agricultural Show included a fly-casting competition for schools, which was hotly contested. The most competent contenders and usual winners came from Monmouth School on the river Wye but occasionally we would win, such as once when three enthusiastic brothers from the same house scored highest. I was very pleased one year when the prizes were won by a local prep school, Prestfelde, led by our son Timothy.

Each house had several tutors working with the housemaster. Once a week they would be on duty and take 'dix', a house assembly after homework had been completed. Finding the right topic on which to speak was never easy for it was supposed to have a religious or at least a moral content on one hand and be sufficiently entertaining to ward off sleep on the other. My preferred choice was to find a series of items, for example, poets who had lived on or near the River Severn from its source in Mid-Wales down to the estuary.

Another activity was to take the year group to spend a night at Talargerwyn, the school's farm house in Snowdonia. For lighting we depended on a diesel generator, which often would not start, and on hurricane lamps and candles in the bedrooms. The school had a lease on Talargerwyn at a very low rent. Eight years before this was due to expire the school was invited to purchase the property freehold for around £36,000, with the prospect that at the end of the lease it would be put on the open market. The governors decided not to buy it as the rent was so low. To me this seemed a foolish decision with the likelihood that it would command a very high price in eight years time and that the school might lose it altogether. I made a fuss and with the support of colleagues asked the governor representing the Common Room to urge a change of mind. This he did and the house now belongs to the school.

Chapter 14

Into the Welsh Mountains for Adventure Training

I am not sure that adventure training is exactly a sport but my participation in what was called 'Basic Year' took as much time and effort as more extensive involvement in traditional sport might have done.

The second or third evening after the beginning of the Michaelmas term in 1973, Donald Wright invited the twelve of us new members of staff to join him for a glass of sherry at his house. He told us that on Thursday afternoons members of staff take part in a variety of school activities such as the CCF, community work, cookery and so on. He explained these to us and invited us to tell him, as we left, what we chose to do. The list included outdoor activities and adventure training, known as Basic Year, and this was the one I chose.

Until 1967 the school ran a Combined Cadet Force which was obligatory for all boys throughout the school. Then, however, it was becoming increasingly apparent that this arrangement was no longer appropriate. National Service had ended and there seemed little point in enforcing military training on this scale. In addition, there was increasing hostility among the boys. The headmaster, Donald Wright, set up a committee of three senior members of staff to come up with a solution. They recommended that participation in the CCF should be voluntary for boys when they reached their third year. In the second year, boys were to undertake training in field craft and camping skills purged of the military element. There would be no uniform or drill, but Army support would continue as if it were part of the CCF. Negotiations secured agreement on both sides and a member of staff, Michael Cross, was asked to set up the Basic Year. He was succeeded by Michael Hall who ironically insisted that participation for all second year boys should be compulsory.

Basic Year was to give me knowledge and experience in areas of which I knew little and accorded well with my love of wild landscapes and mountains. Apart from a journey down the Alto Beni river in Bolivia I had never camped out in my life. Nor had I learnt to use a compass to find my way in open countryside, even in my travels in the Andes and the Himalayas. Basic Year also had deeper objectives and I was to benefit from these as much as the boys taking part.

All boys in their second year at the school were divided into four patrols of six groups, each with five or six boys. They were arranged alphabetically, regardless of houses or any other consideration. This avoided the formation of gangs; it also meant that boys would have experience of looking after each other, with some inevitably weaker than others when it came to challenges in the mountains. Each patrol was led by a master assisted by one or two senior instructors (Upper and Lower Sixth) and three or four juniors in the Fifth Form. Such was my ignorance and lack of experience that for the first year or two I was assistant to a member of staff well able to run the patrol and help me to learn the ropes. Later I became in some respects Michael's deputy. One of my tasks was to organise the way in which boys entered the lecture theatre for meetings; I called out each boy's name when it was his turn to go in and soon got to know every boy in the year group.

Thursday-afternoon activities for each patrol were planned in advance to ensure that all subjects were covered. The simpler activities took place on or near the school site with map and compass, knots, first aid, town tour, bridging a stream using ropes between two trees, training on a climbing wall and an assault course at the Army's base nearby. To begin with, every boy in his second year brought back a bicycle to school and groups were sent off on map and compass exercises in the countryside; sometimes for my group the last checkpoint was our house near the school where boys were given tea and cake. As the years went by it was decided that this was no longer safe because of increased traffic on local roads.

A longer orienteering exercise was also held at Cannock Chase, initially on a Thursday but later on a Sunday to avoid missing lessons. It was on the first Sunday of the Lent term; we began with breakfast in the school dining room at 6 a.m. and were usually late getting back. There were also night exercises, one in the Michaelmas term the other shortly after Christmas. There were two sites for these. The first was on the Army's Nesscliffe training area. During the war, a large number of ammunition bunkers had been put up with rail links to the national system for the storage of munitions up to D-day. The bunkers were still in reasonable repair and the evening began with boys cooking their supper on the platform of one of the bunkers, using ingredients from the school kitchen and Army stoves. The groups would then set off with a plan of the site to find certain numbered huts to which playing cards had been attached. Each group had to collect its particular card to prove that it had found the site rather than picking up information from another group. The whole exercise required a great deal of preparation, but it taught boys to find their way around in the dark. It only once went wrong when it clashed with an Army exercise in the same area. Boys were scared when they came across soldiers in the dark with blackened faces, dressed in camouflage and helmets, and carrying rifles.

The other night exercise was very different in character. It was held on Caer Caradoc, a steep volcanic hill above Church Stretton. Supper was cooked in a small quarry at the foot of the hill, after which groups climbed to the top in the dark to report to a checkpoint there. The view at night was spectacular, across the valley to the Long Mynd with the lights of Church Stretton immediately below. They then had to find their way to a point about a mile away, again in the dark. The use of torches was strongly discouraged; we wanted to train boys to follow footpaths once their eyes had become accustomed to the dark. On moonlit nights, this was no problem. In total darkness it was not so easy, and I was surprised to find that one could walk along a path simply by feeling its shape with one's feet. Once or twice a group would get lost and our return to school would be even later than housemasters were expecting.

More demanding were the Field Days when the entire year group with all instructors and additional members of staff took off on a wide-ranging exercise across the mountains. These required meticulous planning, careful briefing the Thursday before and detailed kit inspection on the day, with boots, waterproofs and survival bags being checked by the patrol master. In the Michaelmas term we went to the Berwyns about an hour's journey from Shrewsbury, with the base in the car park at Llanrhaeadr ym Mochnant. This was for some their first real experience of the mountains and every precaution was taken to ensure safety; groups would follow a set route via several checkpoints manned by instructors and an absolute rule was that a group should never split up. This was my first experience of Field Days: I was attached to a group of boys, one of whom was a keen fisherman and later a tutee; he was good company. In the event of severe weather conditions, there was an alternative low-level exercise which could be invoked at the last moment, but this was rarely used.

Similar schemes were followed in the Lent term in the Radnor

Forest and in summer in Snowdonia, based on the school's farmhouse, Talargerwyn, above the village of Penmachno. Included in the briefing were instructions on the Country Code and respect for the farmers over whose land they would be walking; gates to be shut, care over crossing fences if encountered, no litter to be dropped and so on. Occasionally there would be a hiccough, resolved by an apology. In the early 1990s, however, problems began to arise over the use of land behind Talargerwyn. One day a young farmer drove up to one of the checkpoints and took us to task for being on private land without permission, trespassing, causing damage and so on. I happened to be there, took his address and called on his parents that evening. They resented our using their land without permission and the alleged damage we caused to fences. They would, however, agree to an arrangement, implying some kind of payment. The matter was referred to the School's legal adviser and after further negotiation it was agreed that we would pay this particular landowner £100 as compensation for damage to fences and impact on the land, not as a payment for walking over it.

We had been using the area for training for over twenty years, following public rights of way where possible. When we had complaints, we had dealt with them *ad hoc* in some cases altering routes or moving checkpoints. Paying landowners for use of their land in this case would set a precedent which other landowners might follow; there were many farmers over whose land we operated. We had already been in contact with the Snowdonia National Park Schools Liaison Officer and sought his advice. The issue of public access had also become more prominent in the media and exercises involving large numbers of people were attracting adverse attention. We were not the only organisation to be walking over land in the National Park, although with 170 boys and accompanying staff we were no doubt more intrusive than others. For these reasons the Snowdonia National Park set up a liaison committee and organised a conference to allow an exchange of views among different interests on the question of public access to private land. These included the National Farmers' Union, the Welsh Union of Farmers, the Countryside Landowners' Association, the Forestry Commission and the Ministry of Defence. The School was also represented and a number of controversial matters were resolved.

We sympathised with the farmers but nevertheless regarded our training programme as a very important part of the boys' education. We were concerned not only with map-reading skills, camp craft and survival in the mountains, but also with leadership training; and we did our best to teach them about the countryside and how to behave in it. We were determined that it should continue and the answer was to establish closer liaison with farmers over whose land we would be crossing. The National Farmers Union gave us a list of thirteen farmers and I became the School's Welsh Farmers Liaison Officer. Before the 1993 Talargerwyn Field Day I wrote to the farmers likely to be affected and called on them the day before the exercise. Face-to-face contact was important; we had been warned that Welsh farmers never reply to letters and dislike speaking in English on the telephone. As I called, I followed the advice in a book on Wales, beginning with a general conversation on topics such as sheep farming, before finally broaching the matter of our Field Day. They were without exception friendly and willing to help. Any request was passed on to the boys likely to go on their land. This was not straightforward; some farmers wanted them to go through their farms rather than over pastures, others wanted them to do the opposite. Boys were also instructed on how to cope with angry and aggressive dogs - never turn your back and run away, rather you should stare at the dog and walk slowly backwards until out of the creature's territory.

Perhaps the most important part of the year's programme was overnight camping leading up to the week's camp at the end of the summer term. All the various training activities during the year were supplementary to camping, as Michael Hall in his book *Around the World in Forty Years* explained:

> '*The key activities are camping and hill walking. To be in camp is to be as free as possible of the constraints of 'civilisation', and to walk in the mountains is to invite challenge from the weather, fatigue and so on. I for one prefer fairly primitive camping (most boys when they join have never experienced this): this makes boys self-sufficient and adaptable. Nearly all enjoy this aspect of the training, and like the experience of looking after themselves; cooking, washing in rivers and lakes, coping with days of rain and mud, or with hot and burning sun, away from Mummy, television and the cat, living in a natural (but inevitably still somewhat controlled) environment, discovering new skills... which they would not have experienced without Basic Year.*'

The necessary camp training began with a night at the beginning of the year on a site near Shrewsbury beside a small stream; this would provide boys with practice in putting up a tent and cooking in the open air. A further camp took place at the beginning of the summer term on Cader Idris. It was quite a steep climb from the dropping off point to the campsite at Llyn Cau, a small lake in a cwm a few hundred feet below the summit. Unfortunately one year a boy disregarded instructions about litter, leaving empty Army 'Compo' ration tins under some stones, along with his briefing note making it clear who we were and that we were camping at Llyn Cau. A member of the public came across it and reported it to the Ministry of Defence and the Snowdonia National Park authority; we were ticked off and instructed to find an alternative site. We were able to do this on the southern side of the mountain and follow the route in reverse, reaching Llyn Cau on the way down in the early afternoon of the second day. Although the farmer had agreed to our use of his land, other details were not in place and we again camped at Llyn Cau. A warden happened to reach the summit at the same time as our lot; he reproved some boys for irresponsible behaviour throwing stones off the summit and became aware that we had once again camped at Llyn Cau. It was embarrassing but our explanations were accepted; we had all along maintained good relations with the Park's Schools Liaison Officer. The following year we camped successfully at the alternative site but the farmer was unhappy that some litter had been left and I drove over from Shrewsbury to apologise. There was more than the farmer had noticed; I came across mess tins thrown into the stream.

The week-long summer camp took place in the Brecon Beacons in south Wales. In the earlier years, it was based at the Welsh Regiment's barracks at Cwrt-y-Gollen, near Crickhowell, with two or three nights at an Army camp site at Lower Cantref. We depended heavily on support from the Army who in addition to letting us use their camp sites supplied 'Compo' rations and the use of three-ton lorries. With my heavy involvement in the camp it was suggested that I should learn to drive a lorry and take the test. I took some lessons in Shrewsbury but not enough of them; I failed on several counts, not changing gears correctly using double-declutch and forcing other drivers off the road at a village in Telford. I was given a Certificate of Failure but was glad not to have to drive lorries and so to have more time for other activities on camp.

I was involved in a number of different exercises, but mainly in orienteering. My favourite duty was to man a checkpoint in a remote location, to spend time there reading a good book and to brew up tea for any group that was happy to take a break and stop for a chat. One year I was on a high mountain and noticed a large number of wasps patrolling up and down beside a bank. They were wasp drones waiting for queens to arrive for mating. I caught some and sent them off for identification by an expert at Ripon and York College; they were males of the species *Dolichovespula sylvestris*. It was a rare event and made my day.

A feature of the week's camp was the so-called Monster Exercise. There were four or five small sites scattered across the Brecon Beacons and two or three groups were allocated to them. They had to find their way there with the necessary equipment, set up the tents, cook their meals, pack up the next morning and find their way back to Cantref. Initially they were instructed to draw water from nearby streams but an outbreak of diarrhoea indicated that one of the streams was polluted and thereafter jerry cans of freshwater were taken round to each site. Headquarters was at the Neuadd reservoir, and in the evening, a group of masters and instructors drove down in Michael's Land Rover, Arthur Ransome fashion, to see how the boys were getting on at a site lower down beside an attractive stream. It was a joyful outing, particularly as staff members had enjoyed a refreshing meal beforehand. We ate the same food as the boys, that is Army Composite Rations, or 'Compo', supplemented by the odd addition.

On Sundays, when we were still at Cantref, we would go to church in Llanfrynach as part of the normal programme. If we were not near the village at the time, the School chaplain or his assistant visiting the camp would hold a service of Holy Communion in the open; attendance by the boys was voluntary and I was surprised by the large number who turned out of their tents and came along. My part in this was to help with administering the sacraments and I was given special dispensation allowing me to do so. One year the assistant chaplain had not brought communion wine with him and we resorted to using beer; it seemed strange to be doing this high up in the Brecon Beacons on a rather stormy morning.

We patrol masters and visiting helpers took an active part in running camp. When at base, we had the luxury of a dining tent and a colleague, Barry Storey, cooked delicious meals. He was strict over mealtimes; if we did not appear for breakfast at the specified time we would have to go without and he was rightly insistent that we each did our own washing up. We were also privileged to have our heavy rucksacks taken up to Neuadd in a van or lorry. This attracted some criticism from the boys who were required to carry everything on their backs up the long climb; we justified our apparent laziness by the need to be free to help carry a boy's rucksack in the event of an emergency. This was perhaps not a very convincing excuse but I did not feel too bad about it; the boys attended just the one camp, whereas I took part in thirty-nine during my time at the school, two a year except once when our family had planned a camping holiday across Eastern Europe and I had to get back home early at the end of the first camp.

Much as we enjoyed summer camp, it was hard work and the end of each one was a relief and cause for celebration. Between camps we went for lunch to the Walnut Tree near Abergavenny, a top-class restaurant which provided a magnificent and rather costly meal. I went there sometimes and at others preferred the small inn at Llanthony Priory for a simple Ploughman's Lunch and a pint of beer. At the end of the second camp, when we had seen all the boys off at Abergavenny station, we swam in the stream at Cantref and enjoyed the hospitality of the inn at Llanfrynach, sitting out in the shade of the vines before driving back to Shrewsbury in the Land Rover.

These camps called for rigid discipline if they were to be successful and Michael Hall enforced it fairly and firmly. Arriving late for a briefing meeting or leaving the smallest piece of litter near a tent at night, even a matchstick, was an occasion for putting a boy on 'lats'. In my first year, these consisted of holes in the ground with a screen round for privacy. Later, the Army provided mobile tent latrines, but their buckets still had to be emptied. Beside each one was an aluminium basin of water with soap to improve hygiene. Clearing all this was not a welcome job for the boys, nor for the member of staff who 'volunteered' to supervise it. At the end of camp mess tins were taken in and no boy was allowed to leave until his mess tin, carrying his number, had been handed over spotlessly clean. The level of cleanliness was assured once the first two or three boys had been sent back to do theirs again.

But there were also rewards. These were for those boys or groups who excelled in one way or another and were given Freddo Bar chocolate biscuits. Each one carried a joke on its wrapper. Michael would read it out and call for an answer before tossing it to the lucky recipient. Very soon a number of jokes appeared which clearly were not on the wrapper; most of them had something to do with frogs with which Michael was for some reason associated: 'Q: What happened to the Land Rover when it broke down?' 'A: It was toad away'. or 'Q: What does the frog read on the loo?' 'A: Frogsporn'. A verse from Lewis Carrol's poem *The Hunting of the Snark* is also applicable to Michael's distribution of rewards:

> 'The Bellman perceived that their spirits were low,
> And repeated in musical tone
> Some jokes he had kept for a season of woe -
> But the crew would do nothing but groan.'

It was this mixture of challenges in the mountains, a strict camping regime, appropriate behaviour and a cheerful, humorous atmosphere which made camps an unforgettable experience, whatever the weather.

Camping and climbing in the mountains in all weathers can be dangerous and every effort was made to prevent accident or injury. In running Basic Year Field Days and camps, Michael Hall carried a huge burden of responsibility. He deals with this in a section of his book *Around the World in Forty Years*:

> 'The safety of our activities has always been one of my prime considerations. What we do is potentially dangerous: it would not be challenging if it were not, and I have been aware of the possible consequences of a rash decision. Before every Field Day I have been anxious (I would not have done it if I had not been), and have never been at ease until the last boy has been down off the mountains. I have thought long and hard about the justification for exposing boys to risk. If it is not done then no self-reliance or confidence, in the way we are trying to do it, can be gained. There is a great danger of being over-cautious, with its resulting blandness and lack of challenge. Having said this, and admitting the necessity for some risk, it is our duty to take every sensible precaution, to make emergency arrangements and alternative schemes, to make sure of adequate training and survival equipment, and to be always aware of the possible dangers and hazards involved. We have had some accidents (very few serious ones), and have to balance these against the real value of the challenge we have given to thousands of boys. My touchstone has always been: **if I had to stand on oath in a coroner's court, could I justify my action and decisions?** If there is any doubt, then the opposite decision must be taken. But we must beware of over-doing it: if we always take the 'safe' decision and try to avoid any risks (however remote) at all costs, then the whole thing becomes, in my opinion, pointless: it is just another time-filling activity, enjoyable perhaps but without the essential ingredient of challenge that does so much to build up a boy's self-confidence and realisation of himself.'

During the twenty years that I was involved in Basic Year, I can recall only one case when we had to change the plan for a Field Day. It was in October, 1992, the last year of Basic Year for both Michael and myself. We were due to follow our usual routine for the Berwyns based on all boys reaching the summit of Moel Sych. The previous year, a farmer near the Pistyl Rhaeadr waterfall where some of the groups had been dropped off, had complained and the plan was duly altered to avoid that spot. When the day came, the weather conditions were so bad that we had to resort to the low-level alternative. This had been on the shelf for many years and when it was brought out at a special briefing, it was found that about half the groups would be starting and finishing at the Pistyl Rhaeadr farm. At that stage, there was nothing we could do about it. The farmer understandably complained to the headmaster, Ted

Maidment, in the strongest terms. A letter of apology would not do, so Michael and I were sent out to apologise in person. It was a cold, windy day; the farmer made us stand in his yard while he stood on a milk-churn loading platform and harangued us for some twenty minutes.

After Michael had retired, the task of running Basic Year was handed on to his successor, Mark Twells. At that time, running any such activity was becoming increasingly difficult, not just because of access to land in the Snowdonia National Park but for reasons within the school itself. Boys were under greater pressure academically and participation in Thursday afternoon activities was being eroded. Demands on staff were also increasing and it became ever more difficult to recruit masters prepared to take on responsibility and give up time on a Thursday afternoon. There was also conflict with sport when scheduling the week-end camps at the beginning of the summer term. To start with, it had been agreed that any boy involved in cricket and rowing at a certain level would go on camp on the first week-end of term; those not required for sport would attend camp on the second or third week-end. This was a fair arrangement but in later years sporting demands became more insistent and the odd boy would miss out altogether. Similar pressures were experienced over attendance at summer camp at the end of term. It was a fundamental principle that every boy in his second year at the school should complete the whole year's training; this principle was being undermined.

National regulations also caused problems, especially the rule that there should be one member of staff for every eight boys on exercises out in the mountains; if possible, they should be qualified holders of the mountain training certificate. Many colleagues generously helped out with Field Days and summer camp, but compliance with the regulation was just not possible. Inevitably outdoor adventure training became one of several options on Thursdays along with the CCF, and the Duke of Edinburgh Award scheme came to play a more prominent role.

Michael Hall was arguably one of the most talented and, I dare say, most eccentric members of staff. His whole life was dedicated to serving pupils in addition to his role as Head of Mathematics and running Basic Year. Every Christmas holiday he took a party skiing in Switzerland; at Easter he went on camping trips to Scotland to give experience of outdoor life in winter conditions. After summer camp, he would set off on expeditions to far-flung destinations, often in his vintage Land Rover with a number of enthusiastic boys and one or two members of staff. It is remarkable that in this vehicle he drove across Europe to Turkey and Syria and on another occasion to Morocco. Rachel and I accompanied him

on three such trips, backpacking in Guatemala and Mexico, and taking our car to supplement Michael's Land Rover on journeys to Morocco and Eastern Europe. He also came with us on trips to France and Spain. He will be remembered particularly by his tutees whose interests were so important to him; he encouraged them to read English literature, handing out a list of recommended books, and he entertained them generously.

For his Sixth Form classes Michael good-humouredly set a test on English history and more generally produced learned papers which he called 'Joies de Vivre'. These included 'The Transmission of ancient Mathematics to the Modern World', 'My Top Ten Mathematicians', 'The First Emperor of Mexico', 'Michael Hall's Ten Favourite Buildings'. He was a superb cook and an expert on food and wine, arranging wine tastings for friends and members of staff. He could be difficult at times, yet his contribution to school life, and to ours, was enormous.

The main building at Shrewsbury School (Shrewsbury School)

View from the author's classroom overlooking Shrewsbury town and the river Severn

River Severn at Preston Boats. At low water the remaining posts of the eel trap are shown up in the current

Painting of Montford eel trap by local artist F.W. Seville in the 19th century. This is much as Preston Boats eel trap would have appeared at the time (Shropshire Museums)

The first meeting of the school's Beekeeping Society, James Lawson (left) the author (standing with bowler hat) David Christie (right) and two boys

A meeting at the Jones' apiary in Llanyblodwel

The four stages in taking a swarm

Anthony Jones demonstrating honey extraction at a Speech Day exhibition

Weekend training camp in the snow, April 1981

Overnight camp-site at Llyn Cau, below Cadair Idris

A briefing during summer camp at Cantref in the Brecon Beacons
(Gilbert Roscoe)

Michael Hall about to award a Freddo Bar

Michael's vintage Land Rover with trailer was used to move equipment

Wasps mating on a mountain top in the Brecon Beacons

Statue of Charles Darwin as a
young man (Shrewsbury School)

The author with Robert Hardy at Battlefield. Without his help the site would have been lost to industrial development (Shropshire Newspapers Ltd.)

Solovetsky monastery in the White Sea

Rachel beside a corner tower of the monastery

The family meet up in 2011

Chapter 15

A Time for Change

Any institution, be it school, business or government department, will change to meet changing circumstances; as the saying goes, 'Without change there is no growth.' For some one looking back now on a place where they were once happily employed, it is all too easy to view the past through rose tinted spectacles, muttering 'it was not like that in *my* day'. Those still working there after many years may find change difficult to accommodate. On the other hand, staff arriving at the current time accept what they find and may or may not be happy in their work, only in years to come may they in turn look back and regret subsequent change.

Certainly over the last twenty years Shrewsbury School has seen many changes. The most significant is undoubtedly the decision to go co-educational, first with Sixth-Form girls, and, from 2014, throughout the whole school. Both stages attracted a great deal of criticism and were strongly opposed in some quarters. Shrewsbury had until then been virtually the only boarding school in the Midlands for boys throughout secondary education and some parents had sent their sons there partly for that reason. Other parents, present and prospective, no doubt welcomed the change. Certainly the Sixth Form girls made a great contribution across the board. It was unfortunate that the announcement of the decision was badly handled: members of staff who should have been forewarned knew nothing of the change until it was announced.

A number of colleagues have elaborated on the reasons for this fundamental change. It would appear that in taking this decision the Governing Body was less concerned with educational philosophy than with maintaining the number of pupils entering the school. A colleague more recently retired than myself once told me: 'The school is no longer a Community, it is a Business.' Any school is of course a business in that it has to ensure that income exceeds expenditure. If it does not, it may have to close. I recall one year in the 1970s at a time of deep recession

when members of the Common Room were asked to consider taking a reduction in salary so as to avoid redundancies. This did not actually happen, but it was seen at the time as a possible way of balancing the books.

Some years after my retirement I was approached separately by two parents. They complained to me that they had received a letter from the school stating that their sons would be asked to leave if they failed to achieve satisfactory GCSE results. At that time newspapers were reporting on this matter, linking it to schools wanting to enhance their position in league tables through higher A-level grades. It worried me and I reported the approaches I had received to the Chairman of Governors and the Headmaster. It seemed to me that if a boy was bright enough to gain entry to the school through Common Entrance or other assessment and his parents were committed to pay for his education, then the school should recognise an obligation to see him through. In his reply the chairman claimed that the existence of a 'hurdle' had been policy for many years. He explained that it had little to do with league tables but more with the interests of a child not able to keep up with his peers intellectually.

I was not satisfied with this explanation and wanted to find out the underlying reasons for this arrangement. A number of colleagues in a position to know filled me in on the background. It seemed that a rise in costs and a fall in the number of admissions combined to threaten the school's viability. The standards demanded at Common Entrance were marginally lowered to maintain numbers coming into the school, thus keeping up income. Perhaps because of this, Shrewsbury's position in league tables was slipping, a factor which might influence parents anxious to secure the best possible education for their children. It was in order to counter this trend that a 'hurdle' at GCSE was established; any boy who failed to gain five C grades would be asked to leave; this would hopefully lead to an enhancement in the school's position in relation to league tables and could also be in a boy's interest to study in a more suitable environment rather than end up as a failure. The headmaster at the time decided that, like similar schools, Shrewsbury should no longer take part in league tables which failed to take account of the 'value added' element in the school's achievement, the extent to which pupils improved overall during their stay. Furthermore, the school had much more to offer than just academic excellence.

Boys, and later girls, entering at Sixth Form level, as well as students from overseas, helped financially to make up for a fall in the admission of thirteen-year olds and for a while the requirement for five C-grades at

GCSE was operated with some flexibility. If a boy had qualities in other areas, he might be allowed to stay on. The system suffered from two drawbacks such as the gradual erosion of the quality of GCSE grades on the one hand and on the other the perceived unfairness of a system allowing some to stay on but not others. The solution to the first of these two difficulties was to raise the level required from five grade C's to five grade B's. The second was to impose strict compliance, with no boy failing to make that grade being allowed to remain at the school.

Fortunately the two boys whose parents had complained to me did well enough to stay on into the Sixth Form. Whatever the benefits of a 'hurdle' system may be, I believe that it should be the parents who decide with advice from housemaster, tutors and teachers, not the school. Academic ability and exam grades are not the only reason for a pupil to attend a particular school. All schools, and Shrewsbury especially, have more to offer than the classroom: sport, music, drama, art, outdoor activities, hobbies and so on. A boy who excels in one or more of these areas has much to offer and much to gain. The strict enforcement of the 'hurdle' can also be counter-productive. Parents of a boy of lesser academic talent but with exceptional abilities in sport and other areas may be hesitant to take the risk of possible expulsion on academic grounds and send him elsewhere.

School costs and pressure on staff have risen steadily over the last forty years. When I arrived in Shrewsbury in 1973, the Bursar had four or five assistants to handle accounts and was himself responsible for administering maintenance and grounds staff. This has increased to some thirty administrative staff, with such titles as Human Resources Manager, Human Resources Co-ordinator, Head of Estates, Property Surveyor, Works Department Administrator, Financial Controller, Management Accountant, Fees Ledger Clark and so on. Few of the posts are filled by teachers as a supplementary activity; most are occupied by highly qualified specialists engaged to carry out certain functions in an increasingly technical world. An ever heavier burden of paperwork requires department directors to have deputies and/or secretaries to support them; they all have to be paid for.

A significant proportion of costs is attributable to bureaucratic regulation which has burdened schools and many other organisations with Child Protection, Health & Safety, Risk Assessments and many others. Computers and electronic communication have made matters worse. Nearly all sit at computers to deal with a never ending flood of e-mail messages and other material. In addition, advances in printing and copying and the relative ease of producing documents all result in more

staff time being needed to compile them. Costs have also risen through a widening of the range of subjects taught and of sports available.

To meet these expenses the number of pupils at Shrewsbury rose to 766 in 2014. Girls account for a large proportion of the increase, but there are now a significant number of overseas students from Shrewsbury International School in Bangkok, China, Hong Kong and several European countries; over thirty different nationalities are said to be represented. The School became in effect an international college and the opportunity to meet and work alongside pupils from other cultures is to be commended. It is hardly surprising that the fees for independent schools have risen such that many parents who could have sent their children to private schools twenty years ago can no longer afford to do so, while wealthy overseas students account for a higher proportion of pupils. The Shrewsbury School Foundation runs campaigns to raise money for bursaries to help parents who cannot afford the full fees.

All this represents a serious challenge to schools in the independent sector and they are accordingly in competition with each other. The headmaster of a school in Ely, Alex McGrath, undertook research among other headmasters in an attempt to identify the problems and suggest possible solutions. The results were published in his book *Lifting our Heads: The challenge facing our schools: a call to arms for the independent sector.* Various ideas are put forward; economising on non-teaching activities, persuading older teachers, especially those unwilling to take on extra-curricular duties, to retire in order to recruit in their place younger staff on lower salaries; to alter the terms of employment for staff over, for example, retirement pensions. At Shrewsbury more than a dozen senior members of staff were asked in 2014 to sign a new contract, refused to do so and were dismissed, only to be immediately re-employed under the revised terms.

While major changes inspired by economic considerations or educational philosophy have taken place at Shrewsbury School in the last twenty years, other changes at a day-to-day level have also occurred. A notable one is security. Understandably the arrival of girls on the site required stricter security. At the time of our arrival in Shrewsbury, security by to-day's standards was lax. If one needed to see a boy about something, one could simply walk into his house, look up his study number on a notice board and drop in to see him. One housemaster, who liked to go to bed in good time, would occasionally leave the front door unlocked with a list of boys who were going to come in later. As each one returned, he would tick off his name and the last one to come in would drop the latch.

Despite easy access to houses, theft was unusual, for apart from a radio, boys had nothing much of value in their studies; there were no computers, mobile phones or other electronic equipment worth taking. More likely was the possibility that one boy would be tempted to steal cash from another, a very serious and unpleasant problem for the housemaster who might even have to resort to marking bank notes in the hope of finding the culprit. As time went by, it became necessary to fit combination locks on the boys' entrance doors. With the arrival of girls, access to the site as a whole was tightened up, with some gateways being fitted with locks or removed altogether.

A further example of the more relaxed attitude in the 1970s was the celebration of Ascension Day. At that time the religious aspect was covered in a chapel service the evening before rather than on the day itself, which became a whole holiday when boys had a free hand to do what they wanted. On one occasion I was asked to take boys out after evening chapel to the junction of the rivers Severn and Vyrnwy where they camped overnight and returned to Shrewsbury by canoe the next day. Boys undertook many such activities on their own initiative and without adult supervision; at that time Health & Safety and Risk Assessments had not been thought of.

Catering arrangements also changed over time, with remarkable improvements. Until 1969, boys ate all their meals in their houses. Food was procured by the housemaster or his wife if he was married; there would be a cook but if she failed to show up, it was the housemaster's wife, or even the housemaster himself if he was unmarried, who had to set to with the preparation of meals. All this changed with the opening of a central kitchen and dining hall. For lunch, boys sat at long tables by house, the food was brought in by boys to be dished out by a master sitting at one end. There was no choice and culinary standards, although always adequate, could vary. At the start of the meal, grace was said, every one sat down at the same time and the meal finished after any announcements had been made. Supper in the evening was self-service supervised by a single member of staff, not always a welcome duty when some issue gave rise to ferment among the boys. Then came self-service for lunch as well. This led to a vast improvement in the quality of the food with several choices on offer.

Since the opening of the central kitchens and dining hall, many new buildings appeared on site, some attractive, others controversial to say the least. These included two new boarding houses to accommodate girls, with a sex change for two of the existing boys' houses; a swimming pool, with the old one converted to a sixth form centre; an

indoor cricket-training centre; an indoor rowing tank within what used to be the ferryman's cottage; a new boathouse to replace two old ones which were falling into disrepair; a music centre and most recently a large 'Humanities' classroom block. All this nibbled away at the green areas of the site, just as urban housing nibbles away at the countryside. Obviously it cost millions and was only possible thanks to the generosity of Old Salopians who appreciate the part that the school played in their education and have fond memories of their time at Shrewsbury.

There have been no changes to the Chapel's outward appearance for many years. It is a different story on the inside. When we arrived in Shrewsbury, it had an austere, even gloomy, interior unless the sun was shining through the stained glass windows on the southern wall. Behind the altar, the Reredos was covered in green material; while taking part in a choir rehearsal I looked behind the cloth to find a carved stone statue. This was part of a sculpture depicting the disciples on the road to Emmaus dining with Jesus; the apex had been chopped off, the rest concealed behind the drapes. Some years later under different management, the cloth was taken away and a new section of the sculpture put in to replace the part which had been removed and lost. The chapel was year by year redecorated and painted to give it a much more cheerful appearance trending towards an Anglo-Catholic style. Choir stalls were moved up to the same level as the altar and fitted with cathedral-style candle stands in memory of Chris Argent, organist and choirmaster, who had sadly died at an early age.

This style may not be to every one's taste, but I like to think that it encourages a serious approach to the spiritual well-being of pupils attending services. In the early 1970s one detected an air of resentment among some boys who refused to bow their heads in prayer and would close their hymn books with a defiantly loud thud at the end of a hymn. A succession of outstanding chaplains, particularly the Reverend David Alcock, has significantly changed attitudes. A later chaplain, the Rev. Gary Dobbie, in his introduction to the school's service booklet published in 2014 wrote:

'My job as Chaplain is to convey a spiritual understanding of life, that there is a wider picture, a bigger perspective, another league table of value, in the light of which all our doings will be seen in their true light; that human beings are more than just material entities; that we have a spiritual nature and a spiritual destiny..... Chapel takes us out of the scrum for a short time each week, inviting us to look out, to look up, to look beyond. Above all, it invites us to consider one of the most telling of all questions found in the New Testament: 'What shall it profit a man,

if he gain the whole world, and lose his own soul?'

Remembering my own time at Marlborough and the importance of religion throughout my life, I find this approach most encouraging. I am in no doubt that the ethos of a school is determined in part by its spirituality; pupils may well resent the need to attend chapel at the time but many will recognise its value in later years.

There were also some minor changes which were beneficial although altering the pattern of school life. Much more attention was given to incorporating parents and the general public in the school's activities. Concerts, invariably of a very high standard, were more widely publicised and tickets, if needed at all, were free. The Christmas Carol Service used to be held on the last day of term; attendance was voluntary but most boys came to it. This was followed immediately afterwards by Christmas dinner for all boys and members of staff.

More recently the service has been held on three different days, again open to parents and those with an association with the school and but I doubt whether as many boys go to it now as before. The singing and setting are to my mind up to cathedral standard and it is absolutely right that attendance should be available to a wider congregation. Yet for me, the single service forming part of the end-of-term celebration was very special and I regretted the change; so, I believe, do others. The Michaelmas term is fifteen weeks long and demanding. It starts in late summer, with light evenings and warm weather, but ends in cold and darkness. Boys and masters alike are weary from weeks of intense work and the single service on the last evening was a very special occasion as the term finally ended and the joys of the Christmas holidays began.

There has also been a radical change in the arrangements for Speech Day which is now held on the last day of the Summer Term. Previously it took place at half-term and extended over two days. Parents arrived on Friday afternoon, with a concert in the evening if they so wished. On Saturday the cricket First XI played against a well-known team. Originally an eminent guest gave the speech but later the headmaster took over the role. Tea was served in marquees arranged by houses and the week-end concluded with a traditional call-over at five o'clock.

The available time between events encouraged departments to lay on exhibitions and parents enjoyed looking round them. The most popular venues were probably the Art School and the Library where historic books and documents were set out on display. beekeeping was represented in the Biology building with an observation hive and displays of equipment; one year the spring had been unusually favourable and we laid on a demonstration of honey extraction. In 1982, when the centenary

of the school's move to Kingsland was celebrated, I put on an exhibition of battery-driven clocks in the Physics Department. Since returning from abroad I had become interested in electric clocks and I displayed some that I had collected myself and some I had borrowed from helpful manufacturers like Seiko. Information about different clocks came from the catalogue of an exhibition at The Science Museum in London in 1977, to mark the centenary of the death of the inventor of electric clocks, Alexander Bain.

Later arrangements for holding Speech Day at the end of term provide very little time for visitors to go round exhibitions and less encouragement to departments to lay them on. However, there were good reasons to postpone all this to the end of term. Amongst others it drops the curtain on a term of hard work, exams and sport, much as the Christmas carol service had previously done at the end of the Michaelmas term.

I have been privileged to maintain a link to the school, both through helping to run the Beekeeping Society, also through the annual house singing competition. For many years I attended the competition and would come away with the feeling that the house with the most enjoyable and entertaining performance had not gained the recognition it deserved. When I retired, I suggested to the Director of Music, John Moore, that I should provide a cup to be awarded to the house with the most entertaining performance, even if there were musical shortcomings. The idea was welcomed and since then I have helped with the judging. Obviously I am not qualified musically; my role is to help the judges by running a scoring system for them and giving an opinion over which house should be rewarded for the entertainment value of their performance.

To sum up, I have to recognise that change was inevitable and had given rise to a number of difficulties. My impression, as I view the school from the touch-lines, is that it remains an outstanding and vibrant institution, with greater diversity in the range of pupils attending it and of subjects available for them to study. Sport, music, drama and art continue to flourish, achieving high standards. Life for students, masters and administrative staff is ever more intense and it seems that management has become more autocratic than before. From what I have heard, there appears to be less social life among younger members of staff who prefer to meet up down-town rather than in the school. Bureaucracy and electronics may well be a distraction and an added burden for all concerned. In a way it is still the same school with a wonderful site but totally different as changes brought on by circumstances have affected its character and ethos. David Gee, in his scholarly and comprehensive history of Shrewsbury School *City on a Hill* expertly analyses the nature

of the school's ethos over many years. He points to a number of factors which threaten it and suggests ways in which these threats might be overcome Yes, Shrewsbury School is still a community but a different one. I cannot say whether there remains the same measure of exceptional warmth and cordiality among staff and pupils which I was fortunate to enjoy during my time there. Nevertheless I would wish the school continuing success in the future; it is a great institution.

Chapter 16

Agricultural Committees and Fighting for the Environment

A few years after arriving in Shrewsbury, I was asked by the headmaster, Eric Anderson, if I could help out with a request he had received from one of the governors, Reggie Lloyd. The latter was also a county councillor involved in agriculture and he was looking for a suitable person to serve as impartial chairman of two committees, Agricultural Wages Committee (AWC) and the Agricultural Dwelling House Advisory Committee (ADHAC). Perhaps because of my experience in the Diplomatic Service, it was thought that I would be the right person for the job.

Both these committees were advisory; they did not take decisions but offered advice to higher authority; in the case of wages this was to the Agricultural Wages Board under the Ministry of Agriculture and Food (MAF) and on housing to the relevant district council. The committee comprised three persons, a representative of the NFU who gave professional advice on the farming aspects of a case, a union man representing workers' interests and me as chairman. We got on well together, although obviously there were differences of view between these two and I had to come down on one side or the other in deciding what our advice should be.

The AWC had been set up under the Agricultural Wages Act 1948. It provided for a farmer to employ a worker with some kind of disability on a lower wage than the prescribed minimum. This was expressed as a percentage, and the greater the extent of a worker's disability, the lower his wage. It enabled a farmer to engage less expensive labour, albeit in a limited capacity, while a partially disabled worker could be gainfully employed and receive some remuneration rather than being unemployed and without any income.

In practice we had few cases during my term of office and it was the first one which stands out in my memory. It was a fine autumn day, with a

warm afternoon sun shining over the golden cornfields of the Shropshire countryside some ten miles west of Shrewsbury; peace and tranquillity reigned over the rural scene as we approached the farm. We had been summoned to review the case of a worker who had been injured in an accident. The farmer and his wife told us that he was not able to drive a tractor and was receiving about seventy per cent of the minimum wage to carry out other tasks. When we interviewed the worker, it transpired that he was driving to work on a motorcycle, having recovered from his injuries. In our view he was fit enough to carry out a full range of duties and we accordingly recommended that his wage should be restored to the appropriate level. On arrival I had detected an atmosphere of intense hostility within the family. When we left this was even more pronounced and in stark contrast to the deceptively peaceful and beautiful countryside in which we had found ourselves.

The Agricultural Dwelling House Advisory Committee (ADHAC) was quite different in its remit, although workers' rights were implicit. A number of farms had houses for agricultural workers who enjoyed a right of tenancy under the Rent (Agriculture) Act 1976, which extended also to the family if the worker died. Many workers preferred to continue living in the same cottage they had occupied, possibly all their working life, even after retirement. The farmer might well wish to regain the use of the property and would apply to the local authority for him to be provided with council accommodation instead. In order to do this, he had to show that the dwelling in question was needed to house an essential worker, whose duties required him to live on the spot, for example to oversee cattle about to calve. The request was lodged with the Ministry of Agriculture, who called for an assessment by our committee. Again, the farmer's interests were represented by an NFU member, while the trade union officer had the wishes of the farm worker in mind.

We would listen to both parties and then decide on our recommendation which we sent on to the local housing authority. We had first to establish the validity of the farmer's need for an agricultural worker, bearing in mind the importance of that worker's duties in relation to the farm as a whole; we would also take into account the nearest alternative available accommodation which would enable a worker to fulfil the necessary duties; finally, having established a need, we then had to inform the housing authority of the urgency for finding somewhere else for the present occupant and his family to live. At the back of our minds was always the possibility that repossession of the house was not in fact a primary consideration but that the farmer might in fact wish to sell the property on the open market, having found somewhere else for the worker to live.

Our committee handled three or four cases a year. They were invariably interesting and although the background had been set out in detailed briefing by MAF officers, there were almost always unforeseen circumstances which came to light in our discussions. In some cases the applicant owned the farm on his own account, in others it was part of a large estate. We were surprised to discover that in many cases the farm was owned by an Oxford college. The farmer would usually come himself to explain the difficulties he faced and the need to recruit an experienced worker for a particular task on the farm; in others he would engage a professional consultant to present his case. It was unusual for an applicant not to appear before the committee or engage some one to come in his place.

This occurred in the last hearing I chaired. A farmer in the Oswestry district applied to have a worker re-housed so that a duly qualified replacement could be accommodated. The papers were sent out and a date fixed for the hearing. On the day before, I had a call from the MAF officer to say that the farmer would not be able to attend the meeting as he had to get on with the potato harvest; did I want to have it postponed? This would have caused some inconvenience and I decided that we should go ahead, even if he was not there to explain his problem. At the meeting we were given to understand that the house was intended for his son, at that time living with his parents in the farmhouse nearby. The fact that the farmer could not spare half an hour to meet us led us to believe that the matter was not urgent and we recommended against re-housing.

We heard not long afterwards from MAF that he was exceedingly annoyed with our decision and had complained to his local M.P. The application was resubmitted, to be heard this time by a committee composed of different representatives and a new chair. The committee approved it possibly with a change in circumstances. Not long afterwards I received a letter from a senior MAF officer on the crested blue paper which I recognised from my time in the Foreign Office. I was informed that I had reached retiring age and was thanked for the work I had undertaken in chairing ADHAC for a number of years. I was not pleased; it seemed to me that I had been unfairly moved out for no fault of my own.

*****

When we decided to accept the offer of a job at Shrewsbury School, we only took account of the nature of the job and the ethos of the school, based on advice from a friend. We had no idea what the town of Shrewsbury was like, apart from getting lost as we drove in for an interview. Still less did we know of the surrounding countryside.

Shrewsbury is a remarkable historic town dating back to the early 10th century. It lies in a loop of the River Severn, which surrounds it almost completely; the neck of land to the north is only just over 300 yards wide and is dominated by the castle, erected in 1074 by Henry II. There is an access road at this point and two bridges provide a further way into town, the Welsh Bridge from the west and the English Bridge from the east. There are also three footbridges leading in to the centre. Shrewsbury Abbey lies just across the English Bridge; it was founded in 1083 and although much of it was destroyed in the Dissolution, the main church remains as a local parish church. Unfortunately many historic half-timbered buildings in the centre of town, including three important hotels, were destroyed in the 1960s to make way for shops. Nevertheless, some 660 listed buildings remain as well as important unlisted buildings in the Conservation Area.

We moved into our house five minutes walk from the school in the autumn of 1973. Before long we were troubled by noise from a hotel just down the road. It was a popular venue for parties, especially at week-ends, which went on noisily into the night. A number of local residents got together in an attempt to curtail the nuisance, including myself, but we did not make much progress. One day I came home from school to find a pile of papers in the porch with a note from one of our group suggesting that I should take over management of the campaign. We made little progress at that time and eventually the hotel was demolished, to be replaced by a barracks-like block of flats.

It was not long before other issues of local concern were raised. On the opposite side of the road were several fields which I had visited with groups from my Basic Year programme at the school, as a first step in learning how to use a map and compass. Sadly, the land had been given permission for an extensive housing estate of around 1100 dwellings. We did not want to see all the green land lost to development and we therefore set about trying to secure some open space for the residents of the new estate; in this way we became involved in the planning process.

The County Council had owned the land and prepared a development brief for the whole area, which was divided up into a number of plots available to developers. The brief also laid down that there was to be a local supermarket, a number of shops, various community facilities, along with a school. The implementation of the planning brief was in the hands of Shrewsbury & Atcham Borough Council, who readily gave permission for sections of housing but failed to make any provision for community facilities; the only land left was a marshy area which house builders had preferred to keep away from. By now we had formed ourselves into a

Residents Association and were worried that shops, which were clearly essential for the local community, would never be provided. We held meetings at the nearby Radbrook College but nobody took any notice until we threatened to withhold council tax payments unless something was done to resolve the problem. Fortunately one of our members had contacts with a local firm specialising in small supermarkets, who at once realised the potential for commercial development and plans were put forward. A shopping complex was designed to take account of the difficult site, while the marshy area was turned into a car park. Other community facilities followed.

Then came the question of the school. Council officers considered that there was no suitable spot for this because of drainage difficulties and suggested instead that it be put in the grounds of Radbrook College, a branch of Shrewsbury Technical College specialising in domestic economy. This was clearly a most unsuitable place for a primary school; parents taking their children from the estate would have to turn right into a busy main road and then turn right again into the college. We complained to the councillor in charge of education, Mrs Lesley Owen, who promptly arranged a meeting between ourselves and officers. After hearing both sides of the argument, she asked the latter to think again. As a result, the school was built where it was intended to go in the first place. A community hall and pub followed.

At about this time I was invited to join the Shrewsbury Civic Society's Council of Management. The Society had been established in 1963 in response to a proposal to demolish a row of cottages in the town centre, sharing the fate of many other historic buildings. The cottages turned out to be not cottages at all, but the remnants of a medieval hall. The Society raised money to buy the hall and meet the costs of restoration. The complex of historic buildings known as the Bear Steps provided office accommodation for the Society as well as other organisations like the Campaign for the Protection of Rural England, with a picture gallery and a café on the ground floor Another historic building, the Fellmongers' Hall in Frankwell, was saved in a similar way.

The Society's remit was to protect Shrewsbury's historic legacy and to campaign against further loss of valuable buildings, as well as to advise on roads, transport and leisure provision. When I became involved we were faced with a number of planning issues affecting the town's more general character. One was the lay-out of roads in the English Bridge/ Abbey area. A major road link to the town centre was planned and the problem was to determine the design of a roundabout which would connect it to Abbey Foregate and English Bridge. One idea was for

a small roundabout, the other for a larger one which would require a link through an arch in the railway embankment. The first would cost less, the second would, in our opinion, provide a much better and more efficient arrangement, even if more expensive. The decision lay in the hands of the County Council and I recall writing to the chairman to urge the adoption of our preferred route. In the event it was a tied vote with the chairman casting his deciding vote in favour of the route we had recommended.

We were less successful over a new shopping mall for the town centre. These were a new fashion at the time and one relatively small one had been approved off Pride Hill, the town's main retail street. A second such mall had been proposed higher up Pride Hill, to be called the Darwin Centre. We considered this but decided that there were insufficient reasons to object to it. We should have done. In the first place it was much too large a structure to fit comfortably into the local vernacular and now dominates the north side of the town. Secondly, it would compete with local shops, many of which were housed in historic buildings. If historic buildings were to be properly maintained, the shops within them had to be profitable; large shopping malls threatened the economic viability of small locally owned shops, and still greater was the threat from out-of-town supermarkets offering comparison goods such as clothing and hardware.

One of Shrewsbury's oldest historic buildings is a fine half-timbered residence known, appropriately, as the Old House. It was listed as 'Grade II starred' and would have been Grade I but for the fact that it had been added to in Victorian times. A family headed by a local solicitor had owned it, but a key member of the family had emigrated to New Zealand leaving its future in doubt. They had offered it to the National Trust, who declined on the grounds that there was no endowment to come with it. The Borough Council had also declined to take it on for similar reasons. It was therefore bequeathed to the Civic Society. Just before Christmas one year, we were celebrating at our Bear Steps office when we heard an ambulance blaring as it passed nearby. It was to attend to an accident in which the owner of the Old House had been killed and from that moment the Civic Society became the owners, with the problem of finding the resources to maintain the building. After a few years of use as a flat and premises for the Shropshire Luncheon club, it was sold. Most of the money was invested in bonds, with some kept to cover the costs of our administration.

My Civic Society activities led to a conflict of interest with Shrewsbury School on a couple of occasions. The first was shortly

after the appointment of Ted Maidment as Headmaster in 1988. His first Speech Day was in June 1989 when he made the usual address to parents. I was alarmed when he announced that his ambition was to build a new music school, to be situated in a prime position on land between two boarding houses, Oldham's Hall and Ridgemount, overlooking the town. This was not just an outline idea to be taken further in due course. A distinguished Shrewsbury architect, Leonard Baart, had been asked to produce an outline plan and copies of this were already circulating. To my mind, this was totally the wrong location for a new music school, in the grounds of a listed building with likely impact on the skyline when seen from the town below. In a long letter to the Headmaster, I pointed all this out and suggested that instead it should replace an unattractive building on the other side of the site. This consisted of five or six bed-sits, no longer fully in use, and on the ground floor a Common Room for Sixth Form boys; the latter could be incorporated into the music centre so that its facilities would be available for visitors to concerts as well as for senior boys.

All this was a proper and legitimate complaint. Less proper was a visit I paid to the architect to inform him of my concerns and for this I deserved the ticking-off I had later from the Bursar; I had indeed exceeded my Civic Society responsibilities. Nevertheless, I would certainly have protested against the proposal if it had gone ahead. Fortunately it did not. Instead, the music school was located near the position I had recommended. The ugly block of bedrooms and Sixth Form social centre remained for a while longer, until demolished to make way for a girls' boarding house. The Maidment Music School has been a great success and a major factor in the school's dominant position nationally in school music. All's well that ends well. But so far as I knew, decisions had been taken without any form of consultation or, it seems, inquiry into the relevant planning implications.

The second issue was in 1992, when the Modern Languages department wanted a connection to foreign TV broadcasters via a satellite link. As the department was located in the main school building, the necessary satellite dishes were put high up on the roof. This led to objections from town residents and the Civic Society. I received a note from the headmaster, complaining that the newspapers had been on his back and ending 'I would like to feel, Selby, that you have absolutely nothing to do with this. Please could I be assured of this.'

I was not happy with what appeared to be an implied accusation that I had been plotting against the school's interests. In a long reply I pointed out that I had heard of the Civic Society's disquiet over the impact of

satellite dishes on an important and prominently situated listed building in the Conservation Area. However, I had not been present at any Civic Society planning committee meeting when the matter was discussed and if I had been, I would have had to declare a conflict of interest. In any case planning recommendations and decisions were taken on planning grounds and in the light of planning regulations and local plan policies.

By chance I had met the bursar, who told me that the relevant official from the planning department had been round and had expressed the view that there ought not to be any difficulty over the school's retrospective application. In fact it was refused. It was a pity that planning permission had not been sought before the satellite dishes were installed. Later they were, but hidden and in a manner that did not give rise to any objections. The Modern Languages department was thus able to watch foreign TV programmes after all.

Campaigning on planning matters involves more than just writing in a letter of objection on some proposal. At the centre of the planning system are the Local Plans which lay down how land is to be used, where new housing is to be built and the policies intended to guide development and protect the environment in its widest sense. The plans are set out for public consultation and, at the time, some notice was taken of comments and suggestions. Looking back on the time when I was chairman of the Civic Society, my greatest regret stems from such a consultation. This was a time (as now) when money was to be made by demolishing large buildings and replacing them with a few houses. We had made a number of suggestions but failed to recommend a policy protecting small hotels and B & B businesses. During the few years after the publication of the Shrewsbury Local Plan, three or four such places were demolished, reducing significantly the range of options for visitors wishing to stay in the town with a preference for small-edge-of town accommodation rather than for the larger and more expensive town centre hotels.

It was in connection with the same plan that I took a particular interest in open land attached to Shelton Hospital in Shrewsbury. The hospital had been opened in about 1848 to a design by Gilbert Scott. At the time it was a mile or more outside the town's boundary and treated patients from a wide area of Shropshire and Mid Wales. Many were farmers and to help in their treatment, the hospital bought land and set up a farm which patients would be able to run. It also had several playing fields and the hospital teams performed well; it was even said that in recruiting staff, an applicant's sporting qualifications counted as much as his medical experience. By the 1980s, there were moves to build houses on some of the hospital's playing fields and open space.

When the outline plans for the area were published, they showed that a strip of land behind the Royal Shrewsbury Hospital and next to Shelton Hospital's fields, was to be allocated for housing. We objected both in writing and at the public inquiry, arguing that the area in question immediately adjoining the RSH should be kept in reserve in case the hospital had to expand. The inspector invited a representative from the hospital to attend the next day's meeting. No one turned up and it transpired that the hospital knew nothing of the draft Local Plan. Fortunately the land was saved and is now developed for much-needed hospital facilities and car parking for patients, staff and visitors.

On a day-to-day basis, those campaigning on an environmental issue need to examine a council's weekly list of planning applications in order to identify any which might be harmful to their interests. Those campaigning in this way are often dismissed as NIMBY's (Not In My Back Yard) not just by the applicants but even by government ministers. This is most unfair. Those who object are to be congratulated on taking an interest in the environment, unlike many who cannot be bothered until the bulldozers move in. However, there can be problems. Objections need to be responsible, backed by clearly expressed arguments and based on established planning policies. If planning policies fail to produce the necessary arguments and the proposal's impact is clearly unacceptable, objections should still be lodged. With online technology it is possible to see what other people are saying, both for and against, and it may help to apply to speak at the committee meeting if the matter is submitted to them for the decision rather than being determined by officers under delegated powers.

A knowledge of the complexities of the national planning system is important for any one seeking to engage in the process. The planning system comprises several layers. The topmost is the government in Whitehall and Westminster, the centres for official government departments and Parliament respectively. Between them they lay down the principles of national planning, mainly through Acts of Parliament and statutory regulations. Below them come the regional offices, in our case the West Midlands office based in Birmingham. For most of the time that I was involved, the counties of the West Midlands had their own county-wide Structure Plans which established policy in general terms. Shropshire was divided into six districts, each with its own council. It was these district councils which dealt with planning applications in their respective areas. At this time, Shrewsbury & Atcham Borough Council had two Local Plans, Urban and Rural, covering the town and the countryside respectively. The arrangements were changed in the

1990s when five of the Shropshire district councils were abolished to leave a unitary system for Shropshire and a separate one for Telford.

When the next Shropshire Strategic Plan came forward in 1996 it included provisions to protect areas of particular landscape value and the draft Shrewsbury Local Plan had included an Area of Special Landscape Character covering land on both sides of the river Severn above and below Shrewsbury. Because neither the Borough nor the County was able to justify this ASLC with survey material, the inspector recommended that it be removed, along with the policy protecting it.

The Campaign for the Protection of Rural England considered that this left important areas of landscape value exposed to development applications and decided to undertake its own study, which would serve to comment on landscape designations in future plans and also to object, if necessary, to individual development proposals. A CPRE colleague, Roger Carlyle, and I set about a survey of all the town's fringes. These were divided into 66 plots and each was assessed using the Countryside Agency's *Landscape Character Assessment—Guidance for England and Scotland, 2002.* Roger took several photographs of each plot and masterminded the complicated computer technology which the survey involved. The work took us three years and we received valuable help from the County Council's landscape officers. The Council also arranged to print it for us.

Just how valuable our survey was is debatable. My experience is that councils are reluctant to make use of privately undertaken surveys, even if carried out in accordance with established government guidance. They may commission surveys carried out by their own consultants and when a controversial planning application comes forward they seem to accept the applicant's surveys which are obviously biased in favour of the organisation which is paying for them. Whether officers take note of our assessments without mentioning the origin is doubtful. I have an idea that our report, handed over with due acclaim in 2003, is gathering dust somewhere in the vaults of Shirehall. When a public inquiry was held into housing land allocations in 2014, we complained that no landscape areas worthy of protection had been identified and somewhat tongue-in-cheek we put in a copy of the report as part of our representation. It was ignored.

Particularly contentious in the 1980s was a system of 'Deemed Consents' set out in the Town and Country Planning Regulations 1976. Under this the County Council was able to grant itself planning permission for development on land that it owned and in so doing receive financial benefit. It went further than that. County Councils were under pressure

from the government to operate a policy of 'opportunity purchase' of land 'at a price and at a location which holds out the prospect of significant capital receipts should council use be terminated'. In short, the Council could buy land designated as recreational at a low figure but then change that use and deem itself planning permission for housing in order to achieve a windfall profit.

Just round the corner from our home until 1982 was a playing field of over seven acres used by the town-centre Priory School until it moved to new premises with its own playing field included. It was owned by the County Council, who proposed to give themselves planning permission under the deemed consent regulations for housing development. We opposed this idea vigorously. So did the Borough Council; they presented evidence to show that there was a large shortfall in the provision of public open space, quoting an Inspector's report to that effect. It was a hard battle but in the end we won and the field was saved apart from a strip at one end which had already been earmarked for housing in an earlier plan.

We also had to resist efforts by the County Council to develop the Shrewsbury Battlefield. The Battle of Shrewsbury was fought in 1403 between King Henry IV and a rebel force raised by the Percy's of Northumberland who were dissatisfied with the share of ransom money they received through capturing Scottish military figures and other issues. The Percy forces under the leadership of Harry Hotspur, son of the first Earl of Northumberland, had moved south and in Cheshire recruited knights hostile to the king before moving on to Shrewsbury. King Henry's forces had been in Derby when news of the approaching rebel forces reached them and moved across to Shrewsbury. Battle was joined on fields three miles north of the town and was notable as the first battle on English soil in which the long bow was used by both sides. It was a particularly bloody battle with estimates of the dead around 8,000. It had seemed at one stage that the king had been killed. This was not so and his son, later King Henry V, carried out a flanking movement and attacked the rebel forces from behind. In the course of the battle, he had been struck on the face by an arrow and only skilful treatment by a surgeon saved his life and enabled him to take the throne as Henry V. So heavy was the loss of life on both sides that the king ordered the building of a memorial chapel on the site of the battle, to be manned by twelve priests to offer prayers for the departed. The chapel was later replaced by a church but with the Dissolution the church remained in use as a parish church and was restored in Victorian times.

Around this time, the County Council offered land which they owned

north of the town, including the battlefield site, to the Japanese car manufacturer Toyota for their European plant. In a letter to the Borough Council's Director of Planning we argued that it would have a totally unacceptable impact on the town's urban and natural environment. Fortunately nothing came of it. For Toyota, Shrewsbury came fourth in their order of preferences and they settled on Derby instead. But as I pointed out:

'We believe that the County Council promoted the Toyota scheme, not because it considered that there are planning needs for it, but because it owns the land in question and would stand to make a considerable capital receipt from the transaction. They can use their planning powers under the 1976 regulations to give themselves consent for change of use and it is pertinent to ask by what criteria the council might decide that their use of the land should be terminated.'

The council's Chief Planning Officer later admitted in a letter to the chairman of Shrewsbury Civic Society: 'I agree entirely with your view that such a development would have been inappropriate and out of scale in Shrewsbury. If the town had had the misfortune to be 'successful' in this bid, we would have regretted it for many years to come.' This is all too often the way in which councils, including Shropshire's, conduct their business. If the Chief Planning Officer so thought after the event, how come that he allowed it to be put forward in the first place? He might well have had doubts at the time and in all probability financial considerations had won the day.

The County Council were not to be put off and before long an application came in from a New Zealand firm called Fortex to build a meat packing factory on the battlefield site. Again, fortune was on our side as the firm went into administration before the application came forward.

By chance arrangements had been made at around this time for a visit by Robert Hardy, the actor and historian, to give a lecture on the development of the long bow, a subject on which he is an authority and author of a book. He happened also to be on English Heritage's Battlefield Committee. Up to that time, Shrewsbury's battle had been classified as a skirmish and its location received no protection. Robert Hardy arranged to come back with the director of the National Army Museum in Chelsea to inspect it more closely. The owner of the surrounding land, Mrs Joyce Jagger, was most helpful and arranged for us to view it. Before long the status of the field had been upgraded and full protection provided. As a result, the route of a new link road had to be moved away from

the protected land and the battlefield is now a tourist attraction, with an outstanding interpretative museum attracting many visitors who also enjoy a restaurant and farm shop overlooking the Battlefield church and the field itself.

This was not, however, the end of the story. The battlefield may have been protected but on land next to it came an application to build a waste incinerator. Hitherto, new buildings on the adjoining industrial site were limited to a maximum height of twelve metres in order to protect the setting of the battlefield. The incinerator was to be twenty eight metres high with a sixty five metre chimney emitting a plume of smoke. There was general opposition to the proposal, partly from the health risk of toxic fumes affecting local residents, partly from its impact on the landscape. Shropshire Council had already signed a contract with Veolia for waste disposal and the relevant department favoured the incinerator. Other departments opposed it. English Heritage submitted a formal objection on grounds of landscape impact but withdrew it when money was offered for improving the car park and access paths, and for education. None of these benefits could possibly resolve English Heritage's original objections based on landscape impact. It seemed to us totally wrong that a payment of money should enable the objection to be withdrawn and we campaigned vigorously for it to be resubmitted, but in vain. Nevertheless, after a stormy public meeting the Council refused consent and an appeal was lodged. This led to a lengthy public inquiry and the Inspector approved the scheme (this was at a time when the inspectorate was encouraged by the government to give greater weight to economic considerations as against environmental policies in order to approve proposals which would provide employment).

Another case of objections being lodged and then withdrawn occurred in the Shropshire Hills Area of Outstanding Natural Beauty. A landowner in Herefordshire just across the Shropshire border put forward a proposal to build four large wind turbines. Natural England lodged a formal objection on grounds of impact on the landscape of the AONB but then withdrew it when the developer offered a large sum of money by way of mitigation. In fact, Natural England had hinted in its objection that it would be withdrawn if funds became available to plant trees and provide other environmental benefits for the area. In effect they were fishing for money, using the wind turbine proposal as a pretext in a process now recognised as 'offsetting'.

In both cases the two organisations were withdrawing objections when offered money and this is wrong. The purpose of an objection is to inform officers in their analysis of the proposal and to influence their

recommendations. More importantly, objections are taken into account by members of the planning committee in deciding how to vote on a controversial proposal. If an objection is submitted and then withdrawn, it sends the message that the proposal is in fact acceptable in planning policy terms; councillors may well not study the small print or be aware of behind-the-scenes negotiations and offers of financial mitigation. To us it appeared to be an abuse of the planning system in order to gain benefits which could not possibly meet the reasons behind the original complaint.

Shrewsbury & Atcham Borough Council was also not above reproof. An area of landscape importance bordering the old river bed of the Severn was the subject of a planning application for both market and affordable housing. It was approved with Section 106 agreements under the Town and Country Planning Act 1990 to protect a woodland and public play area from further development. Five years later I noticed that the same area was to be discussed at a council meeting under a heading which excluded the public. It was proposed that more housing should be provided on the land covered by the Section 106 agreements. Unfortunately I did not attend the meeting so as to remind members of this and the proposal went through. I raised the matter with legal advisers who pointed out that the Planning Act stated that councils 'may' enforce compliance but not 'must' do so. In this case, Shrewsbury Borough Council insisted on compliance with a Section 106 agreement requiring a contribution for educational provision but did not see themselves under an obligation to adhere to an agreement which affected their interests.

Despite criticism of local government councils on such issues, I always enjoyed a friendly relationship with officers in both local and county councils built up over the years. The County Council's Chief Planning Officer used to hand on to me a copy of the R.T.P.I. weekly magazine *Planning* which was a great help to me in following current planning matters.

I have not always agreed with my colleagues in the Shrewsbury Civic Society. I come from an architectural/building family and take an interest in the design of new buildings both in the town and the countryside. Shrewsbury has an unusually rich architectural heritage and its old buildings are an essential part of the town's attractiveness. Some of the more recent buildings are ugly and do not fit in with their surroundings. Often the design of a building may be determined by its intended use. Normally a multi-storey car park is a singularly unattractive building, but it does not have to be; both design and materials can be arranged to fit in to the local scene, as has been shown in York. With houses or flats

there is no excuse for poor design. Often the difficulty is that architects wish to create modern structures using modern materials; anything incorporating aspects of existing buildings is dismissed as pastiche.

Design in a particular environment should be like the Roman god Janus, looking both ways, that is modern in concept and, within reason, looking at the materials used in construction; but it should also look back to take account of local vernacular, reflecting the character of its surroundings. In East European countries, previously governed by communist regimes, commercial interests had no part in the design of towns since all was determined by the state; factories and tall, ugly blocks of flats were put up in the outskirts while town centres were left to rot. With the fall of communism, such towns still have a central core of historic buildings now being restored. Shrewsbury has lost much to commercial development; Durham on the other hand, likewise located within a loop of the river Wear, has retained its centre for the cathedral and university, while shopping lies outside the river loop.

The same considerations apply in the countryside. Fortunately a tight planning system with policies to protect green space and limit the random spread of industrial and domestic buildings has, until recently, saved our countryside from disfigurement through inappropriate development. On a recent visit to Italy, I was struck and depressed by the absence of such protection; factories and housing were scattered all over the countryside north of Milan in an unplanned manner. One of the biggest issues in this country has been the redevelopment of disused barns for conversion to housing; nothing is more intrusive in the landscape than a barn converted into a dwelling without regard to the style of the farm to which it pertained. It is only right that these buildings, often of great antiquity, should be put to good use; otherwise they will decay and eventually reach a state of ruin where restoration is no longer feasible.

For most of my time engaged in planning matters, it has been reasonably easy to follow background documentation at county and district level. Lists of planning applications for each district were sent round by post and letters of support or objection could be sent in by the same route, while at county level draft structure plans were similarly available. The first Shrewsbury Local Plan that I became involved with went to a public inquiry lasting a fortnight and the inspector's report on it was between twenty and thirty pages in length. The Local Plan for 1999 had a more extended inquiry lasting for over three months and the final report went to around a thousand pages, with every comment or objection being considered in detail.

The introduction of electronic communication has led to even longer

documentation and the planning system has become more complicated. A paper can be drafted and distributed widely at a computer click but for many it is harder to examine a lengthy document on a computer screen than on a hard copy; to print the whole thing out is wasteful and time-consuming. This works for professional consultants who are adept at searching through documents to extract statements which support the arguments which they are paid to present. Personally I now find it difficult to keep abreast of documentation as it is produced and distributed electronically, even with some thirty years of experience behind me, and I no longer have the time to do this. For those who do not have a computer or are unable to access the necessary information, it is total isolation. This is a denial of democracy and of the right of the individual to have a say in matters which concern them.

Paradoxically, it is the same technology which facilitates the production of printed material and this has led to an ever increasing volume and length of newspapers and magazines, beautifully illustrated with colour photographs. School magazines have doubled in size over the last few years, with every sport or activity described in detail. Newspapers have similarly grown, especially the Saturday editions. Appeals from charities and catalogues from retail firms pour into the letter box. No one has the time to read all this material and waste increases despite pleas to cut back on it.

Does this mean that those fighting for the environment should give up? Far from it. There is much scope for the many organisations engaged in campaigns to co-ordinate their activities. An expert in one aspect of campaigning should specialise in their particular field and advise all organisations with an interest in it. There will be matters where disagreements occur, as in wind farms opposed by countryside groups because of their impact on the landscape but supported by other groups who believe that mitigation of climate change should have precedence. If natural and historic assets are to be protected, one has to keep fighting.

Chapter 17

Weighing the Balance

Being a schoolmaster at a boarding school entails long hours of hard work in and out of the classroom including week-ends. On the other hand there are long holidays; three weeks or so at Christmas and Easter and seven or eight weeks in the summer. Soon after our arrival in Shrewsbury we had decided to look around for a cottage in Wales where we could recover from the term's work and enjoy the wonderful countryside on our doorstep. While I was still in the Foreign Office, we had been tempted by a farm cottage in Scotland but, much as we loved Scotland, that would have involved too much travel.

Our searches in Mid Wales brought up a number of possibilities and a friend of ours, a qualified chartered surveyor, came with us on more than one occasion to assess their condition. One day we came across two properties, one in good condition, the other in a dreadful state of disrepair. Logic would have dictated the former, but the latter, for all its faults, had the advantage of facing south with a view over the Severn valley and an attractive feel to it. It is curious how some properties have a particular character and appeal whereas others do not, and the latter was our choice. It was cheap and earlier offers had fallen through because there was a claim against its owner over damage to surrounding fields. With help from our solicitor these problems were resolved and we had the place done up at some expense.

The long summer holidays also enabled us to indulge our passion for travel abroad and the cottage was let during the summer to contribute towards the cost. The longest was a camping trip through Hungary, Romania and Bulgaria. We still had our Triumph 2000 from our stay in Bulgaria and the car was loaded to the brim, with a large, heavy tent on the roof rack. We had many adventures as these countries were still communist. The highlights of the journey were staying with Paul and Irene Holmer at the Embassy in Bucharest where he was serving as Ambassador. Another pleasure was meeting up with Slavka and Milka in

Sofia, much as we had done while posted there a few years earlier.

On four occasions we exchanged houses with families in the country we wished to visit, for a month on each occasion. Arrangements were made through a firm called Intervac which had been set up some years previously by a teacher. Families wishing to take part would send in particulars of their property to be included in a brochure sent out to all participants. Immediately this arrived, we would look up properties in the country we wished to visit and telephone the one we liked best to draw their attention to our entry and suggest a swap. We arranged for two stays in France, one at Sezanne and the other near Auxerre. The most memorable were a month in Sogndal in Norway and a month near Helsinki. Rachel and I anticipated that as the children left school the latter would be the last opportunity for the whole family to go away together on holiday and so it was.

In later years Rachel and I made a number of trips abroad as part of our rail group. This had been run by Michael Hall for many years and took us by train to just about every country in Europe, often to travel on steam trains on narrow gauge railways. These were great fun but not out of the ordinary in their destinations.

One of our most recent trips was unusual and linked back to the Moscow years. When I was studying Russian in London in 1957, I came across a book in a second-hand bookshop *With Russian Pilgrims* by the Rev. Alexander Boddy, published in 1892. Alexander Boddy was Vicar of All Saints' Monkwearmouth near Durham and a dedicated traveller in the manner popular in Victorian times (he had already travelled extensively in Africa). He described in detail a journey to Archangel and then on to Moscow, with several chapters devoted to a visit to the Solovetsky Monastery on a group of islands in the White Sea. This had been founded in 1470 by two Russian monks anxious to get away to find peace and tranquillity in the far north. It gained military as well as religious importance with the opening of the trade route to Moscow and Russia's wars with neighbouring Sweden from 1570. The monastery was fortified with the construction of massive walls and towers.

Like other Russian forts throughout the world, the monastery became a target for British Navy ships during the Crimean War. In 1854 two British ships, the *Miranda* and the *Brisk*, arrived in the White Sea and bombarded Solovetsky Monastery for several hours. Alexander Boddy includes in his book an account of the bombardment given to him by the Archimandrate Meletii, an account later disputed by the commander of the British expedition, Admiral Ommaney. The last shell fired by the *Miranda* before the ships moved on had torn through the image of the

Virgin above the entrance gate. The monastery interpreted its survival from attack as a miracle and attributed it to the Virgin; it became a pilgrimage destination.

The 1917 revolution saw the destruction of churches across northern Russia, an area which had welcomed and in general supported the Anglo-French intervention. The monastery was closed down and became a concentration camp for political and other prisoners. Although some of the monks remained to help run the estate and provide essential food, it was largely a religious prison and became the scene of martyrdom for dozens of bishops and hundreds of clergy. Alexander Solzhenitsyn's *Gulag Archipelago* was inspired by the camps on the Solovki islands and the horrors experienced there. It later became a training base for the Soviet navy during the war and remained a ruin until the fall of communism saw its gradual restoration as a religious centre.

However, at the time of intervention two icons had been rescued and handed to an officer on a Royal Navy ship in Archangel. In 1992 Michael Bourdeaux was approached by the family of the naval officer with the suggestion that he should take back the two icons to Solovetsky monastery. He travelled there in 1993 and was enthusiastically welcomed by the Archimandrite. It was decided that he should return with the icons in a ceremony which would be the subject of a BBC radio programme. This was arranged but when he arrived on the island, the Archimandrite was away, his deputy knew nothing about it and although the icons were duly handed over, Michael was given a frigid reception. This appeared to be more than an oversight on the part of the monastery; possibly it was due to the criticism by the Keston Institute of the Russian Orthodox hierarchy, which had obsequiously supported the communist regime in Soviet times and afterwards, as against elements of the church which had opposed the hierarchy. Despite the difficulties, the BBC went ahead with the broadcast, making the best they could of a bad job.

Throughout this story a series of chance events have been turning points in my life, such as the outbreak of war and evacuation to Scotland. Then again I was late arriving back to school one autumn term in 1944 which resulted in my studying German rather than mathematics. Later I met Finnish girls in Austria on a German language course which led to me visiting that country. The spin of a coin in St James's Park determined that I should learn Russian rather than Persian in the Foreign Service, and I happened to be on the same skiing holiday as the red-haired Rachel whom I married. If just one of these events had gone the other way, everything after it would have been different.

For me the most important event has been the last, for Rachel has

contributed so much to my life. Our backgrounds are similar, both coming from middle-class families sufficiently well-off to provide us with a good education. Our respective parents held similar perceptions of family life and these we inherited. Staying together as a family has been important and we did not go away on holiday unless we could afford to take the children with us. We had both been brought up as Christians and we had similar tastes in music, food, travel, art and design.

Rachel was happy to accompany me on holidays where she was the only woman in a group of men, as on our railway journeys with bachelor colleagues from the School. Perhaps the most trying for her must have been the holidays we have taken with friends on fishing trips to the north of Scotland, particularly to Altnaharra and later Borgie. We anglers would set off to fish on Loch Hope for sea-trout, each pair with a ghillie, while Rachel was left on her own to spend the day as best she could, walking up and down the loch-side or sketching, plagued by midges or horseflies, but never a complaint. This difficulty was resolved later when another wife and friend also came and they went off on long walks together.

Wonderful holidays though these were, we decided one year not to go back. A friend and I had fished all day with dapping and wet fly on Loch Hope and neither of us had a single touch. Although the landscape was magnificent, the fishing was at times tedious and I decided that sitting in a boat all day and catching nothing was not the sort of thing I enjoyed. The brown trout on small hill lochs were more interesting, but why drive several hundred miles to the north of Scotland to catch small brown trout when those in Wales are larger? Furthermore, I lacked the enthusiasm of younger years. We would go to a lake and I would fish for perhaps an hour or two hours while Rachel walked the dog or read. If I caught a couple of fish, it was enough and unless we needed one for supper, I would put them back.

Were we right to decide to leave the Diplomatic Service in order to teach? The case for so radical a change of direction is never black-and-white and there have been moments when I have asked myself whether the move was wise. One year, life at the school was difficult for various reasons and I had my doubts. I also wished I could have been a diplomat in an East European country when communism collapsed and the Berlin Wall came down. On the other hand, Shrewsbury School has overall been a wonderful community in which to work. The town and countryside surrounding it are exceptional in their beauty and character, and working for their protection has been rewarding, although not always successful. It has been ideal for the family with stability and many local friends. No doubt life in the Foreign Office would have been more prestigious and

offered numerous opportunities to travel. But would it have suited my wife Rachel and me and our children as they grew up? Maybe, maybe not.

In weighing the balance between life as a diplomat and teaching I look back to the day in 1956 when I went to Kensington Town Hall to sit the Civil Service entrance exams. In my diary I had written disparagingly of some of the self-confident young men in their city clothes, behaving with precociousness and affectation, as if they were the cream of the aristocracy and sure to get through. It was of course not I, but they, who mostly went forward to achieve distinguished careers. Of the eight who joined the Foreign Office in my year, three became Ambassadors and were knighted. Should I have been more ambitious and would I have been among them if I had stayed on? I doubt it. They were by intellect, character and temperament better suited to a career in diplomacy than me. My own career has been less distinguished than theirs but it has been enjoyable and rewarding. We have lived a stable family life, our three children have received a sound education and gone on to university and rewarding careers. I do believe we took the right decision.

Further Reading

Angel and Wolseley	The Family Water Naturalist, London (1982)
Applebaum, A.	Gulag; a History of the Soviet camps, London (2003)
Boddy, A.	With Russian Pilgrims, London (1892)
Cunningham, A.	A History of Rannoch, Rannoch, (1989)
Duckers, Peter.	The Crimean War at Sea, Barnsley (2011)
Evans, Stanley G.	A Short History of Bulgaria, London (1960)
Gee, David.	City on a Hill, Wells, (2015)
Hall, F.M.	Around the World in Forty Years Wells, Somerset (2003)
Hardy, Robert	Longbow, a social and military History, Sparkford (1992)
Holliday, Jane	Cocktails and Cockroaches, Authorhouse (2009)
Hopkirk, Peter.	The Great Game; On Secret Service in High Asia London (1990)
Hynes, Noel	The Biology of Polluted Waters Liverpool (1960)
Klein, Herbert	A Concise History of Bolivia, New York (2003)
Macan and Worthington,	Life in Rivers and Lakes, London (1951)
Manson, Jean	Bolivia, London (1961)
McGrath Alex	Lifting our Heads: A Call to Arms for the independent sector. Woodbridge (2013)
Nicholson, Martin	Memoirs of a Kremlinologist and a Family Man, Amazon (2012)
Rankin, Nicholas	Telegram from Guernica, London (2003)

Solzhenitsyn, Alexander	The Gulag ArchipelagoVol. 2 Glasgow (1976)
Ure, John	Shooting Leave- Spying out Central Asia in the Great Game London (2008)
Ure, John	Sabres on the Steppes - Danger, Diplomacy and Adventure in the Great Game London (2012)